Pentecostalism, Secularism, and Post Christendom

Pentecostalism, Secularism, and Post Christendom

Bradley Truman Noel

WIPF & STOCK · Eugene, Oregon

PENTECOSTALISM, SECULARISM, AND POST CHRISTENDOM

Copyright © 2015 Bradley Truman Noel. All rights reserved. Except for brief quotations in critical publications or reviews, no part of this book may be reproduced in any manner without prior written permission from the publisher. Write: Permissions. Wipf and Stock Publishers, 199 W. 8th Ave., Suite 3, Eugene, OR 97401.

Wipf & Stock
An Imprint of Wipf and Stock Publishers
199 W. 8th Ave., Suite 3
Eugene, OR 97401

www.wipfandstock.com

ISBN 13: 978-1-4982-2936-4

Manufactured in the U.S.A.   12/02/2015

This work is dedicated to my students,
past and present,
in the Pentecostal Studies program at
Tyndale University College.

There are few rewards greater than seeing students
become friends . . .
and having the pleasure of observing these friends
contribute to the Kingdom of God
so capably and passionately.

Contents

Abstract | xi
Acknowledgements | xiii
Preface | xv

1 **Introduction** | 1
  Post-Christendom? | 2
  Purpose, Rationale, Methods, and Limitations | 4
  Definition of Terms | 6
  Christians and Cultural Engagement | 9
  Summary of Project | 18

2 **Pentecostalism in North America** | 22
  History, Growth, and Theology | 22
  Theological Antecedents of Pentecostalism | 23
  Azusa Street | 29
  The Global Spread of the Pentecostal Movement | 33
  Characteristics of Early Pentecostalism | 35
  Classical Pentecostal Identity | 37
  The Charismatic Movement and Pentecostal Identity | 41
  Pentecostalism and the Charismatic Movement | 46
  Pentecostalism Today | 48
  Conclusion | 50

3 **Current Societal Context** | 51
  Introduction | 51
  Post-Christendom: An Introduction | 51
  Secularism | 55

Secularization and Post-Christendom in Canada: Summary | 66
Postmodernism | 68
Postmodernity: The Key Tenets | 72
Postmodernism and Evangelicalism: A Critique | 76
Postmodernism: Summary | 82
Conclusion | 84

Part 2

4 **A Sample Pentecostal Denomination** | 87
A Brief History of the PAONL | 88
Recent Decline and Mitigating Efforts | 91
Facing the Decline—Discipleship in the PAONL 2007-2012 | 91
PAONL Provincial Discipleship Survey | 103
Conclusion | 109

Part 3

5 **Theme 1: Generational Issues** | 113
Introduction | 113
Generations within the Church Today | 114
Reflections on Pentecostalism and Generations | 122
Practical Suggestions and a Few Caveats | 125
Conclusion | 129

6 **Theme 2: Creativity and Risk** | 131
Introduction and Biography | 132
Lessons Learned from Aimee | 142
Conclusion | 148

7 **Themes 3 and 4: Being Missional and Influencing Culture** | 150
Introduction: The Missional Conversation | 150
A Brief Synopsis: The Missional Movement | 151
A Pentecostal Assessment of the Missional Church | 153
Summary: The Missional Conversation | 161
Introduction: The Emergent Conversation | 161
A Brief Synopsis: The Emergent / Emerging Church | 162

The Emergent Movement and Pentecostalism | 165
Summary: The Emergent Conversation | 171

8   **Themes 5 and 6: Reclaiming our Supernatural Heritage and Embracing Post-Christendom** | 173
    Postmodernism and Opportunities for Pentecostalism | 173
    Christ and Culture: Niebuhr's Five Options | 180
    Pentecostalism and Post-Christendom | 183
    Niebuhr and Pentecostalism: Conclusion | 188
    Conclusion | 189

9   **Themes 7 and 8: Essence over Distinctives/ Beliefs vs. Values** | 192
    A. Re-thinking Pentecostal Distinctives | 192
    The Displacement of Spirit Baptism in the Academy: Four Reasons | 195
    The Displacement of Spirit Baptism in the Pew | 202
    The Way Forward: Five Suggestions | 204
    Summary | 212
    B. Beliefs vs. Values | 212
    The Pentecostal Challenge | 217
    Ephesians 4—Pastors as Equippers | 218
    Conclusion | 222

10 **Conclusion, Summary and Limitations** | 223
    Summary | 223
    For Further Study | 226
    Conclusion | 226

Appendix One—First PAONL Survey 2007 | 229
Appendix Two—Second PAONL Survey 2009 | 233
Appendix Three—Third PAONL Survey 2011 | 239
Appendix Four—Provincial Survey of PAONL Membership 2012 | 249

Works Cited | 259

Abstract

THE PURPOSE OF THIS practical study is to assist the efforts of North American Pentecostalism as it seeks to navigate the significant changes in cultural attitudes and practices towards Christianity. Via a literary search, we will first explore contemporary Pentecostalism, observing its history, global spread, interaction with the Charismatic movement, and particular theological emphases. Chapter three will investigate changes in Western culture, focusing particularly on the Canadian scene. We will observe the shift from Christendom to post-Christendom, and note the increase in secularism, before concluding with an outline of postmodern thought. Having provided a foundation for our study, chapter four will tell the story of one classical Pentecostal denomination and its struggle to adapt to changing cultural norms in the face of numerical decline.

This work then seeks to interact with eight significant themes that Pentecostalism ought to earnestly consider as it seeks to understand and adapt to post-Christendom. Pentecostals must first consider the varying impact of these changes on the six *generations* (1) currently worshipping together. The story of Aimee Semple McPherson and her willingness to embrace *creativity and risk* (2) is the subject of chapter six. We discuss the lessons Pentecostalism might learn from the *Missional* (3) and *Emergent* (4) church movements, before considering appropriate Pentecostal responses to *Postmodernism* (5) and *post-Christendom* (6) in chapter eight. Chapter nine concludes our study with a plea for Pentecostals to reframe their understanding of *Spirit-baptism* (7) including careful consideration of the key differences in their *beliefs vs. values* (8).

Acknowledgments

THIS STUDY HAS BEEN undertaken as I seek to fulfill God's calling on my life to assist my own tribe—classical Pentecostals—as they navigate cultural shifts that often appear confusing, contradictory, and concerning. I thank God for the privilege of serving in this manner, and offer this study for his glory.

First, and by far most important, special love and gratitude to my wife Melinda, who joins with me on the journey of life, both of us seeking to affect our respective spheres of influence for God's kingdom. She is my primary conversation partner on Pentecostalism and post-Christendom, and I am grateful that, in many regards, her understanding of these topics exceeds my own. Great appreciation is extended also to my family, who in their own ways were supportive and encouraging throughout this process, even while they never could understand why I'd undertake another degree!

The material herein is an adaptation of that which was submitted to Acadia Divinity College for the Doctor of Ministry degree. Deep gratitude is extended to my supervisor, Dr. Anna Robbins. Anna and I go back to our time as students at Acadia, studying the M.A. together in the 1990s. It has been wonderful to again renew our friendship. Her effective and critical analysis of this work is exceeded only by the helpfulness of our conversations together regarding our current places of ministry. A host of others have served as dialogue partners during this process, and have read portions of this work, including A. Holm, D. Kentie, D. Brenton, C. Buckle, C. Andrews, C. Robinson, S. Simms, D. Newman, and A. MacGregor. Your advice, support, and critique have been invaluable. Warm thanks are extended to my diligent editor, Ashley Kentie, whose keen eye and careful attention to detail has made this work suitable for publication. Any errors remaining are mine alone.

Finally, this thesis is dedicated to my students, both past and present, at Tyndale University College. In so many ways, you have become family to Melinda and me. We celebrate with you each victory and mourn each loss. We have learned much from every one of you, and rely on your friendship and support more than you will know. It is our hope that each of you will go further in ministry than we ever could. This study is offered in hopes that it will make your future ministry endeavours increasingly profitable and effective for God's glory.

Soli Deo Gloria

Bradley Truman Noel
Springdale, Newfoundland, Canada
Fourteenth Sunday After Pentecost, 2015

Preface

Prayer before council meetings is banned!
Bakers punished for refusing cakes for gay weddings!
National Cathedral hosts Muslim prayer service!
Scripture verse is removed from local school!

CLEARLY, AS THE SONG goes, times they are a-changing. Further, if one follows social media discussion on the relationship between Church and culture, as I do regularly, you'd be led to believe that the end was not just near, but already here! As a pastor and educator now for almost 20 years, I have followed the changing religious climate in the North America with great interest. Without doubt, a significant shift has occurred, and things long taken for granted by the Church have been summarily dismissed.

From my vantage point, the Church is not always handling this change particularly well. Reactions seem to span the gauntlet from fear, despair and retreat, to militant vows to "take our country back" and other times, complete capitulation to the moral laxness that so pervades our culture. I am particularly interested in my tribe—classical Pentecostalism—and how it is navigating this new world where Christians have gone from tremendous public influence, to being the only group it is still politically correct to mock and disdain—and this all in a span of just 50 years.

My intended audience is therefore varied. I trust that denominational leaders and educators will find the following assessment to be cogently framed and the suggestions given worth contemplating. The times are difficult, and courageous leadership is essential. Further, my hope is that Pentecostal pastors and other leaders will find in these pages both a challenge to "watch our lives and doctrine closely," but also comfort in knowing that the present turn from Christendom may well present the church with the greatest opportunity she has ever seen. Finally, I pray that this book will speak encouragement to the many young pastors, just starting in ministry, for whom a post-Christendom world is the norm. You are by far the most comfortable with the changes in Western culture; I trust this work will give you practical and theological assistance as you enthusiastically participate in God's mission, already in progress!

— 1 —

Introduction

MUCH LIKE THE CHURCH of the first century, the church in North America is now struggling to find its place in society. The writers of the New Testament often admonished those to whom they wrote about the importance of influencing, rather than being influenced by culture; the North American church finds itself struggling with similar issues. Unlike the early church, however, which faced a culture that never was Christian (in any sense) to begin with, the North American church of the twenty-first century must learn to find its place in a culture that, just a few decades ago, seemingly embraced the Christian worldview—but does so no longer. In recent times the church in Western Europe and her offspring elsewhere in the United States, Canada and Australia have faced an unprecedented decline in ecclesial participation and cultural influence; as I will demonstrate below, this has often happened more quickly than church leaders had previously imagined possible.[1]

While all denominational groups have faced similar challenges negotiating the new religious context, attempts to mitigate the decline have varied widely. Several mainline denominations, for example, have focused on bridging the widening gap between church and culture in part by adjusting doctrine and practice to better suit prevailing attitudes in society. Others, largely from more fundamentalist or holiness backgrounds, have been tempted to retreat within the four walls of the church, as they await the Lord's return and subsequent removal of the saints from this "world of sin." As members of the latter group, Pentecostals have likewise grappled with an appropriate response to a culture that in many ways scarcely resembles

---

1. It is important to note that the trend towards post-Christendom does not affect all of the world's Christians, particularly those in Africa, Asia, Latin America. While Christians in the United States have long hoped in American "exceptionalism," we may observe though America may be a few decades behind in this trajectory, cracks in American Christendom are now openly visible. See Murray, *Post-Christendom*, 15.

the more "Christian" culture that existed in 1906—the year Pentecostalism exploded upon the religious world of North America.

The challenge is particularly significant at this stage in Canadian Pentecostal history, for as we shall observe, the religious scene in Canada is replete with examples of denominations that, though robust as recently as 1960, have found their membership plummeting, some by over 50 percent. Pentecostals, long known for their incredible growth, have also watched their increase slow and, in some cases, join the others in a downward slide. In the coming chapters I will argue that failure to address the considerable changes in Canadian culture in the last fifty years will spell disaster for Pentecostalism in Canada. Further, with the United States facing its own version of the post-Christendom narrative sooner rather than later, American Christians may be able to make the adjustments necessary to embrace the post-Christendom context, and do so before facing the significant numerical decline experienced by the Church in Canada and Europe. As such, the Canadian experience is presented herein as a harbinger of the wider cultural and religious shifts occurring in North America as a whole.

Post Christendom?

At issue in this study is whether Canada is in fact becoming a society that in the last century has shifted from being largely beholden to Christendom to a post-Christendom posture that is increasingly secular in orientation. We are thinking here of the shift in attitudes and practice among the Canadian populace that just a few decades ago reported high percentages of weekly church attendance and saw a large majority self-identify as Christian. As chapter 3 will demonstrate, both of these markers have demonstrated significant decline in the last half-century. With the American statistics closely following those of Canada, albeit belatedly, lessons learned from the Canadian experience may well be readily applicable to our southern neighbours. To assist with our exploration of this trend and our discussion of post-Christendom later in chapter 3, we will first pause and explore what a "Christian country" might look like in the context of Canadian society. John H. Redekop[2] helpfully summarizes the options:

1. *A Christian country is one in which there is an official or unofficial fusion of church and state.* This was a common situation in medieval Europe; John Calvin established just such a situation in Geneva in the 1530s.

2. Redekop, "Is Canada Becoming a Post-Christian Country?" The five definitions come from this helpful source. Redekop is a retired professor of political science, who has taught at both secular and Christian universities in Canada.

In our day, this fusion of political and religious (Muslim) institutions may be found in some Arab countries, including Iran, Saudi Arabia, and Pakistan, and when considering Christianity, the United Kingdom and many European countries are examples.

2. *A Christian country is one in which Christianity is the dominant faith and the government, while separated from the religious structures, ensures that the values of the dominant Christian religion are upheld, at times with coercive force.* We may note examples of this in early French Canada, and most of Roman Catholic Latin America until the 1960s.

3. *A Christian country is one in which Christianity is the dominant religion and its values are reflected in the laws of the land but the government does not use coercive power to assist religious organizations.* Some laws, such as the prohibition against Sunday shopping, and the use of the Bible in courts, may incorporate Christian values. Government does not promote Christian values but typically grants Christian groups the freedom to do so. The tradition in Canada of the Gideons distributing New Testaments to grade five students is emblematic of this. This definition reflects the situation in Canada from about 1840 until the Charter of Rights and Freedoms was enacted in 1982, elevating minority and individual rights, which Redekop believes significantly changed the Canadian landscape and ushered in further examples of secularism.

4. *A Christian country is one in which Christianity is the dominant religion but while some government policies may still incorporate certain religious values, these are generally described by governments, the media, and educators in secular terms.* The basic government stance is that no religion is to be given preferred treatment for the government itself is secular by definition. To demonstrate that they are not in any way pro-Christian, governments, media, and educators sometimes give preferred treatment to minority, non-Christian religions. Redekop believes this was the case in Canada from about 1982 until about 2000. While we may dispute the dates used to provide a timeframe, the outcomes described have been observed in Canadian political and religious life.[3]

---

3. I think for example of the recent decision by a school within the Toronto District School Board to provide prayer space for Muslim students, permitting the restrictions that girls pray behind the boys who occupy space at the front, while menstruating girls are not allowed to pray at all. Urback, "Girls should not be segregated."

5. *A Christian country is one in which Christianity, although mostly in a nominal form, is still the dominant religion, and its principles and ethos still impact society. Governments, courts, media, and the schools, however, at all levels strive to remove from the public institutions of society anything that is obviously Christian, for example, Christian celebrations of Christmas and Easter.* Religion, especially Christianity, is relegated to the margins as a purely private matter. This has been the situation in Canada since about 2000, though the seeds of this may be observed in Canadian culture from the 1980s; many battles are currently underway in the United States on this front. According to this criterion, a country is Christian only because most of its people identify with that faith, whether seriously or only superficially, not because Christian values and practices enjoy public support or endorsement.

Though there are other ways of approaching this classification, I believe that Redekop's categories bring clarity to the discussion without binding us to his method of delineation. His approach assists us as we seek to understand the historical journey Canada has traversed in terms of Christianity. Though scholars may wish to challenge minor details used to describe each category, or perhaps the specific years assigned to each period, there is nearly unanimous consensus based on statistical evidence alone that Canada has experienced profound movement as a nation towards post-Christendom in the last half-century. In chapter 3 I will demonstrate that in the last fifty years Canada has transitioned in its relationship with Christianity from Definition 3, through Definition 4, to Definition 5. As such, it is incumbent upon Pentecostals to evaluate both their understanding of new cultural realities, and their efforts to evangelize successive generations of Canadians.

Purpose, Rationale, Methods, and Limitations

The goal of this work is to serve as a primer for pastors and other Pentecostal leaders as they endeavour to understand trends towards secularism and post-Christendom, and from that vantage point create new ways of engaging North American culture. I strive therefore to provide a study of both Pentecostalism and current cultural trends. From this I will offer a number of suggestions via eight themes that I believe Pentecostals must consider on a going forward basis. It is my hope that this study will become a stimulus both for discussion and action. A great deal has been written on the shift to a post-Christian culture in Western society. Many volumes have also been written on the rise of Pentecostalism from a small revival in

1906, to the worldwide movement of 600 million it is today. Little, however, has been written on the intersection of the two. This work seeks to address that lacuna, and will explore Canadian Pentecostalism's efforts to come to terms with changing cultural realities, and in so doing, provide timely commentary on the situation in the United States. We will accomplish this largely through a literature review from which we will explore the changes occurring in Canadian society as they impact religious groups, and thus situate Pentecostalism within these transitions. We will also gain a sense of who Pentecostals are, what they believe, and how their orthodoxy may be observed in their practice.

To further clarify how Pentecostals self-identify, we will avail of research completed in a smaller Pentecostal denomination, the Pentecostal Assemblies of Newfoundland and Labrador (PAONL). Via a survey given out to the entire membership of this classical Pentecostal denomination in Canada's most easterly province, we will observe how these classical Pentecostals view themselves, both in their efforts to evangelize and their sense of personal and corporate identity. From this, we may draw conclusions regarding classical Pentecostalism in Canada as a whole.

The limitations of this study arise first from our inability to speak as precisely as we might wish. Tracking cultural changes in a society relative to its attitudes towards religion and morality, for example, is not an exact science, despite the abundance of surveys and statistics. While we may note, for example, that far fewer Canadians or Americans attend Sunday worship regularly than did 50 years ago, or that many more individuals of both countries now approve of gay marriage than was the case in the mid-20th century, can we say with certainty that this represents the secularizing of society? Though this work will argue in the affirmative, the topic is still open for debate. Further, Pentecostalism as a whole is now variegated to the point that an all-encompassing synopsis of classical Pentecostalism is nearly impossible. While we may tease out commonalties in the worldwide movement, the geographical differences and variation of traditions alone make absolute conclusions unreliable. For this study therefore, we will focus on Pentecostalism in North America, with particular emphasis on the Canadian experience.

Additionally, as our objectives are broad, our path will necessarily traverse considerable ground. We must explore Pentecostalism, in terms of its history, theology, and global growth before turning to questions of identity. Significant attention must be given to questions of secularism, postmodernism, and post-Christendom in Canada, via both statistical and anecdotal evidence. To put "a face in the window" as it were, we will devote a chapter to understanding the struggle of one small Pentecostal denomination to find its place within current Canadian religious culture while acknowledging its own recent decline. Finally, as there is no singular solution to the present challenges facing Pentecostalism amidst increasing secularism, we offer a series of themes, or foci, that Pentecostals must soberly visit. Though these may appear varied, and perhaps unconnected, each speaks to a facet of the ongoing struggle Pentecostals face as they endeavour to relate to culture.

Finally, limitations of space dictate that we are not able to explore all of Western Pentecostalism, let alone the global reach of the Pentecostal movement. This study will focus largely on Canadian Pentecostalism, as I believe that on the continuum of change as per post-Christendom and secularism, it finds itself midway between Western Europe (twenty years further ahead in this process) and the United States (twenty years behind.)

Definition of Terms

Before pressing further, it is wise to pause and define the terms we will use in this study. Though each will be fully unpacked in turn, a framework for understanding the core concepts contained herein is beneficial.

"*Modernity* is characterized by the triumph of Enlightenment, exaltation of rights of humans and the supremacy of reason. Modernism assumed that human reason was the only reliable way of making sense of the universe. Anything that could not be understood in scientific terms was either not true or not worth knowing."[4] At its essence, *Postmodernism*[5] is a worldview consisting of anti-foundationalism[6], disbelief in pure objectivity, and deconstruction of "certain" knowledge, primarily characterized by a reaction to the prevailing worldview of Modernism. *Relativism* is the general philosophical belief that no absolutes exist. In terms of ethics, it indicates that no criteria for ethical judgment can be claimed and that morality varies

---

4. Jaichandran and Madhav, "Pentecostal Spirituality in a Postmodern World," 44–45.

5. For a sample of sources attempting to define postmodernity, see Finger, "Modernity, Postmodernity," 353–68; Gitlin, "The Postmodern Predicament"; Percesepe, "The Unbearable Lightness of Being Postmodern"; Van Gelder, "Postmodernism as an Emerging Worldview," 412–17.

6. *Foundationalism* may be defined as "Philosophical or theological approaches affirming specific truths as bases and criteria for all other truths." See McKim, *Westminster Dictionary*, 108. For the Christian, the belief in the God who created humanity and the universe, and who revealed himself in Jesus Christ and through his Word, is foundational.

with the culture. Closely related is *Pluralism*, which may be understood as the outworking in society of relativistic moral values.[7]

On the church front, we will explore several contemporary approaches. Though individuals involved with the *Emergent/Emerging* church are often loath to self-define, Missiologist Ed Stetzer has helpfully summarized three streams. *Relevants* describe those leaders who are trying to contextualize their worship, music, and outreach to emerging culture. They are often deeply committed to biblical preaching and other values common to conservative evangelical churches and are simply trying to communicate the message of Christ in a manner that will connect with their generation. *Reconstructionists* believe that the current form of church is increasingly irrelevant even while often holding to an orthodox view of Scripture and theology. They are not about tweaking what exists in terms of buildings, budgets or programs—all are expendable. Finally, *Revisionists* are questioning and are in many cases redefining all aspects of church life, including doctrine long held to be orthodox. In addition to sweeping changes to form, the nature of the Gospel itself is being debated.[8]

As will be explored in chapter 7, many other contemporary writers on the Christian church are heavily into the *Missional* conversation. At its core "missional" simply means an approach to evangelism and discipleship whereby one seeks to partner with God who is already at work in the community, as opposed to waiting for the lost to "come to church" and, therein, find salvation. Though largely promoted and championed by seasoned leaders, the missional approach has been welcomed eagerly by younger believers, many of whom have a more natural affinity for community involvement than do their elders.

When we speak of *post-denominationalism*, we describe a context where "it is far less important whether you are Methodist or Baptist, or even Catholic, than where you fall along the continuum of fundamentalist to evangelical to progressive (liberal) to secular or unaligned."[9] Finally, *post-Christian* is a term first used by Mary Daly in her 1973 book, *Beyond God the Father: Towards a Philosophy of Women's Liberation*. In general, it may be understood as an epoch where "history has ended, there is no form of the old belief in progress or linear eschatological time, and where Christian stories have lost their strength, and the institutions continue to evaporate in crisis, not knowing how to respond . . . " A 'post-Christian culture' may involve not only fragmentation of a previous Christian coherence but may

---

7. Ibid., 211, 235.
8. Stetzer, "First-Person."
9. Thistlethwaite, "The U.S. Is Post-Denominational."

be characterized by the presence of Christian symbols that have lost any reference to their original meaning.[10] Stuart Murray Williams writes, "*Post-Christendom* is the culture that emerges as the Christian faith loses coherence within a society that has been definitively shaped by the Christian story and as the institutions that have been developed to express Christian convictions decline in influence."[11]

As this study focuses in particular upon Pentecostalism, a few words about this group will conclude this section. By *Global Pentecostalism*, we mean the worldwide movement of both Pentecostal and Charismatic groups. The modern Pentecostal movement is now just over 100 years old, and continues to see impressive growth worldwide. Allan Anderson counts the total number of Pentecostals/Charismatic in the year 2014 as just over 631 million, some 108 years after the beginning of the modern Pentecostal movement in 1906. 800 million Pentecostal/ Charismatic believers worldwide are projected by the year 2025.[12]

When we talk of *Pentecostals*, we are referring specifically to *Classical Pentecostals*. Classical Pentecostals are those that trace their roots to the turn of the century, and the Azusa Street revival. "Classical" was added in about 1970 to distinguish Classical Pentecostals from *Charismatics*. Essentially, Pentecostals believe that the outpouring of the Holy Spirit on the 120 at Pentecost as is recorded in Acts 2 should be normative for all Christians. As those in the Upper Room were already believers, according to Pentecostals, Spirit Baptism thus occurred as a second act of grace, following salvation; this is the Pentecostal doctrine of *Subsequence*. Further, most Pentecostals strongly hold to belief in *Initial Evidence*; the key proof associated with this Spirit-baptism is *glossolalia*, as it was in Acts.[13] For the purposes of this study, *Charismatics* are those who have received the Pentecostal experience of Spirit-baptism, usually with *glossolalia*, but have typically remained in one of the mainline Protestant denominations, or Roman Catholicism.[14] *Charismatic* refers to " . . . all manifestations of Pentecostal-type Christianity that in some way differ from classical Pentecostalism in affiliation and/or doctrine."[15] Not all of the charismatics remained in traditional denomi-

---

10. "Post Christian Society: What Is Meant by the Term "Post-Christian?"

11. Murray, *Post-Christendom*, 19.

12. Anderson, "Transformation of World Christianity."

13. For more on the history and impact of the Azusa Street revival and the subsequent Pentecostal movement see Robeck, *The Azusa Street Mission and Revival*; Hunter and Robeck, *The Azusa Street Revival and Its Legacy*; Owens, *The Azusa Street Revival*; Hyatt, *Fire on the Earth*; Valdez, *Fire on Azusa Street*; Dayton, *Roots of Pentecostalism*.

14. Hocken, "Charismatic Movement," 477–519.

15. Ibid., 477.

nations; many of the largest charismatic churches in North America, for example, are affiliated only with loose networks of other "independent" charismatic churches.

Canadian Pentecostalism refers to the variety of Pentecostal groups in Canada that arose out of the Azusa Street revival, the largest of which is the Pentecostal Assemblies of Canada.[16] Discussion of *Pentecostalism in Newfoundland and Labrador* will be limited to just one denomination for the purposes of examining a specific Pentecostal denomination in light of the concerns arising from this study. As such, this project will focus upon the Pentecostal Assemblies of Newfoundland and Labrador, a sister organization to the Pentecostal Assemblies of Canada, but one that was founded decades before Canada's tenth province joined the Canadian confederation in 1949.[17]

As one can imagine, the naming and dating of the various generations alive today is not a precise science. Scholars are typically agreed only on the dating of the Boomer generation that immediately follows World War II in 1945; apart from the Boomers, even the names of each generation vary widely from author to author. For the purposes of this paper, we will use the following dates and monikers: *Seniors* (born before 1925); *Builders* (born between 1925 and 1944); *Boomers* (born between 1945 and 1964); *Generation X* (born between 1965 and 1983); *Millennials* (born between 1984 and 2001); and *the newest (and unnamed)* generation, born since 2001. Based on this dating, the median age of each generation in 2015 is: Senior—100, Builder—80, Boomer—61, GenX—42, Millennial—24, with the newest generation comprised of children, the oldest of whom is just 14 years of age.[18]

Christians and Cultural Engagement

As will be observed, Western Christians are not in agreement on biblical teaching regarding cultural engagement. Though I understand the interaction between the church and the society in which it is placed to be axiomatic, a brief discussion to clarify our understanding of what is meant by "cultural engagement" and how a rationale for this effort can be found in Scripture, may be prudent.

---

16. See www.paoc.org, and Miller, Canadian Pentecostals.

17. See www.paonl.ca, and Janes, *History of the Pentecostal Assemblies of Newfoundland*.

18. As we will observe in chapter five, there are a variety of approaches to naming and dating the generations.

Definitions

A discussion on the merits of Christians engaging culture cannot be entertained with much productivity unless we first establish what we mean by both *culture* and *engagement*. Definitions are important, because we may observe that definitions themselves are culturally bound attempts to understand something, to the extent that even by defining we may add weight to a particular argument. What then is *cultural engagement*? To be sure, culture exists in the entire realm of human activity. Whether we are riding the bus, reading the newspaper or latest online article, enjoying a game of golf for leisure, interacting with friends on a social networking site, investing in the stock market, watching the many advertisements on television, or simply raising our children to be good citizens, we are engaging the culture around us. All of human activity involves cultural engagement on this level; everything we do may be seen to support cultural norms or repudiate the same. There is no neutral position. Cultural engagement must therefore refer to more than simply living and performing human activities in the world around us. Rather, we wish to discuss cultural engagement as the ". . . deliberate, thought-out, philosophically-consistent activity of vocational and societal living that is proactively designed to reflect a biblical perspective on the world."[19]

Derek Brown asks the correct question:

> Does the Bible speak with clarity on the matter of how to live in 21st century society, and is it right for Christians today to spend significant time and sustained energy on deliberately seeking to shape how they and other people live and relate together and use the environment in response to this supposed biblical mandate, as a legitimate witness to the gospel of Jesus Christ? Or is such an activity a dangerous diversion from the true biblical position of doing what is necessary to sustain life whilst focusing on the only truly worthwhile purpose of helping individuals to become Christians and so in some future day after death, to enter into the wonderful promise of eternal life through Jesus Christ our Lord?[20]

There are a variety of responses to this question, as we will discuss more thoroughly in chapter 8. As this point, it will suffice to highlight two different approaches. First, Christians are called only to preach the Gospel of Jesus Christ and him crucified, for the forgiveness of sins and eternal

---

19. Brown, "Is Cultural Engagement Biblical?"
20. Ibid.

life to those who will accept this message. As the Bible rarely comments on secular culture, and fails to give contemporary believers instruction for cultural engagement, Christians are to stick with the task given us by Christ—winning souls. Any attempt to engage the culture with the Gospel eventually ends with the culture having transformed the message of the Gospel, and is a dangerous distraction from the primary and important goal of the Christian life.

In the second approach, a proper understanding of creation reveals that all of society is God's and that we must differentiate the concept of culture as part of God's original design, from the practice of culture defined as it is by the stain of sin upon all human endeavours, and its need of the light of the Gospel. Engaging the culture need not be synonymous with conforming to the culture. Rather, the Christian recognizes that a properly biblical worldview entails that as the believer embraces life, every activity, thought and plan, is subjected to the Lordship of Christ. In so doing, Christians automatically speak into the culture around them, shining light in dark places, doing a small part to re-align culture with God's design, every day in every way. In this sense, all of life and human activity engages culture, and is part of a rounded understanding of worship. With this understanding, for example, the Christian in business seeks not only to pray for her fellow workers and share with them the good news of Christ, but she also seeks to apply the biblical principles of justice and mercy in the workplace, and to consider matters such as stewardship and generosity.[21] In this approach, Christians seek to influence both the individuals in their lives, and also the societal structures of which they are a part.

My understanding of cultural engagement aligns with viewpoint two, above. I believe that Christians are called to live out the Lordship of Christ in all areas of work, play, and mission, and in so doing, engage the culture around them with the light of the Gospel. We may influence both individual and societal structure, bringing the principles of biblical living to bear upon each as we view all of life as worship. By way of caveat, however, I believe it is important to retain the priority of the mission to the individual over and above structures, policies, or governance. I share the discomfort of those who suggest that Christians in some circles have reversed the proper focus, and now spend more time and energy bringing a Christian worldview to bear upon governments and laws than on ensuring their neighbour has heard about Christ. While we may surely have a voice within culture, and may speak to themes of love, compassion, and justice clearly, we must also

---

21. Ibid.

remember that Christ's kingdom is first in the hearts of believers, which then influences the structures of which they are a part.

Pentecostal Theology of Social (Non) Engagement

As will be observed, Pentecostals have not had a cohesive theology of social engagement. In fact, it can be argued that the only theology relative to engaging culture Pentecostals have recognized is one that posits a basic position of separation from "the world" and an isolationist outlook. In *Beyond Pentecostalism: The Crisis of Global Christianity and the Renewal of the Theological Agenda*, Wolfgang Vondey argues that early Pentecostals saw themselves primarily as a "missionary movement" led by the Holy Spirit. The absence of support structures and organizational plans for these missionary endeavours eventually severely hampered the growth and effectiveness of this new movement. Pentecostals therefore moved towards the organization and structures associated with an understanding of being a "church" only reluctantly, and primarily to facilitate their missionary efforts. If Pentecostalism remained simply a movement as many hoped, some wondered whether it was valuable to discuss ecclesiology at all. Vondey notes,

> In this debate, classical Pentecostalism avoided the crucial question of culture in defining its own ecclesiality and thereby, sidestepped the debate on the impact of modernism, modernity, and cultural formation, supporting the separation of the religious realm from the arena of politics, economics, and the secular, and strengthening the autonomy of culture. As a result of the underdeveloped account of the theological identity and ecclesiological role of culture, the organic ecclesiality of Pentecostalism as a movement, its pneumatological basis, and its eschatological orientation have remained largely underdeveloped.[22]

For example, David Milley studied the doctrine of "Separation" in the Pentecostal Assemblies of Newfoundland and Labrador, the denomination that we will focus upon in chapter 4. He observed that the core message of the foundress of the denomination, Alice B. Garrigus, was one of separation. Milley notes,

> There was such a strong stand taken to separate the church from the world that anything that appeared to be of the world was condemned . . . The Pentecostal Assemblies of Newfoundland stressed separation even to the point of isolation. Association

22. Vondey, *Beyond Pentecostalism*, 158.

with the world, and the organizations of the world were considered to be contrary to standards of separation, and therefore isolation was the preferred choice of action.[23]

A few examples will suffice. The issue of modesty in dress, particularly for women, was deemed sufficiently important to be a topic of discussion and subsequent motions in the General Conferences of 1931, 1932, 1933, 1939 and 1941—five times in ten years. Concern for modesty was such that changes to the building code of individual assemblies were recommended to protect the modesty of altar workers. The 1929 and 1934 General Conferences discussed burial of the dead, clarifying that Pentecostal workers were not to participate in funerals held in churches of other denominations, or bury in sacred burial ground those known as members of "secret societies."[24] By 1936 leaders were apprehensive that drift from strict standards of separation was already occurring in the young denomination. That year the wife of the General Superintendent, Mrs. Eugene Vaters, in an article entitled "Hold Fast . . . Repent," wrote, "God does not want us to let go of the old lines of separation we took in him. He does not want us to take unto ourselves again that which once we put away from us."[25]

In 1936, the PAONL General Conference also ruled against participation in, " . . . any outings or occasions whether indoors or out of doors in which games, rings, races, plays, selling or sport or revelling of any kind are permitted." It declared, " . . . we discourage the participation on the part of our people, young or old, in promiscuous gatherings in which such things are done, or in such gatherings of any other church or society." Any Pastor who became "lax in vigilance" and permitted such things among his people, "shall be held responsible." The following year pastors voted to establish one day a year for the congregations to share a common meal, but one that would specifically exclude those outside the church. The meal was to be, ". . . away from the general public; . . . without revelry, excessive feasting, or evidence of the holiday or picnic spirit." Milley notes, "In retrospect it would appear as though they were permitted to have a meal, but not to have fun."[26]

By 1941, General Conference banned the wearing of flowers or feathers as adornment, and sought to move towards uniformity, ". . . in sister worker hats, and other platform and out-door apparel." In 1947, a dress code for the annual camp meetings was established, and by 1951, an actual uniform consisting of a "plain navy dress" and "plain navy hat and dark stockings"

23. Milley, *Message of Separation*, 11.
24. Ibid., 14.
25. Ibid.
26. Ibid., 16.

was adopted for female workers. While the reader may wonder about the relationship between social engagement and the colour of women's stockings, we emphasize that all of this was intended to create a further separation between the church and the world. As Garrigus complained in a 1946 letter to the General Superintendent, "What a shame that one cannot hardly tell a baptized one from the world—bobbed dresses and bobbed hair have proved to be too great a temptation to withstand . . ."[27]

These examples serve to demonstrate the commitment of one Pentecostal denomination to separation from the world, in matters as seemingly minor as the uniformity of women's hats, to participation in social events sponsored by community clubs or other church groups. In fact, the leadership explicitly believed and taught that the blessing of the Lord in terms of revival of numbers and individuals was directly tied to the quality of separation practiced by church members. While the focus in recent decades within the PAONL has shifted from an isolationist approach[28] to one that focuses more upon internal criteria for being "set apart," the message of separation from the first half of the denomination's history still has a lingering effect, particularly within older generations. From my conversations with members of other classical Pentecostal denominations, it appears that neither the stories of isolationism and legalism, nor the continuing effects into the present day, are unique; similarities abound throughout North American Pentecostalism.

Biblical Mandate

Before leaving this section, we will first pause and consider the Scriptural support for a proper cultural engagement. As others have penned comprehensive treatments of this position,[29] we will simply outline in broad strokes the biblical rationale for engaging culture. Genesis 1:28 is often viewed as providing the original mandate for interaction with creation: "God blessed them and said to them, 'Be fruitful and increase in number; fill the earth and subdue it. Rule over the fish in the sea and the birds in the sky and over every living creature that moves on the ground.'" Though much has been written on the notion of "subduing the earth" in the recent focus on ecological concerns, we may note foundationally that humanity was encouraged to go

---

27. Ibid., 18.

28. Kent Duncan demonstrates a similar transition in the American Assemblies of God. See Duncan, "Emerging Engagement."

29. See for example, Wright, *The Mission of God*; Brueggemann, *The Word That Redescribes the World*.

into the earth and interact with its inhabitants. In this first command given by God, his intention is clear: we shape culture as an exercise of faithful obedience to our creator. Brown notes,

> Read again the extract from Genesis 1 above, and the meaning is clear: cultural shaping or engagement (ruling over the animals, engaging in farming etc.) is not a secular exercise, to be done in some God-ignoring manner. As we are reminded in Psalms 8, cultural shaping or engagement for the Christian means obeying God's pattern for life in how we live day by day in everything. It means denying the false claims of dualism which have restricted Christian activity to the spiritual realm, and it means celebrating the purpose and meaning of the Good News of the gospel in all that we do. Not only is cultural engagement inescapable; the calling for the Christian to engage and shape the culture in a biblically faithful manner also is inescapable.[30]

Jeremiah 29 provides more specific instructions for God's people who live in a context that is not immediately welcoming or shares an affinity in beliefs. With his people in Babylonian exile, God directed:

> This is what the Lord Almighty, the God of Israel, says to all those I carried into exile from Jerusalem to Babylon: "Build houses and settle down; plant gardens and eat what they produce. Marry and have sons and daughters; find wives for your sons and give your daughters in marriage, so that they too may have sons and daughters. Increase in number there; do not decrease. Also, seek the peace and prosperity of the city to which I have carried you into exile. Pray to the Lord for it, because if it prospers, you too will prosper." Yes, this is what the Lord Almighty, the God of Israel, says: "Do not let the prophets and diviners among you deceive you. Do not listen to the dreams you encourage them to have. They are prophesying lies to you in my name. I have not sent them," declares the Lord.

In this passage we observe God's direct command for his people to settle into the foreign culture, accomplishing everything normally associated with human living, all the while seeking the prosperity and peace of the culture in which they found themselves. We see in this letter to the exiles something of Jesus' later description of God's people as those who are *in*, but not *of*, the world.[31] Although the exiles are to go about their lives, and seek the peace and prosperity of their adopted culture, they are not to be

30. Brown, "Is Cultural Engagement Biblical?"
31. John 17: 14–15

swayed by the lies of those who suggest that God is acting immediately to remove them from this foreign culture. J. A. Thompson writes, "Jeremiah by these words cast the people completely adrift from all those things on which they depended and which they regarded as essential to their own well-being: a nation-state, kingship, an army, national borders, the temple. Without all these Yahweh could give the nation new perspectives and a new understanding of their calling."[32] The parallels to the collapse of Christendom in the West are striking; God will provide both a new perspective and a new understanding of the Christian calling once our reliance upon the structures of Christendom ceases.

From Jesus' teaching, I believe we have a clear mandate to engage culture. In Matthew 5, following the Sermon on the Mount, Jesus describes believers as both the "salt of the earth" and "the light of the world." In Jesus' mind, it is inconceivable that salt can be non-salt, or that light would be hidden or would fail to shine. Implicit in Jesus' command to "let your light shine before others" is the challenge to engage the darkness, wherever it may be found. Donald Hagner observes, "The disciples . . . are thus of vital importance for the accomplishment of God's purpose in the world. They constitute the salt and light without which the world cannot survive and remains in darkness. Their mission is accomplished, however, not only in word . . . but in the deeds of their daily existence."[33] Douglas Hare, in observing the common use of the phrase "salt of the earth" today, notes that it is difficult for us to now grasp the power of the original use of this phrase. "We can perhaps catch its force better by substituting another seasoning: 'You are red hot pepper for the whole earth!' In this way we are reminded that the statement refers not to *status*, as if it said 'You are the world's ethical elite,' but to *function*: 'You must add zest to the life of the whole world.'"[34] In a warning to those who would contextualize to the point of assimilation, Hare states, "Any church that adapts itself so completely to the secular world around it that its distinctive calling is forgotten has rendered itself useless. Its vaunted salt has become tasteless and uninteresting."[35] Further, and contrary to popular thought, the key point of the Great Commission[36]

---

32. Thompson, "The Book of Jeremiah," 546.
33. Hagner, "Matt 1–13," 102.
34. Hare, "Matthew," 44.
35. Ibid., 45.

36. Matt 28:18–20 "Then Jesus came to them and said, "All authority in heaven and on earth has been given to me. Therefore go and make disciples of all nations, baptizing them in the name of the Father and of the Son and of the Holy Spirit, and teaching them to obey everything I have commanded you. And surely I am with you always, to the very end of the age."

is not commanding believers to "Go" but to "make disciples." Literally, we may understand Jesus saying, "*Going* into all the world," or "Having gone therefore, into all the world," that is, since you are going anyway, "make disciples"—the command.[37]

The narrative of Paul on Mars Hill provides another excellent example of the biblical injunction to engage culture. In Acts 17:22-31 we read of Paul's discussion with "the men of Athens" concerning their worship of "the Unknown God." We may quickly observe that Paul was interacting with these individuals in the public square, an open area surrounded by government buildings, businesses and temples, where citizenry could gather to discuss political matters. Paul did not wait for the curious to seek out proper teaching at the Christian place of worship, but sought an audience with the Athenians on their own turf. Well-trained in the rhetorical styles of his day, and familiar with their Epicurean and Stoic philosophers, he was able to engage these seekers of Athens on their own terms, in a manner readily accessible. Paul's explanation of the Gospel was replete with references to their own poets and philosophers, and is a model of how we may translate Christ's message to those holding a decidedly non-Christian worldview. William Larkin notes, "Paul's preaching at Athens shows us how God's messenger made inroads into the very center of a culture's religious and intellectual life. A fearless proclamation of Jesus and the Resurrection within the framework of God's work as transcendent Creator, immanent sustainer, and righteous savior may have brought mockery, but it also yielded adherents."[38]

In 1 Corinthians 9 Paul describes his efforts to contextualize the Good News of Christ:

> Though I am free and belong to no one, I have made myself a slave to everyone, to win as many as possible. To the Jews I became like a Jew, to win the Jews. To those under the law I became like one under the law (though I myself am not under the law), so as to win those under the law. To those not having the law I became like one not having the law (though I am not free from God's law but am under Christ's law), so as to win those not having the law. To the weak I became weak, to win the weak. I have become all things to all people so that by all

---

37. Some scholars note that as a circumstantial participle that depends on the imperative, "going" gains imperatival force of its own. We may conclude that though Jesus assumes the disciples are going, and commands them to make disciples, the force of his statement suggests that refusing to go is not an option. See Kurtzhan, "Exegesis of Matt 28:18-20."

38. Trites and Larkin, "The Gospel of Luke Acts," 549.

possible means I might save some. I do all this for the sake of the gospel, that I may share in its blessings.

We may not translate Paul's efforts at contextualization into a perception that he was willing to transform the message itself into whatever was most palatable to his listeners. Ben Witherington observes, "Furthermore, his accommodating behavior has clear limits. He does not say that he became an idolater to idolaters or an adulterer to adulterers. But in matters that he did not see as ethically or theologically essential or implied by the gospel, Paul believed in flexibility."[39] He insisted that his message was simply one of "Jesus Christ and him crucified"[40] and encouraged Timothy to "Watch your life and doctrine closely,"[41] for the time will come when people will not put up with "sound doctrine" and will listen only to that which tickles their fancy.[42] Indeed, Paul learned how to present the Gospel in a manner accessible to a variety of cultural settings, without negating the core of Jesus' message, or softening the call to repentance, sacrifice, and death to self. We would do well to model the same, recalling the admonition from the writer of Jude: "Dear friends, although I was very eager to write to you about the salvation we share, I felt compelled to write and urge you to *contend for the faith* that was once for all entrusted to God's holy people."

Summary of Project

With a clear biblical command to share the Good News, and mindful of Paul's efforts at contextualization while holding firm to the faith so long ago entrusted, this study seeks to assist Pentecostalism as it endeavours to navigate an increasingly post-Christian culture—contending for the faith, as it were, in a context both similar and dissimilar to the first century. I trust this project will serve as both a primer on current realities and a stimulus for discussion and action going forward. To accomplish this, chapter 1 has first explored briefly the religious changes in Canadian culture in the last one hundred years, via a consideration of the various options for understanding in what sense a country might be considered "Christian." Essential terms have been defined and a foundational background for the topics to be covered has been laid. Chapter 2 will commence the contextual focus of Part One. It will first move to examine Pentecostalism both in a historic

---

39. Witherington, "Conflict and Community in Corinth," 213.
40. 1 Cor 2:2
41. 1 Tim 4:16
42. 1 Tim 4:3

and theological sense. We will trace the growth of global Pentecostal from the Azusa Street revival of 1906, to the movement that today numbers more than 600 million souls. The peculiarities of Pentecostal doctrine will be considered, as will praxis that has developed over the decades in a very real Pentecostal subculture.

Chapter 3 will explore the current societal context in Canada that Pentecostals must learn to engage properly. To begin, we will continue our discussion of post-Christendom begun in chapter 1, via a comprehensive survey of the state of religious faith in Canada. Through this we will seek to discern whether Pentecostals in Canada are indeed facing a secularist culture moving towards post-Christendom, as many are proclaiming. We will then move to an examination of postmodernism, and its role in the rapidly changing face of North American religious culture. Pentecostals may in fact be in an excellent position to engage a culture steeped in the tenets of postmodernism, but only if they recognize postmodern thought for what it is, and respond appropriately.

Part Two examines the Pentecostal Assemblies of Newfoundland and Labrador (PAONL) specifically as an example denomination for the project. Desiring to observe the trends discussed above in a particular Pentecostal denomination, significant attention will be given to exploring the impact of post-Christian thought on the Pentecostals of Newfoundland and Labrador. Further, we will seek to observe the reaction (or lack thereof) to changing cultural tides by this classical Pentecostal body.

Having provided sufficient background for our discussion, and having observed the situation of the PAONL, we will then move to eight themes that I believe must be considered as Pentecostals move forward. We will give concrete examples of ways Pentecostals can engage Western culture, while remaining confident that we remain *in*, but not *of*, the world around us. Part Three and its focus on practical application and solutions begins with chapter 5, which examines the various generations that currently compose Pentecostalism in the West. At present, up to six generations currently worship together at a typical Christian gathering: children, Millennials, Generation X, Baby Boomers, Builders, and Seniors. The contribution and significance of generational traits will be examined for each of the generations, with particular attention paid to the impact of each on Canadian Pentecostalism. This chapter therefore engages our first theme—Generational Issues.

We then move to chapter 6 for a look back at an early Pentecostal pioneer who was a master at engaging culture—Aimee Semple McPherson. The founder of the International Church of the Foursquare Gospel—a classical Pentecostal denomination—McPherson packed a 5300 seat auditorium three times daily in 1920s Los Angeles. Despite being located next to what many considered the sin and entertainment capital of the United States—Hollywood—McPherson was able to combine cutting edge media presentations of the timeless gospel with a willingness to share the good news with many of the "untouchables" of the day. She is an exceptional example of the importance of a correct approach to our second theme—creativity and risk. Her attitudes and approach are worth examining, for she was incredibly successful in the same arenas that much of contemporary Pentecostalism today languishes.

Chapter 7 will then shift focus to the present, and inquire about the promise of the recent Missional conversation for classical Pentecostalism in this hour. Arguing that the contemporary church has become far too inward focused, Missional authors insist that believers must re-envision the purpose of the Church, and cast a new vision of community involvement and outreach. "Come out from among them and be ye separate"[43] has been replaced, as it were, with the simple command to "Go ye into all the world . . ."[44] Given Pentecostalism's penchant for withdrawal from all things "worldly" in their pursuit of holiness, theme #3, the Missional conversation, will bring a significant and timely message to Canadian Pentecostalism.

On the religious front, chapter 7 will continue by examining the cultural significance of the Emerging/Emergent[45] Church movement. Though not quickly visible, or even accepted throughout much of Canadian evangelicalism, the Emergent Church nonetheless has a significant voice and is influential in the younger generations of Canadian Pentecostals. This chapter will serve to explore theme #4—Pentecostals as Influencers of Culture.

Chapter 8 will seek to address themes #5 (reclaiming our supernatural heritage) and #6 (embracing post-Christendom). We begin by coming back to the groundwork on postmodernism began in chapter 3, but now with an eye towards a proper Pentecostal engagement of a culture influenced by postmodern thought. This chapter concludes with a discussion on the importance of engaging culture where we find it. We will examine the increasing need for Western Pentecostalism to seize the opportunities afforded the church through the decline of Christendom and growth of secularism. Though many Christians and churches are quite aware of the changes in culture recently, some seem confused or afraid of the loss of a Christian dominance in culture that has provided comfort throughout their lifetime.

---

43. 2 Cor 6:17

44. Matt 16:15

45. The term *Emerging church* is used generically to reference those churches actively seeking to reach communities influenced by postmodern thought. *Emergent churches* were specifically connected to the Emergent Village organization. See Carlson, "Emerging Vs. Emergent Churches."

Fewer have recognized the tremendous possibilities that accompany the death of Christendom, and we will seek to assist in that regard.

Concluding our efforts to explore practical steps Pentecostalism can take to once again engage and impact for Christ the culture around it, chapter 9 will address our final two themes. Few doctrines are as important to Pentecostals as that of Spirit Baptism. On the doctrinal front, Pentecostalism must therefore closely examine its "distinctive doctrines"—subsequence and initial evidence. While some classical Pentecostals have held to these understandings of Spirit-baptism with a dogmatism one would think reserved for only the most foundational pillars of the gospel, others have expressed considerable reservations about the traditional expressions of the practice, if not dogma, that have arguably made Pentecostalism into the worldwide force it currently is. I will argue that neither the retreat into increasingly dogmatic positions nor the abandoning of that which has been most highly cherished by Pentecostalism, will benefit the movement well into the future. Pentecostals must consider the importance of theme #7, and reflect on the difference in the *essence of Pentecostalism, versus doctrinal distinctives*.

How will Pentecostals bring change to such a key doctrine for identity? I believe they would do well to consider our final theme—the difference in *belief* and *values*. While beliefs as such are important, only those things we actually value impact our behaviours. It is possible that on a number of core doctrines, Pentecostals are simply giving mental assent to that which they traditionally valued quite highly. The results are problematic and telling.

Part Four will conclude with a final chapter on conclusions from our study. A summary of lessons learned will be given, and we will explore the various limitations of this study. Finally, areas of research will be suggested for those who wish to pursue these topics with further study.

— 2 —

Pentecostalism in North America

History, Growth, and Theology

THOUGH PENTECOSTALISM MAY SEEM to differ in many respects from other expressions of western Christianity, the distinctives are often less extensive than they appear. As heirs of the Reformation, Pentecostals are theologically orthodox by Protestant standards, and uphold key doctrines including justification by faith, the authority of Scripture, the deity of Christ, and the Trinity.[1] Pentecostalism's strong emphasis on a second work of grace does, however, differentiate it from other conservative Protestants. All evangelical groups believe and teach the necessity of a conversion event, during which the unregenerate individual is met by the grace of God and regenerated by the Holy Spirit. Pentecostals however, teach the importance of a second experience, that of the Baptism in the Holy Spirit, distinct from the reception of the Spirit at conversion.

To begin setting the context for our study of Pentecostalism and its reaction to an increasingly secular environment, we must first provide sufficient background to the Pentecostal movement. This chapter will explore theological precursors to Pentecostalism, before examining the Azusa Street revival itself. Following that we will discuss the first century of the Pentecostal movement, including the global reach of Pentecostalism and the rise of the Charismatic movement. We will conclude with an overview of the "distinctives" of Pentecostal doctrine, and how these beliefs have contributed to a particular Pentecostal praxis and subculture.

---

1. Spittler, "Theological Style among Pentecostals and Charismatics," 296. The exception here would be the small minority of Pentecostals who hold to Oneness views. See Reed, *In Jesus' Name*; Boyd, *Oneness Pentecostals and the Trinity*.

Theological Antecedents of Pentecostalism

We begin by exploring the historical background[2] of the second work doctrine at both the academic and popular levels. Starting with the writings of John Wesley, the furtherance of the idea can be clearly found in the thought of the Holiness movement, and that of evangelists Dwight Moody and Reuben Torrey. In each of these Pentecostalism is rooted. In the coming pages we will observe the shift in focus of this doctrine from that of entire sanctification to empowerment for service.

John Wesley

The first historical occurrence of the doctrine of a second blessing is debated among scholars[3], though in all such discussions, the writings of John Wesley figure prominently. Wesley's belief in a second work of grace came through his study and preaching on the doctrine of sanctification. Beginning in 1739 and continuing until 1777, he issued and repeatedly revised his beliefs concerning perfection in a tract entitled, "A Plain Account of Christian Perfection as Believed and Taught by the Reverend Mr. John Wesley."[4] This 81-page document has become a veritable manifesto for various holiness groups since it was written.[5]

Harald Lindstrom argues that prior to his conversion in 1738, Wesley believed in perfection as something the Christian was commanded to strive for but could never procure. After his conversion and realization that justification is obtained by faith alone, he saw sanctification as something that might be achieved in similar fashion. Each is a gift of God, unattainable by any other means than *sola fides*.[6]

Most scholars agree that Wesley did perceive sanctification as an act of God, subsequent to salvation, completing the process of holiness begun at

---

2. This section is abbreviated from Noel, "The Historical Roots of the Second Work Doctrine."

3. See Dunn, "Spirit-Baptism and Pentecostalism." Dunn believes the move toward two distinct works began with the Puritans, from whom Wesley borrowed the idea. This was not conclusively demonstrated, nor referred to in the other works consulted. For further reading on the Holy Spirit in Puritan thought, see Nuttall, *The Holy Spirit in Puritan Faith and Experience*.

4. Wesley, *The Works of John Wesley*, 366–446.

5. Dieter et al, *Five Views of Sanctification*, 37.

6. Lindstrom, *Wesley and Sanctification*, 133.

conversation.[7] The clearest and most convincing evidence of Wesley's second work doctrine are the words of Wesley himself:

> But does God work this great work in the soul gradually or instantaneously? Perhaps it may be gradually wrought in some . . . but it is infinitely desirable, were it the will of God that it should be done instantaneously; that the Lord should destroy sin 'by the breath of his mouth,' in a moment, in the twinkling of an eye. And so he generally does; a plain fact, of which there is evidence enough to satisfy any unprejudiced person. *Thou* therefore look for it every moment! Look for it every day, every hour, every moment! Why not this hour, this moment? Certainly you may look for it *now*, if you believe it is by faith. And by this token you may surely know whether you seek it by faith or by works. If by works, you want something to be done *first, before* you are sanctified. If you seek it by faith, you may expect it *as you are*; and if as you are, then expect it *now*. It is of importance to observe that there is an inseparable connection between these three points—Expect it *by faith*, Expect it *as you are*, and Expect it *now*![8]

Clearly, Wesley believed in entire sanctification as a work wrought by God, in an experience subsequent to salvation.[9] This is the first step in tracing the Pentecostal doctrine of the baptism of the Holy Spirit as a second work of grace. Once it was clear that the "moment" of entire sanctification was emphasized in Wesleyan thought, the question naturally arose as to whether it was appropriate to describe this moment in terms of the baptism of the Holy Spirit. Wesley's designated successor, John Fletcher, was keen on using the phrase[10], but Wesley appears to have resisted. He insisted that, "the phrase in that sense is not scriptural and not quite proper; for they all 'received the Holy Ghost' when they were justified."[11] For Fletcher's part, he agreed to disagree on this issue, commenting,

---

7. See Synan, *The Holiness-Pentecostal Movement in the United States*, 19; Dieter et al, *Five Views of Sanctification*, 17; Cannon, *The Theology of John Wesley*, 242; Flew, *The Idea of Perfection in Christian Theology*, 329–41; Lindstrom, *Wesley and Sanctification*, 132–33. Typically, not everyone agrees with the preceding statement.

8. Wesley, "The Scripture Way of Salvation," 53.

9. Though not all are in agreement; in particular those who wish to claim Wesley but not Pentecostalism. See McPherson, "John Wesley's Views of Spirit Baptism."

10. Dunn, "Spirit-Baptism and Pentecostalism," 399.

11. Telford, *The Letters of the Rev. John Wesley, A.M.*, 214–15. Hollenweger, though, concludes, perhaps in an assumption, that Wesley equated entire sanctification with the baptism in the Holy Spirit. See Hollenweger, *The Pentecostals*, 21.

You will find my views on this matter in Mr. Wesley's sermons on Christian Perfection and on Scriptural Christianity; with this difference, that I would distinguish more exactly between the believer baptized with the Pentecostal power of the Holy Ghost, and the believer who, like the Apostles after our Lord's ascension, is not yet filled with that power.[12]

Fletcher's ideas were the beginning of what would later become a significant Pentecostal doctrine and are the first hint of the change in focus from holiness in Methodism, to power in Pentecostalism.

The Holiness Movement

When Methodism was transplanted to American soil the doctrine of entire sanctification came with it. In the earliest recorded Methodist sermon in the United States, dating back to 1766, Captain Thomas Webb declared, "The words of the text were written by the Apostles after the act of justification had passed on them. But you see, my friends, this was not enough for them. They must receive the Holy Ghost after this. So must you. You must be sanctified . . ."[13] This is the initial tying together of the second work with the baptism of the Holy Spirit in America. As Methodism spread, so did this theology.[14]

Phoebe Palmer

Meetings known as the "Tuesday Meeting for the Promotion of Holiness" became, over a sixty-year period, a magnet for those interested in holiness, both as a movement and for themselves.[15] A leader in the holiness movement, Phoebe Palmer was the first to popularize the vocabulary associated with Pentecostalism. She began to use the phrase "baptism of the Holy Spirit," which she felt was synonymous with "entire sanctification."[16] Her teaching that a Pentecostal baptism of the Holy Ghost was every believer's privilege and duty was widely circulated.[17]

12. Tyerman, *Wesley's Designated Successor*, 411.
13. Hurst, *The History of Methodism*, 1252.
14. Noll, *A History of Christianity*, 173. See also Richardson, "Methodist Revivalism," 21–36.
15. Noll, *A History of Christianity*, 182.
16. Riss, *A Survey of 20th-Century Revival Movements*, 18.
17. Ibid.

In her "shorter way" to holiness, she outlines three steps, each of which focuses on the human decision: 1) entire consecration; 2) faith, that is, believing we have already received that which we have asked for; 3) and testimony to the fact that we have received it, whether or not we have felt anything. The difference between Palmer's attitudes and Wesley's early thought are tremendously significant. Whereas Wesley had originally believed in holiness as a life-long pursuit, full of hard work and many failures, Palmer seems to be a forerunner of the "name it and claim it" theologies. Holiness is now a matter of the proper human steps, secured by faith, not by hard work and perseverance. Palmer's influence on Pentecostalism can hardly be overemphasized. Indeed, she has been called, "the missing link between Methodist and Pentecostal spirituality."[18]

Charles G. Finney

In the decades before the U.S. Civil War[19], Charles Grandison Finney (1792–1875) emerged as the best-known revivalist in the United States.[20] As such, he impacted the religious thought of America in several ways that would help to prepare the way for Pentecostalism.[21] Conventionally, in the Calvinistic pattern of the First Great Awakening under Edwards, salvation was firmly in the hands of God alone. Under Finney, however, the focus began to change dramatically. His revivalism was for the "whosoever will" and stressed the free will of humanity. Conversion was understood less as a process, and more as a crisis experience, gained in a moment of time.[22] This transformation in the understanding of conversion helped prepare the way for a similar move in the doctrine of sanctification.

> These developments were a necessary prelude to what would follow. Once "crisis" overwhelms "process" to make sanctification primarily an event occurring at a definite point in time—that is, when sanctification has been largely absorbed into entire sanctification—and once the teleological thrust of Christian perfection is transmuted into an initiatory experience that usually follows rapidly on conversion, the stage has been set

18. Knight, "From Aldersgate to Azusa," 86.
19. The US Civil War occurred from 1861–1865.
20. Noll, *A History of Christianity*, 174. See also Finney, *Memoirs*.
21. While beyond the scope of this work, detailed information on Finney's revival measures may be found. See Finney, *Lectures on Revivals of Religion*.
22. Douglas and Clouse, *New 20th Century Encyclopedia of Religious Knowledge*, 715. See also Sweet, *Religion in the Development of American Culture*.

for the re-emergence of the Pentecostal formulation of entire sanctification.[23]

John L. Gresham, in *Charles G. Finney's Doctrine of the Baptism of the Holy Spirit,* argues that Finney laid new emphasis on the doctrine of Spirit-baptism. Not only was the baptism essential for sanctification, but also for *empowerment for service*. "Finney's later discussions of the baptism in the Holy Spirit revolved around those two themes: sanctification and usefulness. The baptism was presented either as a cleansing, liberating experience or as an act of empowerment for ministry."[24] Finney wrote, "If filled with the Spirit, you will be useful. You cannot help being useful. Even if you were sick and unable to go out of your room, or to converse, and saw nobody, you would be ten times more useful than a hundred of those common sort of Christians who have no spirituality."[25] This tendency to interpret the baptism of the Holy Spirit in terms of sanctification *and* power for service is an important theme, and one that will be of great significance for early Pentecostalism.

Pre-Pentecostal Doctrine

Perhaps the most influential spokesman on the Baptism of the Holy Spirit was Dwight L. Moody (1837–1899). In his book *Secret Power*[26] Moody outlines what he believes is the cause for the lack of spiritual effectiveness in believers of his time—a failure to be empowered by the Holy Spirit. He distinguishes clearly between the reception of the Spirit at conversion, and the subsequent empowering for service. Unlike the later Pentecostals, he does not seem to clearly expound the notion of *one* future empowering, or Spirit-baptism. Moody leaves open the possibility of many occurring over the course of a lifetime, empowering and energizing the Christian for service.

> The Holy Spirit dwelling in us is one thing; I think this is clearly brought out in Scripture. And the Holy Spirit upon us for service is another thing. I think it is clearly taught in Scripture that every believer has the Holy Ghost dwelling in Him . . . But I want to call your attention to another fact. I believe, today, that

---

23. Dayton, *Theological Roots*, 70.

24. Gresham, *Charles G. Finney's Doctrine*, 15. See also Knight, "From Aldersgate to Azusa," 88.

25 Shelhamer, *Finney on Revival*, 114. See also Anderson, *Vision of the Disinherited*, 41. Anderson believes that Finney placed more emphasis on power than perfection.

26. Moody, *Secret Power*.

though Christian men and women have the Holy Spirit dwelling in them, yet He is not dwelling within them in power.[27]

Another well-known advocate of the Pentecostal view of sanctification and empowerment came from Reuben A. Torrey (1856–1928),[28] the long-time associate of Moody. While Torrey did not support the doctrine that would become the "initial evidence" position of Pentecostals, he nonetheless clearly expounded their views concerning the purpose of Spirit-baptism. He taught that "the baptism with the Holy Spirit is a definite experience of which one may and ought to know whether he has received it or not,"[29] and "it is evident that the baptism with the Holy Spirit is an operation of the Holy Spirit distinct from and additional to His regenerating work."[30]

In addition, he wrote:

> The purpose of the baptism with the Holy Spirit is not primarily to make believers individually holy. I do not say that it is not the work of the Holy Spirit to make believers holy, for as we have already seen, He is "the Spirit of holiness," and the only way we shall ever attain unto holiness is by His power. I do not even say that the baptism with the Holy Spirit will not result in a great spiritual transformation and uplift and cleansing . . . *but the primary purpose of the baptism with the Holy Spirit is efficiency in testimony and service.*[31]

We have now traced the doctrine of a second work, subsequent to conversion, through the writings of John Wesley, and into the theology of the forerunners of Pentecostalism. We have seen the gradual connection

---

27. Ibid., 47–51.

28. Torrey wrote several books on the Holy Spirit, including *The Person and Work of the Holy Spirit*, and *The Holy Spirit: Who He Is and What He Does*.

29. Torrey, *The Person and Work of the Holy Spirit*, 147.

30. Ibid., 149.

31. Ibid., 155–56. By the time the Spirit of God began to fall on worshippers at Azusa Street in 1906, the religious world was well prepared to understand the occurrence in terms of "the baptism of the Holy Spirit." The dominant issue for many involved in the debate, however, consisted of integrating the "perfection" and "cleansing" motifs of Wesleyanism, with the increasing theme of "power" in Pentecostalism. The solution of some, such as Mrs. Palmer and others, involved combining the two. She suggested that "holiness *is* power" and that "purity and power are identical." See Palmer, *The Promise of the Father*, 206; Palmer, *Pioneer Experiences*. Charles Finney tended to understand the baptism in terms of both sanctification *and* power, as has been demonstrated above. Others such as E.P. Ellyson and Russell Bryum taught that when the Holy Spirit came in His fullness, He cleansed the vessel from abiding sin, and through His indwelling presence, empowered the believer for active service. See Ellyson, *Doctrinal Studies*, 106; Bryum, *Holy Spirit Baptism and the 2nd Cleansing*, 18.

between the baptism of the Holy Spirit and the second work. The movement from sanctification as the purpose of this work to empowerment for service was also unhurried, taking shape in the thought and teachings of individuals such as Mrs. Palmer, Charles Finney, D.L. Moody, and R.A. Torrey. From this rich background the theological ground had been tilled for the planting of the Pentecostal movement, with its unwavering emphasis on an empowering baptism of the Holy Spirit subsequent to conversion. Clearly, the foundation had been laid for the Pentecostal movement to interpret the occurrences of Azusa Street in terms of the Baptism of the Holy Spirit as an empowering for service and witness. To Los Angeles, and the revival that helped spread Pentecostalism across the globe, we now turn.

Azusa Street

Charles Parham may rightly be called the founder of Pentecostal theology,[32] for it was he who first developed the distinctive Pentecostal doctrine[33] of glossolalia as the initial evidence of Spirit-baptism.[34] For Parham, tongues-speech was the necessary evidence that one had been baptized in the Holy Spirit; without this evidence, one could not consider the experience valid.[35] He stated that, "Speaking in other tongues is an inseparable part of the Baptism of the Holy Spirit distinguishing it from all previous works; and no one has received the Baptism of the Holy Spirit who has not a Bible evidence to

---

32. The following is briefly summarized from relevant sections of Noel, *Pentecostal and Postmodern Hermeneutics*.

33. As has been demonstrated, a number of prominent individuals had set the groundwork in place for this "new" doctrine, including Wesley, Finney, Palmer, Moody, and Torrey. Beginning with Wesley's teaching of a second blessing for sanctification, this gradually moved into a focus on power for witness.

34. Noel, *Pentecostal and Postmodern*, 18. Some scholars distinguish carefully between the founder of Pentecostal theology, as such, and the founder of the Pentecostal movement. Harry Letson suggests that it was Seymour's "vision, leadership, teaching and drive," which "kept the whole thing on track." Letson concludes that while Seymour is the founder of modern Pentecostalism, it was Parham who initiated a new paradigm shift within Christianity known as Pentecostalism. See Letson, "Pentecostalism as a Paradigm Shift." Walter Hollenweger would settle the matter by suggesting that the choice depends on one's understanding of the essence of Pentecostalism. If it is found in a particular doctrine about a particular experience, Parham is key. If, however, the essence lies in the oral, missionary nature of Pentecostalism, that was able to break down barriers and bring equality to the marginalized, then Seymour gets the nod. See Hollenweger, "The Black Roots of Pentecostalism," 42–43.

35. Jacobson, *Thinking in the Spirit*, 18–19. On Parham, see also Goff, *Fields White Unto Harvest*.

show for it."[36] In 1905, Parham launched a Bible school in Houston, Texas, as an outlet for his preaching of the Pentecostal message. Among his notable students during this period was William J. Seymour, who due to local segregation laws was only permitted to listen to the lectures from the hallway outside the classroom. Despite this challenge, Seymour became the leader of the Azusa Street outpouring in Los Angeles just one year hence.[37]

As the pastor of the Azusa Street Revival, Seymour effectively oversaw the revival that spawned the Pentecostal movement today. In February 1906, Seymour received an invitation to pastor in Los Angeles, and armed with Parham's Spirit-baptism theology, arrived shortly thereafter. He began a series of Bible studies at the home of Richard and Ruth Asbury at 214 Bonnie Bray Street, and within weeks, several of the participants, including Seymour, had experienced the Baptism of the Holy Spirit with the "Bible evidence" of speaking in tongues.[38] Soon Seymour was forced to look for more spacious accommodations, and quickly settled upon the former sanctuary of an African Methodist Episcopal Church at 312 Azusa Street. A description of the mission from the time of the revival is worth quoting at length:

> The center of this work is an old wooden Methodist church, marked for sale, partly burned out, recovered by a flat roof and made into two flats by a floor. It is unplastered, simply whitewashed on the rough boarding. Upstairs is a long room, furnished with chairs and three Redwood planks, laid end to end on backless chairs. This is the Pentecostal "upper room,"v where sanctified souls seek Pentecostal fullness, and go out speaking in new tongues and calling for the old-time references to "new wine."
>
> There are smaller rooms where hands are laid on the sick and they recover, as of old. Below is a room 40x60 feet, filled with odds and ends of chairs, benches, and backless seats, where the curious and eager sit for hours listening to strange sounds and songs and exhortations from the skies. In the centre of the big room is a box on end, covered with cotton, which a junk man would value at about 15 cents. This is the pulpit from which is sounded forth what the leader, Brother Seymour, calls old-time repentance, old-time pardon, old-time sanctification, old-time power over devils and diseases, and the old-time Baptism with the Holy Ghost and fire.
>
> Meetings begin at 10 o'clock every morning and are continued until near midnight. There are three altar services daily.

---

36. Parham, *Kol Kare Bomidbar*, 35.
37. Goff, "Parham, Charles Fox."
38. Robeck, "Seymour, William Joseph." Also see Borlase, *William Seymour*.

> The altar is a plank on two chairs in the center of the room, and here the Holy Ghost falls on men and women and children in old Pentecostal fashion as soon as they have a clear experience of heart purity. Proud preachers and laymen with great heads, filled and inflated with all kinds of theories and beliefs, have come here from all parts, have humbled themselves and got down on the straw matting, and have thrown away their notions, and have wept in conscious emptiness before God and begged to be "endued with power from on high," and every honest believer has received the wonderful incoming of the Holy Spirit to fill and thrill and melt and energize his physical frame and faculties, and the Spirit has witnessed to his presence by using the vocal organs in the speaking forth of a "new tongue."[39]

The Spirit of God was reported to have moved mightily in their midst and many people received the baptism in the Holy Spirit. News of these events spread throughout Los Angeles and people came from a variety of churches to participate. Some churches lost so many members that they closed their doors and attached themselves to the revival. Meetings were not typically planned; leadership relied instead on the leading of the Holy Spirit. Attendees reported extensive times of praise and worship with special attention given to prayer. Preaching was "as the Spirit led" and wasn't reserved for clergy alone; anyone who felt led could speak.[40]

The Azusa Street revival began primarily with the working class but grew to include all manner of individuals coming from completely variegated backgrounds. People from many different denominations attended, people of every racial background were welcome, and both genders worshipped together and took on leadership roles. This caused no small amount of negative feedback for the Pentecostals, as this came at the height of segregation and before women had won the right to vote. Indeed, it may be argued that in the initial days Pentecostals differed from other denominations as much in their egalitarian views as they did for their belief in manifestations of the supernatural, including glossolalia.[41]

The Press were especially harsh in their descriptions of this new religious movement. The description from the *Los Angeles Times* on April 18, 1906, begins with the headings "*Weird Babel of Tongues. New Sect of Fanatics is Breaking Loose. Wild Scene Last Night on Azusa Street. Gurgle of Wordless Talk by a Sister.*" The article itself wasn't any more encouraging:

39. "Way of Faith."

40. Hollenweger, "The Black Roots of Pentecostalism," 42–43.

41. Robeck, *The Azusa Street Mission and Revival*, 137. Also see Synan, *The Century of the Holy Spirit*, 54–55.

> Meetings are held in a tumble-down shack on Azusa Street, near San Pedro Street, and the devotees of the weird doctrine practice the most fanatical rites, preach the wildest theories and work themselves into a state of mad excitement in their peculiar zeal. Colored people and a sprinkling of whites compose the congregation, and night is made hideous in the neighbourhood by the howlings of the worshippers, who spend hours swaying forth and back in a nervous racking attitude of prayer and supplication. They claim to have the "gift of tongues" and to be able to understand the babel.
>
> An old colored preacher, blind in one eye, is the majordomo of the company. With his stony optic fixed on some luckless believer, the old man yells his defiance and challenges an answer. Anathemas are heaped upon him who shall dare to gainsay the utterances of the preacher.
>
> "You-oo-oo gou-loo-loo come under the bloo-oo-oo boo-loo," shouts an old colored "mammy," in a frenzy of religious zeal. Swinging her arms wildly about her, she continues with the strangest harangue ever uttered. Few of her words are intelligible, and for the most part her testimony contains the most outrageous jumble of syllables, which are listened to with awe by the company."[42]

The revival at the Azusa Street Mission burned brightly until mid-1908, and arose once again in 1911, but thereafter ceased forever. At its peak, the small Mission would be packed to capacity by the faithful, those seeking their own Pentecostal baptism, and critics who had come to solidify their opposition to this noisy and undignified movement. The word began to spread far and wide of what was happening at this little mission, and even spread to other countries. In fact, a part of each service at Azusa Street was kept for reading letters of what had happened after other churches began to pray and seek for their own baptism of the Holy Spirit. Out of the Azusa Street Mission came many leaders empowered for ministry by the Holy Spirit, who founded Pentecostal churches of their own across America, as well as many leaders of other denominations who took the Pentecostal message back to their own church and led their people into the Pentecostal revival as well. From Azusa Street, the Pentecostal message and experience spread rapidly throughout the earth.[43]

---

42. Synan, *The Century of the Holy Spirit*, 58–59.

43. For more on the history and impact of the Azusa Street revival and the subsequent Pentecostal movement, see Robeck, *The Azusa Street Mission and Revival*; Hunter and Robeck, *The Azusa Street Revival and Its Legacy*; Owens, *The Azusa Street Revival*; Hyatt, *Fire on the Earth*; Dempster, *The Globalization of Pentecostalism*; Valdez Sr, *Fire*

The Global Spread of the Pentecostal Movement

In the decades following the Azusa Street revival, Pentecostalism spread to nearly every corner of the world. Azusa was undoubtedly important: for several years after 1906 the revival continued without ceasing, and from this flowed Seymour's *The Apostolic Faith* periodical, which at its peak reached an international circulation of 50,000. A recognized authority on the globalization of Pentecostalism, Allan Anderson, notes that at least twenty-six denominations trace their origins to Azusa Street, including the two largest: the Church of God in Christ and the Assemblies of God. "In a real sense, the Azusa Street revival marks the beginning of classical Pentecostalism and [from there], the revival reached to other parts of the world."[44] Anderson writes,

> From its beginning, North American Pentecostalism placed an emphasis on evangelism and missions. People came from as far away as Europe and went back there with the "baptism"; and Pentecostal missionaries were sent out from Azusa Street, reaching over twenty-five nations in two years, including places as far away as China, India, Japan, Egypt, Liberia, Angola and South Africa. This was no mean achievement and the beginning of what is arguably the most significant global expansion of a Christian movement in the history of Christianity.[45]

Interestingly, while much of the growth can be attributed directly to Azusa, Pentecostalism also sprang up in various locations with no connection to the revival in Los Angeles. Some scholars have argued while the Azusa revival was certainly of central importance, the 'myth' of Azusa Street is that it alone was responsible for the spread of Pentecostalism worldwide.[46] Though the Azusa revival clearly had the greatest impact on the growth of Pentecostalism worldwide, there were several "Pentecostal" revivals prior to 1906 that are not as widely recognized. During the Welsh revival of 1904–5, for example, ". . . the Pentecostal presence and power of the Holy Spirit was emphasized, and meetings were hours long, spontaneous, seemingly chaotic and emotional, with 'singing in the Spirit' (using ancient Welsh chants), simultaneous and loud prayer, revelatory visions and prophecy, all emphasizing the immediacy of God in the services and in personal experience."[47] The revival at Pandita Ramabai's Mukti Mission in Kedgaon, northeastern India,

---

on Azusa Street; Dayton, *The Theological Roots of Pentecostalism*.

44. Anderson, *An Introduction to Pentecostalism*, 42.
45. Ibid.
46. Anderson, "The Origins of Pentecostalism."
47. Anderson, *An Introduction to Pentecostalism*, 36.

included, "tears of repentance and confession, emotional and prolonged prayer meetings, powerful demonstrations of the Spirit including healings, prophecy, and speaking in tongues and interpretation . . . "[48] Frank Bartleman, a participant in the Azusa revival, later wrote, "The present worldwide revival was rocked in the cradle of little Wales. It was brought up in India, following; becoming full-grown in Los Angeles later."[49] We note the order here is reversed from the common perception of Azusa outwards to the rest of the world. Likewise, the "Korean Pentecost" of 1907–8, unaffiliated with Azusa, was likened by an eyewitness to the Day of Pentecost in Acts 2, and included the typical Pentecostal practices of healing the sick, miracles, and casting out demons.[50]

Further, while recognizing the significant role of Azusa in the worldwide spread of Pentecostalism, Allan Anderson emphasizes that all "Pentecostalisms" were not "made in the USA" via the influence of Western missionaries; local pastors played an equally significant, but often unrecognized role. He writes,

> Despite the undeniably courageous work of the early Pentecostal missionaries from the West, the equally important contribution of African, Asian, Latin American, Caribbean, and Pacific evangelists and pastors at the beginning should also be acknowledged. This involves recognizing that much of Pentecostalism's rapid expansion in the twentieth century was not only due to the labours of missionaries from North American and Western Europe to Africa, Asia and Latin America, but was especially the result of the spontaneous contextualization of the Pentecostal message by thousands of local preachers who traversed these continents with a new message of the power of the Spirit, healing the sick and casting out demons.[51]

Both through the Azusa Street revival, and through seemingly spontaneous revivals around the globe, Pentecostalism was by the 1930s, a global movement.

---

48. Anderson, "To All Points of the Compass."
49. Bartleman, *Azusa Street*, 152.
50. Anderson, "The Origins of Pentecostalism."
51. Ibid.

Characteristics of Early Pentecostalism

Although descriptions of Pentecostalism in the early years are varied, there are widely agreed upon features that accurately characterize the movement in its first decade. William and Robert Menzies, long-time Pentecostal scholars and missionaries, have helpfully summarized these into eight distinguishing marks.[52] First, as might be expected, Pentecostals were known for their emphasis on *Baptism in the Spirit* with glossolalic evidence. Though an unpopular doctrine throughout Christendom that caused no small amount of antagonism towards the new movement, early Pentecostals were passionate about their experience in the Holy Spirit, and biblical teaching about that experience. Many Pentecostals identified closely with the recipients of the initial outpouring of the Spirit in Acts, and expected similar treatment.[53] As will be discussed, their participation in the "Latter Rain" of the Spirit's outpouring was for many the fulfilling of biblical prophecy.

In line with this, early Pentecostals demonstrated an incredible *commitment to evangelism and missions*. With their understanding of the prophesied Latter Rain, and Spirit baptism as an empowerment for witness, Pentecostalism exhibited a sense of urgency for reaching the lost with the Gospel of Jesus Christ. This missionary zeal formed in part the impetus for the organization of early Pentecostals into denominations, largely for the support of foreign missions. Further, the recognition of the need to reach beyond themselves would form one of the marks that distinguished early classical Pentecostalism from the charismatic movement some sixty years later.

Third, with a clear sense of God's immediate presence among them, Pentecostals naturally sought divine intervention in the world around them, eagerly praying for the sick and suffering. *Strong faith* was a cherished possession among early Pentecostals, and such was often achieved only through intercessory prayer. Early testimonies are laced with answers to prayer, and stories of those who surrendered the comforts of their lives for the call of God to ministry opportunities at home and abroad.

Continuing with their understanding of the Latter Rain, and God's willingness to intervene in their immediate situations, Pentecostals possessed great *expectancy* in the soon return of Christ—a premillennial, literal, physical return. Just as God cared for their personal needs, so he would soon

---

52. The following summary is taken from Menzies and Menzies, *Spirit and Power*, 22–25.

53. Early Pentecostal leader P.C. Nelson, wrote, "We esteem this gift so highly that we are willing to suffer reproach and loss for the sake of the wonderful privilege of receiving the Holy Spirit in the way the hundred and twenty did at Pentecost." Nelson, *Bible Doctrines*, 90.

care for world history. The world order was, in their minds doomed from the beginning, and they had but a short time to reach as many who were lost as possible before God stepped in to make matters right once again. Their expectancy included not just the end times, but also each worship service; Pentecostals typically abhorred liturgy, preferring instead allow the Spirit to lead each service. Every gathering was therefore another opportunity for the Body to receive something from God specifically tailored to their immediate need.

Fifth, Pentecostals had experienced the presence of God in such a tangible manner through the baptism of the Holy Spirit that the *reality* of Heaven and the soon return of Christ were ever present in their lives. As Menzies notes, "Pentecostals had tasted of the glory of God's presence and longed to see him face to face."[54] Holiness became an authentic quest for these believers because the sense of God's nearness led naturally to a lifestyle that would not offend the Holy Spirit. Unfortunately, when behaviours both encouraged and objectionable were codified and passed down to younger generations, this eager desire for holiness arising from a personal sense of God's presence was often replaced by formal legalism and rigid religious restrictions.

Pentecostal services from the earliest days were marked by *enthusiastic worship*, complete with concert prayer, the raising of hands, exuberant clapping, dancing "in the Spirit," and other ecstatic manifestations such as trembling, crying, shaking violently, or "falling under the power." Though these behaviours did not endear early Pentecostals to other, more formal Christians, they bore slurs such as "Holy Rollers" with a sense of pride. Pentecostal preaching, though sometimes short on exegesis, was passionate and cherished truths proclaimed with great volume and energy.[55] Gifts of the Spirit could be expected to interrupt any service, and attempts at pre-planning worship services were often met with the belief that doing so would quench the flow of the Holy Spirit in their midst.

Seventh, Pentecostals naturally cultivated *rich fellowship* among those of similar persuasion, ostracized as they were by both the religious and secular worlds. In the earliest days, other Pentecostals believers were often viewed more like close family than their own non-Pentecostal families—families that more often than not had rejected these new religious zealots. For many early Pentecostals, their worship gatherings and communion with other like-minded believers became quite literally the centre of their lives.

---

54. Menzies and Menzies, *Spirit and Power*, 23.

55. It is worth noting that even today, in the Pentecostal denomination of which I am a member, volume and passion in preaching are sometimes confused for biblical substance—and anointing.

Finally, it is important to note the commitment of early Pentecostals to *biblical authority*. Experiential by nature, and not given to excessive rationalism, Pentecostals had experienced personally truths such as Spirit baptism and divine healing taught by Scripture, and therefore had little reason to doubt that the rest of Scripture was authoritative and trustworthy also. The mantra "The Bible says it, I believe it, and that settles it," would accurately express the sentiments of Pentecostals relative to the Scriptures. Of note here is the Pentecostal understanding of the Scriptures as authoritative in all matters of faith, belief, and practice, without the strictures of doctrines such as inerrancy. Pentecostals knew the Bible to be trustworthy because they had personally experienced the reality of its message.

Classic Pentecostal Identity

The Latter Rain

To comprehend the Pentecostal reaction to, and understanding of, the Charismatic movement, we must first get a sense of Pentecostal identity; that is, how Pentecostals viewed themselves on the world (and church) stage. Although a surprise to some, early Pentecostals did not see the Baptism of the Holy Spirit as evidenced by glossolalia as the sum total of their distinctive doctrine; it was much larger than that. As Faupel notes in *The Everlasting Gospel: The Significance of Eschatology in the Development of Pentecostal Thought,* Pentecostals saw themselves as the *Latter Rain* outpouring of God's Spirit, marking His soon return. Spirit-baptism was a sign that this was the case, and an empowering to witness in the last vital days before Christ's return. Tongues were simply the external initial evidence that this had in fact occurred. Faupel writes,

> The Latter Rain covenant motif provided the Pentecostal movement with its philosophy of history thus providing the general framework within which it saw its own role . . . Within this context, glossolalia played a crucial role. To the adherents, its initial occurrence signified that the second Pentecost had come, inaugurating the Latter Rain era.[56]

---

56. Faupel, *The Everlasting Gospel,* 32, 42. With Faupel on this understanding is Land, who also argues that eschatological passions were central to the Pentecostal movement. See Land, *Pentecostal Spirituality.* Frank Macchia is more cautious. While Macchia states of Spirit baptism that, "the doctrine dominates early Pentecostal concerns more than is generally admitted," he finds Faupel's "eschatological narrative of the outpouring of the Spirit at the heart of Pentecostal distinctives rather compelling as a historical thesis." He would then wish to see the Pentecostal understanding of Spirit

This understanding is confirmed in the writings of early Pentecostals such as George Floyd Taylor, who dedicated an entire chapter of his c. 1907 work *The Spirit and the Bride* to explaining the early and latter rains,[57] and David Wesley Myland's *The Latter Rain Covenant with Pentecostal Power and Testimonies of Healings and Baptism*, published in 1910.[58]

A.B. Simpson, in a 1907 editorial for *Christian and Missionary Alliance* magazine, encouraged his readers to expect a 'Latter Rain' outpouring.[59] Charles Fox Parham also discussed this motif as early as 1911:

> A careful study of the subject in the Old Testament proves that the early rain fell upon newly sown seed, to sprout it and to grow it; and that the latter rain fell on the fields at the time the grain was in the milk state to full it for the harvest. This is true of the Pentecostal work today. Christianity was in the milk state.
>
> ... At Topeka, God baptized his true ones with the real Pentecost . . . where-after the Holy Spirit fell in Pentecostal power . . . This has been true of this Latter Rain. Wherever it has gone it has been like "rain upon new mown grass," filling the wheat for His "Glorious Harvest."
>
> The purpose of this Latter Rain is two-fold: The preaching of this "gospel of the Kingdom" to all the world "as a witness," and the fulling of the grain for the harvest."[60]

Pastor Eugene Vaters, the second General Superintendent of the Pentecostal Assemblies of Newfoundland and Labrador, writing in 1924, agreed:

> . . . we have a new thing, that claims distinction from everything else, and which is called, in many instances, "The Latter Rain." There are, it seems, as many shades and shadows within what is known as "Pentecost" as there are in the whole of the Church outside it. Perhaps this is one of the strongest evidences in its favour in being called "The Latter Rain." . . . [W]e see the same power manifested as at the *beginning*—in both gifts and

---

baptism "expanded and invigorated by the eschatological nature of the Pentecostal vision of the latter rain rather than subordinated to it." Macchia's concerns here will be addressed more thoroughly in chapter nine. See Macchia, *Baptized in the Spirit*, 40.

57. Taylor, *The Spirit and the Bride*.

58. Myland, *The Latter Rain Covenant*.

59. "We may . . . conclude that we are to expect a great outpouring of the Holy Spirit in connection with the second coming of Christ and one as much greater than the Pentecostal effusion of the Spirit as the rains of autumn were greater than the showers of spring. . . . We are in the time . . . when we may expect this latter rain." See "What is meant by the Latter Rain?," 38.

60. Parham, *The Everlasting Gospel*, 31.

graces—in this movement; but, we have seen things, also, which we could not place with the *Holy Spirit*. There are many spirits, embodied and disembodied, but there is one only Holy Spirit, and an honest heart need not be long in doubt about His manifestations. Meanwhile if the claim be true, and we do not doubt it, that it is indeed "the latter rain," then "harvest" is very near, which Jesus called, the end of the age; and, we may expect the return of our Lord at any time.[61]

These earliest Pentecostals therefore did not long wonder whether they had correctly interpreted their place in Christendom as recipients of the greater 'Latter Rain' outpouring of the Holy Spirit; one need only witness the many miracles occurring within Pentecostalism to recognize the Divine stamp of approval on this 'Full Gospel' message. An article in *The Apostolic Faith*, the official newspaper of the Azusa Street Mission, noted:

> The signs are following in Los Angeles. The eyes of the blind have been opened, the lame have been made to walk, and those who have accidentally drunk poison have been healed. One came suffering from poison and was healed instantly. Devils are cast out, and many speak in new tongues. All of the signs in Mark 16:16–18 have followed except the raising of the dead, and we believe God will have someone to receive that power. We want all the signs that it may prove God is true. It will result in the salvation of many souls.[62]

Kenneth Archer concludes:

> In sum, the 'Latter Rain' motif provided the Pentecostals with a persuasive apologetic account for the existence of their community. The 'Latter Rain' motif provided the basic structure for the Pentecostal story. The Pentecostal story brought together the Full Gospel message and extended the past biblical 'Latter Rain' covenant of promise into the present Pentecostal movement. The Pentecostals, then, understood themselves as the prophetically promised eschatological movement, which would bring about the unity of Christianity and usher in the Second Coming of Christ.[63]

---

61. Janes, *History of the Pentecostal Assemblies of Newfoundland*, 61–62.
62. October, 1906.
63. Archer, "Pentecostal Story," 10.

From the Latter Rain to the Initial Evidence

As noted above, in the years immediately following the Azusa revival, Pentecostal leaders such as Myland and Taylor focused their attention on an explanation of the Latter Rain, and Pentecostalism's place in history. Almost simultaneously, it would seem, public fascination with Spirit baptism and glossolalia seized the spotlight from the less glamorous eschatological discussions.

From the very beginning therefore, in line with their understanding of the Latter Rain, Pentecostals gave special emphasis to Spirit-baptism as an event subsequent to conversion, with the initial physical evidence of speaking in tongues. Early Pentecostals were not known as great theologians; they were far more eager to experience the Spirit personally, and then relate this experience to every soul encountered. Pentecostals did record their theology; however, it was simply designed to "meet the need" of the time, explaining who Pentecostals were and what they believed. Douglas Jacobson, in *Thinking in the Spirit*, notes:

> Most leaders of the early Pentecostal movement were, of course, suspicious of theology done in the traditional way. Too often, they thought, theology had lost touch with the Spirit and had become dry and brittle, incapable of conveying the living truth of God's love to anyone. William Seymour, for example, cautioned the members of his Azusa Street Mission against getting caught up in merely "talking thought" lest the power of God decline in their midst . . . At the same time, each [leader] was convinced that thought was a necessary part of Pentecostal faith—theology was necessary and unavoidable.[64]

In the first decades Pentecostal leaders focused more on a very literal reading of Scripture than on great theological investigations, which did not further endear them to theologians of other denominations. Writing about Spirit-baptism, early Pentecostal leader Donald Gee wrote,

> You may stumble at first over the teaching that the scriptural evidence of the baptism in the Holy Spirit is speaking with other tongues and that it should be expected in every case as an initial sign. I firmly believe that if you ponder this with an open mind before the Lord, you will come to see from the examples of the recorded cases in the New Testament . . . that it is really so. This sign unquestionably marks the divine choice for a simple,

---

64. Jacobson, *Thinking in the Spirit*, 2.

universal, and supernatural evidence to seal the baptism with the Holy Spirit.[65]

As Pentecostals attempted to defend and explain their doctrine and practice, their attention shifted from strong identification with the Latter Rain motif and resultant eschatological implications. Pentecostal identity clearly became aligned with a defense of Subsequence and Initial Evidence; these became the "Distinctive Doctrines" and chief identity markers of Pentecostalism. Longtime Pentecostal pastor and speaker, Carl Brumback (1917–87) expanded a series of radio sermons from 1942 to 1944 into one of the earlier and more significant defenses of Pentecostalism, in *What Meaneth This? A Pentecostal Answer to a Pentecostal Question*.[66] A telling insight into the Pentecostal mentality at this time is seen in Donald Dayton's suggestion that "Carl Brumback's classic *apologia* for Pentecostalism is basically a defense of glossolalia."[67] The importance of this observation should not be missed.

With an understanding of early Pentecostal belief and practice in hand, we now move to the Charismatic movement, and its impact upon classical Pentecostal identity.

The Charismatic Movement and Pentecostal Identity

For almost sixty years Pentecostals remained unique to a degree in their focus on present-day manifestations of the Holy Spirit, including the gifts of the Spirit, and Spirit-baptism with the "evidence" of glossolalia. In the 1960s, however, the church world in North America was turned upside down when believers in a variety of mainline denominations began to experience manifestations of the Spirit that were heretofore the domain of Pentecostalism. This section will explore the rise of the charismatic movement, and the resultant impact upon Pentecostalism.

Mark Sidwell summarizes the essential differences between the Charismatic movement and the Classical Pentecostal movement:

> It is sometimes difficult today to see any distinction between Pentecostalism and the Charismatic movement, but there are differences. Pentecostals have remained in their distinctive denominations. They belong to clearly Pentecostal bodies, such as the Pentecostal Holiness Church or the Assemblies of God.

---

65. Gee, *Pentecost*, 16–17.
66. Brumback, *What Meaneth This?*
67. Dayton, "The Limits of Evangelicalism," 38.

Charismatics, on the other hand, generally belong to churches in the major denominations. Normally, Pentecostals insist on speaking in tongues as the mark of the Holy Spirit's baptism, but Charismatics are sometimes open on this question.[68]

We will now briefly survey the arrival of the Charismatic movement in a number of the larger mainline denominations.

Episcopalian / Anglican Churches

It was on Sunday April 3, 1960 that Dennis Bennett shocked St. Mark's Episcopal church in Van Nuys, California with his announcement that not only was he baptized in the Holy Spirit, but 70 other members of the church were also speaking in tongues alongside him.[69] Prior to this, people had heard of such occurrences, but only in the Pentecostal denominations, and views of the baptism of the Holy Spirit were held with contempt or skepticism, more so than curiosity and acceptance.

When Bennett stepped out in 1960, he faced a great deal of persecution and criticism, often publically; this experience is considered by many to be the official beginning of the Charismatic movement in the United States. Quebedeaux notes, ". . . this Episcopal priest became a modern-day Alexander Boddy and was himself responsible for much of the early growth of Charismatic Renewal—especially among Episcopalians, Lutherans, and Presbyterians."[70] The initial reaction from those in his congregation however, was not encouraging. The assistant priest refused to work with him and according to Bennett, one of the congregants yelled out, "We are Episcopalians, not a bunch of wild-eyed hillbillies!" "Throw out the damn tongue speakers!" yelled another.[71]

The effect of the Charismatic movement on the Anglican Church has not had an undisputed impact through all the Episcopal dioceses, with each diocese differing in style and worship. In 1973, the Episcopal Charismatic Fellowship[72] was founded, which promotes awareness of the charismatic movement. Today, the Church of England continues to be profoundly

---

68. Sidwell, "The Dividing Line." Also see Anderson, *An Introduction to Pentecostalism*, 9–15. Anderson notes, "Pentecostals have defined themselves by so many paradigms that diversity itself has become a primary defining characteristic of Pentecostal and Charismatic identity." (10).

69. See Bennet, *Nine O'clock in the Morning*.

70. Quebedeaux, *The New Charismatics*, 57.

71. Synan, *The Century of the Holy Spirit*, 153.

72 The Episcopal Charismatic Fellowship is currently entitled *Acts 29 Ministries*.

impacted by charismatic movements, including the "Toronto Blessing" of the early 1990s.[73]

Lutheran Church

The Charismatic Renewal within the Lutheran Church happened shortly after Dennis Bennett went public about his experience with Spirit-baptism. Harold Bredesen preceded Bennett in receiving baptism of the Holy Spirit in 1947 but did not lead others to this experience until the early 1960s. He has been credited with leading many important Christian leaders of the time into Spirit baptism, including Pat Robertson, John Sherrill, and Pat Boone.[74] In 1963, "Eternity" magazine used the phrase "The New Pentecostalism" for this movement. Bredesen published a response objecting to the "Neo-Pentecostal" label, preferring the term "Charismatic Renewal."[75]

Another influential leader within the Lutheran Church was Larry Christenson, who received the baptism of the Holy Spirit in 1961. Christenson made the decision to remain a pastor within the Lutheran Church, despite some hesitation to do so and later investigation by his peers and superiors. When Christenson's congregation became a major center for charismatic renewal in the Lutheran Church, he and participating members were subject to investigations by "a team composed of a psychiatrist, a psychologist, and a theologian."[76] A further investigation by the Missouri Synod encouraged openness to whatever forms of grace God might bestow upon his church, while noting that Lutherans traditionally viewed these charismatic manifestations as having been limited to the era of the early church.[77] Today, although there are still groups seeking to keep the renewal alive within the Lutheran Church, the general emphasis appears to be declining within the denomination as a whole.

Presbyterian Church

Following Bennett's public announcement in 1960, all mainline denominations observed experiences of the baptism of the Holy Spirit in their

---

73. See, for example, Warnock, "The Toronto Blessing"; Beverley, *Holy Laughter and the Toronto Blessing.*
74. Synan, *The Century of the Holy Spirit*, 159.
75. Hocken, "Charismatic Movement," 480.
76. Christenson, "The Charismatic Movement."
77. For further reading see *The Charismatic Movement and Lutheran Theology.*

ranks, including leaders within the Presbyterian churches. Robert Whitaker received the baptism of the Holy Spirit in 1962, George C. "Brick" Bradford in 1966 and J. Rodman Williams in 1965. All three of these Presbyterian leaders greatly influenced the Charismatic movement in Presbyterian denominations.

After the case of Bennett became highly publicized, however, some pastors had a more difficult time remaining in their parishes due to the profound skepticism surrounding charismatic manifestations. Brick Bradford's experience received a poor reception within the Presbyterian Church; he was placed under intense investigation, and was told he needed mental counseling. In 1967, Brick was removed from his position as Pastor.[78]

Another Presbyterian Pastor, Robert Whitaker, was forced to make a stand on his beliefs. When investigated by the local presbytery for his refusal to "cease and desist" speaking in tongues, praying for the sick, and casting out demons, he was removed from his pastorate. After appeals to the various State and National levels of Presbyterian governance were dismissed, a long court battle ensued. Positive results came out of this legal suit for the Charismatic movement as a whole. Pastors in the Presbyterian denomination were protected from being removed from their positions based on their involvement in the Charismatic movement. Charismatic Presbyterians continue to be leaders in the worldwide renewal movement.[79]

Vinson Synan notes:

> The Episcopalians, Presbyterians, and Lutherans represented the respectable centre of American Protestantism. That highly educated churchmen such as Bennett, Bradford, and Christenson could speak in tongues, call themselves 'Pentecostals,' and remain in their churches blasted away all the stereotypes that had held sway in American religious life for decades.[80]

Eastern Orthodoxy

The Charismatic movement never gained ground in Eastern Orthodoxy as it did in Western denominations. As Synan notes, "Orthodoxy has always claimed to be charismatic in its worship and piety. At no time has it held to a theory of the cessation of the gifts of the Holy Spirit. Signs and wonders, including prophecy, healing, and miracles, have traditionally been accepted

---

78. Synan, *The Century of the Holy Spirit*, 170.
79. Ibid., 171.
80. Ibid., 175.

as part of the heritage of the church."[81] In some cases, Orthodox leadership have relentlessly harassed charismatics, believing their presence denied Orthodox claims that they have never lost the Spirit or charismata. Individual priests, such as Fr. Eusebius Stephanou, Fr. Athanasius Emmert, and Fr. Boris Zabrodsky, founder of the Service Committee for Orthodox Spiritual Renewal (SCOSR), which published the "Theosis" Newsletter, were some of the more prominent leaders of the Charismatic Renewal in Orthodoxy.[82]

Roman Catholic Church

The modern Charismatic movement in the Roman Catholic Church began on February 18, 1967. A number of students from Duquesne University in Pittsburgh, Pennsylvania were at a retreat and during prayer received the baptism of the Holy Spirit. This event forever changed the face and nature of the Catholic Church, even to this present day. The Roman Catholic Diocese of Lafayette, Louisiana in an article entitled, "History of the Catholic Charismatic Renewal", notes that many of the students, ". . . had profound 'baptism in the Spirit' experiences and they shared these experiences with others in prayer . . . There followed a wildfire movement of the Spirit so profound that it led to the National Service Committee here in the U.S. and the International Catholic Charismatic Renewal Services in Italy."[83]

There were several leaders of great significance that provided early direction to the Charismatic movement within the Catholic Church. Cardinal Leon Joseph Suenens, Pope Paul VI and Pope John Paul II were the influential voices during this time. As a result, the charismatic movement within the Roman Catholic Church received less negativity, skepticism or criticism by opponents. In recent times, for example, Cardinal Angelo Sodano, with the Pope's blessing, read aloud that following in the steps of Pope John Paul II, "His Holiness [Benedict XVI] wishes to continue this [renewal], so that the gifts that the Lord dispenses to his Church will be fully appreciated and oriented in the best way for the building of the Body of Christ . . ."[84]

In an August 2013 article entitled, "Pope Francis discovers charismatic movement a gift to the whole church," the *Catholic News Service* quoted Pope Francis as having changed his mind over the years about the charismatic movement:

---

81. Ibid., 199.
82. Ibid., 198–200. See also, "The Charismatic Movement and Orthodoxy."
83. "History of Catholic Charismatic Renewal."
84. "Benedict XVI Signals Support for Ecclesial Movements."

> "Back at the end of the 1970s and the beginning of the 1980s, I had no time for charismatics," the pope told reporters on the plane returning from Rio July 28. "Once, speaking about them, I said: 'These people confuse a liturgical celebration with samba lessons!'"
>
> "Now I regret it," he said. "Now I think that this movement does much good for the church, overall."
>
> "I don't think that the charismatic renewal movement merely prevents people from passing over to Pentecostal denominations," Pope Francis said. "No! It is also a service to the church herself! It renews us."
>
> "The movements are necessary, the movements are a grace of the Spirit," the pope added, speaking of ecclesial movements in general. "Everyone seeks his own movement, according to his own charism, where the Holy Spirit draws him or her."[85]

The Catholic Charismatic Renewal (CCR) has already celebrated its 40th anniversary, and it is reported that more than 100 million Catholics share the charismatic experience worldwide.[86] It appears the Catholic Church is committed to seeing the Holy Spirit operate to the fullest capacity of the believer, and is dedicated to consistent renewal.[87]

Pentecostalism and the Charismatic Movement

As one might expect, for a movement that so clearly self-identified with the particular experience of glossolalia via Spirit-baptism, the spread of the charismatic movement throughout the mainline church was not always easy to comprehend. Macchia writes,

> In the past, Pentecostals viewed these churches as the chief opponents of the latter-day bestowal of supernatural signs and wonders. Apparently, without the permission of Pentecostals,

---

85. Rocca, "Pope Francis Discovers Charismatic Movement."
86. "Benedict XVI Signals Support for Ecclesial Movements."
87. Worth noting, though beyond the scope of this study, is the tremendous influence Pentecostalism has had worldwide in less formal categories. It is widely recognized, for example, that much of the significant growth in Christianity throughout Asia, Latin America, and Africa may be considered a form of Pentecostal/Charismatic spirituality, even if unaffiliated with a particular Pentecostal denomination. This is less evident in North America, where denominationalism still reigns, even to a sectarian extreme. Further, much of urban evangelicalism clearly has traits associated with "small-p" Pentecostalism. For examples see Vondey, *Beyond Pentecostalism*; Miller and Yamamori, *Global Pentecostalism*; Westerlund, *Global Pentecostalism*.

the Spirit of God was suddenly being felt in Charismatic Renewal among members of major Protestant churches and, most surprisingly for Pentecostals, in the Roman Catholic Church ... Pentecostals had not only to wrestle with the dramatic work of the Spirit in the mainline churches, they also had to come to terms with the possibility that the movement may serve as a source of renewal for Pentecostal churches.[88]

In his 1972 work *Charismatic Bridges*, widely respected Pentecostal historian and theologian Vynson Synan noted that the charismatic movement was forcing an "agonizing reappraisal" of what it meant to be Pentecostal. Commenting on the sixth annual International Conference on the Charismatic Renewal in the Catholic Church, he opined, "They were singing 'our' songs and exercising 'our' gifts. It was more than I could take."[89] Though he quickly recognized the Charismatic movement as a continuation of the outpouring of the Spirit began at Azusa Street, Synan's comments provide insight into the struggle.

Ronald Kydd views the impact of the Charismatic Renewal upon Canadian Pentecostalism as "significantly negative." In brief, he outlines three concerns. First, Charismatic worship was highly influenced by the youth culture of the time, and one of its dominant themes was self-gratification. While those who remained attached to the mainline denominations were protected by the established liturgies, Pentecostalism was not so fortunate. As a result of their interaction with Charismatic worship, Pentecostals have begun to view worship as what they could receive from it, rather than what God receives. Second, Kydd believes that Pentecostals failed to learn from the excellent theologians attached to the Charismatic movement, except (to their detriment) in the areas of shepherding and demonology. Third, though Pentecostals by the 1950s and 60s were beginning to move beyond a spirituality that largely centred upon crisis experiences, interaction with a Charismatic movement that was experiencing God profoundly through experience, reinforced and hardened that earlier orientation.[90]

The reappraisal of Pentecostalism vis-à-vis the Charismatic movement focused primarily upon three concerns.

1. Spirit-baptism, including glossolalia, was no longer the "exclusive" purview of classical Pentecostalism. For a movement that identified so closely with their position in the Latter Rain outpouring of the Spirit, and evidenced by their glossolalia, bearing witness to believers

---

88. Macchia, "God Present in a Confused Situation," 33.

89. Synan, *Charismatic Bridges*, 25.

90. See Kydd, "The Impact of the Charismatic Renewal," 63–65.

of all theological and denominational stripes speaking in these same tongues was a shock, to say the least.

2. Charismatics did not strictly adhere to the Pentecostal dogma of tongues as the singular and initial evidence of Spirit baptism, but remained open to other possible signs. Pentecostals scholars of the time felt that this would weaken the Initial Evidence doctrine to the point where it would be of no value. In tangling with Gordon Fee over Fee's use of "normal" instead of the preferred "normative" when describing whether glossolalia was indeed the initial evidence of Spirit baptism, William Menzies declared, "The use of *normal* in this connection is indeed compatible with the views of some contemporary evangelicals, but it is too weak to be made into a doctrine. Repeatability is hardly a preachable item . . . This reductionist point of view . . . is somewhat short of a thoroughgoing Pentecostal theology [and] is apparently a position held today by a number of evangelicals."[91]

3. Charismatics often favoured church renewal over the Missions fervor within Pentecostalism's eschatological framework of understanding. For those Pentecostal churches that were losing touch with their eschatological roots, the Charismatics offered an alternative spirituality, albeit one that caused great consternation among traditional Pentecostals.[92] The influence of the Charismatic movement upon Pentecostalism in this regard will be further addressed in chapter 9.

Pentecostalism Today

Though the movement has drifted from its original eschatological focus, Pentecostalism generally continues to place great emphasis on experiencing the supernatural. That the leadership of the Assemblies of God (USA) was invited to join the formation of the National Association of Evangelicals in 1942 demonstrated general Evangelical acceptance of Pentecostalism, some 35 years after Azusa Street.[93] Though North American Pentecostalism has

---

91. Menzies, "The Methodology of Pentecostal Theology," 9–10. Interestingly, Fee responded by pointing to the millions of Charismatics worldwide, who do not hold dogmatically to glossolalia as initial evidence, but who speak in tongues following Spirit baptism nonetheless. Gordon Fee, Interview by author, 5 December, 1997.

92. Macchia, "God Present in a Confused Situation," 35.

93. Menzies notes, "Evangelicals, many of whom had been led to believe that Pentecostals should be classified as a cult, had come to recognize that apart from Pentecostal teaching about baptism in the Spirit with the accompanying sign of speaking in tongues, Pentecostal teaching was squarely in line with orthodox Christian theology."

never been closer to Evangelicalism in many regards, key differences remain. In her description of the variety of Pentecostal churches worldwide, Sociologist Margaret Poloma notes, "What these churches share is not single structure, uniform doctrine, or ecclesiastical leadership, but a particular Christian world-view that reverts to a non-European epistemology from the European one that has dominated Christianity for centuries."[94] Paul W. Lewis agrees: ". . . the nature of Pentecostal experience within Biblical hermeneutics is tied with certain elements which inform Pentecostal experience, and ultimately these beliefs, experiences, and hermeneutics, demonstrate a Pentecostal epistemology. This Pentecostal epistemology is a non-Enlightenment enterprise, and places Pentecostal thought in a very different framework from conservative Evangelicalism . . ."[95]

Poloma quotes Pentecostal pastor and theologian Jackie David Johns to further illustrate. Johns notes: "At the heart of the Pentecostal worldview is transforming experience with God. God is known through relational encounter which finds its penultimate expression in the experience of being filled with the Holy Spirit. This experience becomes the normative epistemological framework and thus shifts the structures by which the individual interprets the world."[96]

Johns lists six special foci of the Pentecostal[97] worldview, several of which will be observed to have particular relevance to a postmodern[98] world:

Menzies and Menzies, *Spirit and Power*, 29.

94. Poloma, "The Spirit Bade Me Go," 5.

95. Lewis, "Towards a Pentecostal Epistemology," 95. Menzies agrees: "This yearning for Evangelical acceptance came, however, at a price, seen most clearly in the area of hermeneutics. Blind adherence to the full panoply of standard Evangelical principles of hermeneutics caused Pentecostals to fall unwittingly into a trap. The reason lies in the restrictive rules that govern the Evangelical hermeneutical enterprise, restrictions that rule out the possibility of a Pentecostal outcome [. . .] Evangelicals operated with one set of hermeneutical rules; Pentecostals operated with a different approach. It was not until the 1970s that this problem was clearly understood. It is important to take into account significant changes in Evangelical hermeneutical theory since 1970, changes that make it easier for present-day Evangelicals and Pentecostals to speak similar language." Menzies and Menzies, *Spirit and Power*, 33–34. Though appreciative of Menzies' optimism, it is my contention that Pentecostal presuppositions concerning Scripture are sufficiently distinct as to warrant a hermeneutic that retains much of the Evangelical enterprise, while acknowledging a distinctive Pentecostal hermeneutical approach. See Noel, *Pentecostal and Postmodern Hermeneutics*.

96. Johns, "Yielding to the Spirit," 74–75.

97. As noted earlier, Charismatics, whether within established denominations or the independent variety, differ little from the following description of Pentecostalism.

98. The significance of postmodern thought for Pentecostalism will comprise the

- First, the Pentecostal world-view is experientially God-centered. All things relate to God and God relates to all things.

- Second, the Pentecostal world-view is holistic and systemic. For the Spirit-filled person God is not only present in all events, he holds all things together and causes all things to work together.

- Third, the Pentecostal world-view is transrational. Knowledge is relational and is not limited to the realms of reason and sensory experience.

- Fourth, in conjunction with their holiness heritage, Pentecostals are concerned with truth, but not just propositional truth. Pentecostals were historically anti-creedal.

- Fifth, the Pentecostal epistemology of encounter with God is closely aligned with the biblical understanding of how one comes to know . . . This understanding is rooted in Hebrew thought and may be contrasted with Greek approaches to knowledge. The Hebrew word for "to know" is *yada*. In general, *yada* is knowledge that comes by experience.

- Finally, the Scriptures hold a special place and function within the Pentecostal world-view. Pentecostals differ from some Evangelicals and Fundamentalists in their approach to the Bible. For Pentecostals the Bible is a living book in which the Holy Spirit is always active.[99]

Conclusion

This chapter has surveyed Pentecostalism from its theological and historical precursors, to the Azusa Street revival, earliest theological convictions, and its subsequent spread globally. The genesis of the Charismatic movement was explored, as was the shift in Pentecostal identity from eschatological to pneumatological, which created an identity crisis of sorts as the Charismatic movement gained momentum. We concluded with a brief discussion on Pentecostal values and theology today. Although necessarily succinct, as volumes have been written on each aspect of Pentecostalism's first century, this chapter has served to provide the background necessary to begin the exploration of Pentecostalism in relation to the post-Christendom and increasingly secular culture of Canada. To further assist with the contextual analysis, chapter 3 will explore the twin challenges of secularism and postmodernism.

---

second half of chapter 3.

99. Johns, "Yielding to the Spirit," 74–75. This succinct summary is taken from Poloma, "The Spirit Bade Me Go," 5–6.

— 3 —
Current Societal Context

Post-Christendom: Secularism and Postmodernism

Introduction

HAVING EXPLORED PENTECOSTALISM WITH a view to providing a solid background to the movement as it seeks to navigate changing societal trends, we now move to an exploration of the changes in question. Recognizing that an exhaustive survey of cultural vagaries is beyond the scope of this chapter, we will begin by establishing that increasing secularism with resultant moves towards a post-Christian context is indeed a reality in Canada. Though disputed by some, I believe we can demonstrate that Canada has changed considerably in the last 50 years, from a country that was widely Christian in belief and practice to one that is significantly more secular. Going deeper, we then wish to explore in greater detail an example of the changes Pentecostalism must navigate in the coming years, via a discussion of postmodern trends that have gained increased prominence in Western culture in the preceding decades. A seismic shift has occurred in several of the philosophical presuppositions that undergird much of Western culture, and these impact Pentecostalism directly.

Post-Christendom: An Introduction

Before delving more deeply into our discussion on secularism and postmodernism, we will first be well served to consider briefly the concept of *Christendom*. We will trace its history, and acknowledge that in Western Europe and Canada, presently, and with the United States seemingly on the threshold, we are now living in a culture marked by *post-Christendom* attitudes and beliefs. Our guide for this synopsis will be Stuart Murray, who has penned the excellent work, *Post-Christendom: Church and Mission in a Strange New World*.[1]

Christendom may be understood as the central and influential place in society held by the Church for much of time since the early 300s, to the point that the Western world considered itself both formally and officially Christian. Most scholars[2] trace the origins of Christendom to Constantine's granting of special favours and powers to the church following his conversion to Christianity in 313 AD. As a privileged and protected religion, Christianity achieved unrivalled cultural dominance that would profoundly shape European society and culture (and those that arose from it) for years to come. Christendom may be understood as Christianity supported by two key pillars: Church and State.[3]

Alan Hirsch observes the following characteristics of Christendom; these will be readily observed in much of Christian tradition in the West today.

1. Its mode of engagement is attractional as opposed to missional/sending. It assumes a certain centrality of the Church in relation to its surrounding culture. (The missional church is a "going/sending one" and operates in the incarnational mode.)

2. A shift in focus to dedicated, sacred buildings/places of worship . . . It became more static and institutional in form. (The early church had no recognized dedicated buildings other than houses, shops, etc.)

3. The emergence of an institutionally recognized, professional clergy class acting primarily in pastor-teacher mode. (In the New Testament church, people were commissioned into leadership by local churches or by an apostolic leader.)

4. The paradigm is also characterized by the institutionalization of grace in the form of sacraments administered by an institutionally authorized priesthood. (The New Testament church's form of communion was an actual [daily?] meal dedicated to Jesus in the context of everyday life and the home.[4]

---

1. Murray, *Post-Christendom: Church and Mission*.
2. Though a full exploration of the history of Christendom is beyond the scope of this work, the reader may consult Brown, *The Rise of Western Christendom*; Herrin, *The Formation of Christendom*.
3. As G.K. Chesterton supposedly remarked, "The coziness between church and state is good for the state and bad for the church."
4. Alan Hirsch, *The Forgotten Ways*, 276–77. Cf. Gibbs, *The Rebirth of the Church*,

Michael Craven notes that, "even though the legal structures of Christendom were removed in North America (i.e. the separation of Church and state), the legacy of this Constantinian system remained by means of powerful traditions, attitudes, and social structures that could be described as 'functional Christendom.'"[5] When we speak of post-Christendom, therefore, we posit the understanding that "the church no longer occupies this central place of social and cultural hegemony and Western civilization no longer considers itself to be formally or officially Christian."[6]

Murray succinctly outlines a number of changes that will occur as Western culture moves from Christendom to post-Christendom; the reader may well observe personal faith realities in this list. In offering these verbatim, our understanding of Christendom itself will be enhanced. We may expect the following transitions:

- *From the centre to the margins:* in Christendom the Christian story and the churches were central, but in post-Christendom these are marginal.
- *From majority to minority:* in Christendom Christians comprised the (often overwhelming) majority, but in post-Christendom we are a minority.
- *From settlers to sojourners:* in Christendom Christians felt at home in a culture shaped by their story, but in post-Christendom we are aliens, exiles and pilgrims in a culture where we no longer feel at home.
- *From privilege to plurality:* in Christendom Christians enjoyed many privileges, but in post-Christendom we are one community among many in a plural society.
- *From control to witness:* in Christendom churches could exert control over society, but in post-Christendom we exercise influence only through witnessing to our story and its implications.
- *From maintenance to mission:* in Christendom the emphasis was on maintaining a supposedly Christian status quo, but in post-Christendom it is on mission within a contested environment.
- *From institution to movement:* in Christendom churches operated mainly in institutional mode, but in post-Christendom we must become again a Christian movement.[7]

4–5.

5. Craven, "The Church in Post-Christendom."
6. Ibid.
7. Murray, *Post-Christendom: Church and Mission*, 20.

In chapter 8 we will detail a Pentecostal response to the secularism outlined below that we may observe readily in post-Christendom. Before discussing this transition in the Canadian context, however, we will conclude this section by clarifying what post-Christendom is *not*.[8] First, post-Christendom does not comprehensively describe the culture that will replace Christendom. Just as postmodernism does not fully describe what will remain as the foundations of Modernism weaken, post-Christendom points to what may be without dogmatically asserting what is to come. Second, post-Christendom is not the same as pre-Christendom. Far too many vestiges of the Christian story remain within our culture throughout literature, the arts, and music—to name but a few—to view the coming era as synonymous with the past. Third, and important for our next discussion, post-Christendom does not mean secular. In many ways, the demise of Christendom has precipitated the rise of secularism, but we may also note that increasing secularism has hastened the demise of Christendom. Further, as we will note below, the "secularization thesis" often championed in the last 50 years, did predict the fall of Christendom[9], but failed to allow for the many forms of spirituality and religious beliefs that have arisen or increased in strength even during, or perhaps due to, the fall of Christendom. As Murray notes,

> In post-Christendom, however, renewed interest in spirituality is generally not related to Christianity, which is associated with oppressive dogmatism and seen as spiritually inhibiting. The fervent hopes many Christians express that resurgent spirituality might represent new opportunities for the churches have not yet been realized. Most people interested in spirituality in post-Christendom are looking elsewhere for insights and resources. Post-Christendom is not secular, but neither is it Christian.[10]

Fourth, we must remember that post-Christendom is not the same as postmodernism. As we shall observe near the end of this chapter, postmodernism represents a critique of modernism, and is widely viewed as the most significant philosophical shift since the Enlightenment. As was true with secularization, postmodernism is to post-Christendom both cause and consequence. In chapter 8 we will explore ways in which both postmodernity and secularization offer opportunities of growth for Pentecostalism. Finally, we should note that post-Christendom is not the experience of all

---

8. This section is adapted from Murray, *Post-Christendom: Church and Mission*, 3–19.

9. Bruce, *Religion and Modernization*.

10. Murray, *Post-Christendom: Church and Mission*, 12.

the world's Christians, but rather of those in Western Europe and other societies with roots in that culture. Wolfgang Vondey notes, " . . . the 'church' of Christendom is a thoroughly Western concept oriented along a premodern, prescientific, and preglobal worldview. Christendom marks the confines of a 'Christian' world in contrast to the 'global' world. The 'church' in this world is not attuned to the awakening of Christianity in the cultures of the East and in the Southern Hemisphere."[11] This narrative therefore has far less to do with the church and culture in Asia, Africa, or Latin America, where official Christendom never did take root as it did throughout the Western world.

Having explored the realities of post-Christendom, we will now move to a discussion on secularism. These sections are intended to provide the background necessary for thoughtful consideration of the challenges Pentecostalism faces in contemporary culture. In chapter 8, we will consider how Pentecostals may respond properly to the opportunities for growth afforded by post-Christendom and the increase in secularism.

Secularism

Evidence of Secularism in the Canadian Context

Europe, once the source of almost all Christian missionaries, now finds itself the recipient of the same from South East Asia, Africa, and Latin America.[12] According to the *Pew Forum*, Europe in 1910 was home to 66.3 percent of the world's Christians; by 2010 this number had shrunk to just 25.9 percent.[13] Murray notes, ". . . sixty percent of Christians now live in Africa, Asia, or Latin America, and a reverse missionary movement is underway."[14] In December 2010, Michael Valpy and Joe Friesen began their five-part *Globe and Mail* series on the future of faith in Canada with the declaration, "What we've seen is a sea of change in 40 years, a march towards secularization that mirrors what's happened in Europe."[15] Without the state churches and vestiges of cultural Christianity that have been a permanent fixture on the European and British landscape, might secularization in Canada actually be more profound and arrive more quickly? Is Canada following rapidly on the heels of Europe?[16]

---

11. Vondey, *Beyond Pentecostalism*, 146.
12. Veale, "Korean Missionaries Under Fire." See also Hook, "Further Fervor."
13. "Global Christianity."
14. Murray, *Post-Christendom: Church and Mission*, 223.
15. Valpy and Friesen, "Canada Marching from Religion to Secularization."
16. Helpful here is Bowen, *Christians in a Secular World*.

Known as the "Secularization Theory," this was for many years the standard assumption. "The seminal thinkers of the nineteenth century— Auguste Comte, Herbert Spencer, Emile Durkheim, Max Weber, Karl Marx, and Sigmund Freud—all believed that religion would gradually fade in importance and cease to be significant with the advent of industrial society."[17] Norris and Inglehart observe, however, "Secularization theory is currently experiencing the most sustained challenge in its long history."[18] They give two clear examples. First, Peter Berger, once a strong advocate for secularization,[19] recanted his earlier claims: "The world today, with some exceptions . . . is as furiously religious as it ever was, and in some places more so than ever. This means that a whole body of literature by historians and social scientists loosely labeled 'secularization theory' is essentially mistaken."[20] Similarly, prominent sociologists of religion Rodney Stark and Roger Finke declare, "After nearly three centuries of utterly failed prophecies and misrepresentations of both present and past, it seems time to carry the secularization doctrine to the graveyard of failed theories, and there to whisper 'requiescat in pace.'"[21]

Is secularism dead? There has been considerable discussion surrounding "Christian America" and the lament experienced in conservative Christian circles over their perceived loss of this reality in recent decades.[22] Far less, however, has been made of the current state of religion in Canada[23],

---

17. Norris and Inglehart, *Sacred and Secular*, 1.
18. Ibid.
19. See, for example, Berger, *The Sacred Canopy*.
20. Berger, *The Desecularization of the World*, 2.
21. Stark and Finke, *Acts of Faith*, 79. Newbigin agrees, describing the theory of secularization as a "myth" and "quite simply untrue." Newbigin, *The Gospel in a Pluralist Society*, 212.
22. Though tangential to the purpose of this study, it is worth noting that scholars are divided on the state of Christendom in America. I believe that the United States is entering post-Christendom, even if it is delayed somewhat from the Canadian or European timetable. Stuart Murray notes that Christendom in America is "persistent and resilient." Norris and Inglehart observe that the United States remains an "outlier" among other industrialized nations, but even in America there has been "significant movement towards secularization." Voddie Baucham bluntly states that we already see a "post-Christian America," while the title of Gabe Lyons' work is self-explanatory. See Lyons, *The Next Christians*; Murray, *Post-Christendom: Church and Mission*, 187; Norris and Inglehart, *Sacred and Secular*, 25; Baucham, *The Ever-Loving Truth*, 4.
23. For more on religion in Canada, see O'Toole, "Religion in Canada"; Thiessen and Dawson, "Is There a 'Renaissance' of Religion in Canada?"; Beaman and Beyer, *Religion and Diversity in Canada*; Kilbourn, *Religion in Canada*; Gauvreau and Christie, *Christian Churches and Their Peoples*; Grant, *The Church in the Canadian Era*; Beaman, *Religion and Canadian Society*; Crysdale and Wheatcroft, *Religion in Canadian Society*.

and whether Canada is indeed entering an era of post-Christendom, or whether it was ever, in fact, "Christian" at all.[24] In fact, Peter O'Toole notes, "although the importance of Canadian religion has been, with few exceptions, greatly underestimated by both sociologists and historians, its crucial role in the nation's development now appears, if somewhat belatedly, to have attained more widespread recognition."[25] While the Christian religion is without question a significant part of the Canadian narrative, scholars have not generally viewed Canada[26] as "Christian" in the way they have our American counterparts;[27] while the role of Christendom in America is regularly observed, the same cannot be said of the Canadian context.

Mark Noll

One scholar who seeks to address this misunderstanding is church historian Mark A. Noll. In his concise work, *What Happened to Christian Canada?*[28], Noll argues that by the middle of the 20th century, Canada was in fact "far more Christian" than our American neighbours. Unsurprisingly, however, the last 50 years have witnessed an incredible shift on this front. Noll's argument is worth exploring, and to that end we now turn.

His first lines betray his intentions:

> By asking "what happened to Christian Canada," I begin with an assumption that there once was a Christian Canada which is now gone. That assumption is intentional. It is intended to highlight not only the dramatic changes that have taken place in Canadian religious life over the last sixty years, but also substantial contrasts between the religious histories of Canada and

---

24. Some scholars have already ceded the fact. See, for example, Studebaker and Beach, "Emerging Churches in Post-Christian Canada." Also, the first chapter of *The Church in an Age of Crisis* is entitled, "A Post-Christian America." See White, *The Church in an Age of Crisis*.

25. O'Toole, "Religion in Canada," 120.

26. Brian Stiller, past President of the Evangelical Fellowship of Canada, in warning of a contemporary desire to return nostalgically to some past golden age of "Christian Canada", suggests that it's dangerous to speak of Canada ever having been Christian. See Stiller, *Was Canada Ever Christian?*.

27. See for example, O'Toole, "Religion in Canada," 121. For more on the differences in American and Canadian evangelicalism, see Reimer, *Evangelicals and the Continental Divide*; Reimer, "A Generic Evangelicalism?"

28. Noll, *What Happened to Christian Canada?*

the United States, which otherwise are so similar in so many respects.[29]

As is apparent, Noll is concerned to demonstrate the significant changes in Canadian religious life in the last half century. Four historical snapshots serve at the beginning to reinforce this message. On September 15, 1959, Georges Vanier was sworn in as Canada's new Governor General, and immediately began his acceptance speech with a prayer invoking the aid of "Almighty God." Fifty-six years later, on September 27, 2005, Michaëlle Jean in accepting the same position offered a progressive address that stressed toleration and the exaltation of individual liberty. At no time, however was there a mention of the deity.[30] Upon reflection, Canadians would perhaps be less surprised by Jean's exclusion of God from her remarks, than by Georges' inclusion.[31]

Second, Noll notes that Prime Minister Pierre Trudeau, in re-patriating the Canadian constitution from Great Britain in 1982, faced opposition from his own party over his inclusion of a solitary reference to God. It was removed, and not reintroduced until a "broad ecumenical coalition lobbied for formal recognition of Canada's traditional Christian posture."[32] We note with irony that though the new Charter in its preamble states, "Canada is founded upon principles that recognize the supremacy of God and the rule of law," the Charter itself has accomplished everything except recognition of the supremacy of the deity. Under the new Charter, multiculturalism, enforced toleration, and public religious neutrality have found increasingly privileged status in Canadian jurisprudence, each serving to "de-christianize" public spaces, including those where religious foundations were once the norm.[33]

Third, the educational system in Canada provides another example of significant cultural change. Throughout Canada's history, many provinces

---

29. Ibid., 7–8.

30. Noll observes that in contrast to similar U.S. events, campaign speeches by both Bush and Kerry in the 2004 Presidential Election were considerably more overtly religious than in Eisenhower's era.

31. Noll, *What Happened to Christian Canada?*, 8–9.

32. Ibid., 10.

33. See Egerton, "Trudeau, God, and the Canadian Constitution." Although the jury is still out, there is some evidence that Canadian multiculturalism may slow the relegation of religion to the private sphere as influential immigrant communities, passionate about their own non-Christian religions, seek to incorporate their religious and public lives. While politicians may be hesitant to participate publically in holy days that are Christian in origin, the same cannot be said for their willingness to be seen at events and celebrations organized by Muslim or Hindu communities, for example.

had provided for a confessional educational system, operating alongside public schools, each stream publically funded. Gidney and Miller note, "the centrality of Christian doctrine in Ontario's public schools, albeit in non-denominational Protestant form, was alive and well in the mid-twentieth century . . . [and] finally ousted only through a prolonged, contested process."[34] Further, "in this particular part of the public arena . . . Christianity has not only been disestablished but banished."[35] Newfoundland provides another example, having entered into Canadian Confederation in 1949 with an explicit guarantee of its government-funded but denominationally administered school system. By 1997 however, after repeated efforts, the provincial government finally succeeded is wresting control from the churches, establishing a public school system for the first time in the province's 500-year history.[36]

Finally, Noll notes how easily the legalization of same-sex marriage passed through the Canadian parliament in 2005, in contrast to the protracted battle still occurring throughout the United States. "In Canada, the redefinition of marriage, which had been unthinkable short decades ago, has been widely, if not universally, accepted. In the United States, the unthinkable has become the contested."[37]

Markers of Religious Decline in Canada: Anecdotal Evidence

An article posted on the webpage of the Canadian Broadcasting Corporation recently asked a pertinent question: "Are We Living in Post-Religious Times?"[38] It may certainly seem so to those following current events; anecdotal evidence abounds. Canadian headlines scream of weakening Church influence and the arrival of post-Christendom. From Saskatoon: "'This isn't

34. Gidney and Millar, "The Christian Recessional in Ontario's Public Schools," 275.

35. Ibid., 289.

36. See Ferrin, "From Sectarian to Secular Control of Education," 411–30; Rideout, *History of Pentecostal*. Also, Dawe, "Denominational Education in Newfoundland and Labrador." This example is particularly poignant for me personally; I attended a Pentecostal school from K–12, and watched my father, as Assistant Superintendent of the Pentecostal School Board, fight this battle throughout my early adult years.

37. Noll, *What Happened to Christian Canada?*, 13. Kurt Bowen notes three areas of his own: secular mass media seem disinterested in covering anything but the most fringe or bizarre of religious news; the Government has almost entirely assumed responsibility for social welfare from the churches; and in many provinces the religious educational system has been transformed into a purely secular entity. Bowen, *Christians in a Secular World*, 11.

38. Davidson, "Are We Living in Post-Religious Times?"

supposed to be a Christian country': Atheist to get human rights hearing against politician's dinner blessing."[39] Even the Gideons, a charity long known for freely and cheerfully passing out Bibles to fifth grade students, has gotten caught in the crossfire: "Ontario tribunal bans Bible distribution unless school board also gives out atheist texts."[40] Trinity Western University, the largest faith-based school of its kind in Canada, has recently proposed the establishment of a new law school. The "Community Covenant Agreement"[41] employed by the school, which promotes biblical lifestyles, and prohibits sexual intimacy outside of marriage, (including the expression of same-gender attraction), has become a flash point. The response has not been kind. Lawyers with national recognition took to the media to proclaim their disagreement: "A law school at Trinity Western University will impose a queer quota," read one headline in a national newspaper.[42] The Canadian Council of Law Deans (CCLD) circulated a letter addressed to the Federation of Law Societies of Canada, describing the TWU Lifestyle Covenant as "fundamentally at odds with the core values of all Canadian law schools."[43] An editorial in one of Canada's two national newspapers proclaimed, "No gay-free law school should stand in Canada."[44]

Quebec, long the bastion of Catholicism in North America,[45] is currently in the midst of an unprecedented debate over secularism in the public sphere. In a province that recently instituted a ban on turbans at soccer pitches—and was forced to retreat—the provincial government in Quebec has recently proposed the verbosely titled, "Charter Affirming The Values Of State Secularism and Religious Neutrality and of Equality Between Men and Women, and Providing a Framework for Accommodation Requests." This legislation would prohibit overt religious symbols from all public spaces, including on the persons of public employees, including teachers, and daycare workers. "In the exercise of their functions, personnel members of public bodies must not wear objects such as headgear, clothing, jewelry or other adornments which, by their conspicuous nature, overtly indicate

---

39. Gerson, "This Isn't Supposed to Be a Christian Country."
40. Baklinski, "Ontario Tribunal Bans Bible Distribution."
41. "Community Covenant Agreement."
42. Ruby and Chan, "Clayton Ruby and Gerald Chan."
43. McGill, "Counterpoint." At the time of this writing, five of ten Provincial law societies in Canada have voted to exclude future grads from Trinity Western from practicing law in their jurisdiction.
44. "No Gay-Free Law School Should Stand in Canada."
45. In Quebec, post WWII weekly attendance at Mass was recorded as an incredible 90 percent. Noll, *What Happened to Christian Canada?*, 14.

a religious affiliation."[46] Even for a country widely believed to happily embrace secularism, this has proven to be a hard pill to swallow.[47]

Christians may wonder, in the midst of a society that has come to worship multiculturalism, whether the outcry against this proposal has far more to do with restrictions against turbans, niqabs, kippas, and hijabs, than with crucifixes. At least one community in Quebec has announced it will not apply the "racist" new charter. In their Council resolution, included under "Unanimously Resolved" was the following: "*That* we believe the wearing of a Kipah, Sikh turban, or Hijab, is not an impediment to carrying out ones' duties as employees of the State. These symbols do not diminish the wearer, they do not impede the wearer and they are not prejudicial to those with whom the wearer of a religious symbol interacts . . . "[48]

Even my home province of Newfoundland and Labrador, long considered one of the more conservative provinces in Canada, has not been immune to changing tides. A local clergyperson was recently invited to share the meaning of Easter at school assembly.[49] The school board was forced to review its policies after a parent contacted the media, noting she was "appalled" at the presentation of religious themes in a public school.[50] With the demise of the province's denominational school system just 18 years ago, religious imagery remains a common feature of many schools. In recent months, a large cross adorning St. Matthew's school was removed because of a complaint from a single parent.[51] One imagines that "Holy Spirit High School" in St. John's will shortly be targeted for renaming.

Markers of Religious Decline in Canada: Statistical Evidence

Reginald Bibby is a well-recognized Canadian sociologist who has charted the course of Canadian religious involvement for almost 40 years and authored a series of books reporting his finding and interpreting the results.[52]

46. "Charter Affirming the Values of State."
47. "Quebec Religious Symbols Ban Proposal Roundly Condemned."
48. "Town of Hampstead Won't Apply 'Racist' Quebec Charter."
49. As we have noted, Newfoundland and Labrador had a publically funded, but denominationally administered, school system until 1997. The first of these challenges to religious overtones in the newly "public" system are just emerging.
50. Kean, "Religious School Assembly Concerns Parent."
51. "School Cross to Be Removed after Parent Complaint."
52. See, for example: Bibby and Posterski, *Teen Trends*; Bibby, *Fragmented Gods*; idem, *Restless Gods: The Renaissance of Religion in Canada*; idem, *The Boomer Factor*; idem, *The Emerging Millennials*; idem, "Continuing the Conversation on Canada."; idem, *Beyond the Gods & Back*.

In many ways, his is the most complete set of data available on the subject, spanning the period from 1975 to 2008—eleven national surveys in all. Leaving interpretation aside momentarily, we will first explore Canadian attitudes towards Christianity by the numbers, availing both of Bibby's work within Canada, and other surveys since 2000 that have enabled us to view Canada in a global perspective.

A quick look at the statistics included in one of Bibby's latest works[53] is enough to give us considerable pause for thought:

Canadian Weekly Church Attendance:

- 1945—60 percent
- 1975—31 percent
- 2005—25 percent

Quebec Roman Catholic Monthly-Plus Adult Attendance:

- 1965—83 percent
- 1985—50 percent
- 2005—21 percent

National Membership in the Anglican Church:

- 1941—800,000
- 1961—1,350,000
- 2010—500,000

National Membership in the United Church:

- 1941—700,000
- 1961—1,000,000
- 2010—500,000

---

53. The five charts detailing this information may be found in Bibby, *The Resilience & Restructuring of Religion in Canada*, 5, 9.

Canadian Church Service Attendance:

- Weekly—19 percent
- Monthly—9 percent
- Yearly—30 percent
- Never—42 percent

Bibby has released four major works on the Canadian religious[54] scene. The first, *Fragmented Gods*, was released in 1987. Bibby notes, "At that time there seemed to be considerable support for the secularization thesis. With few exceptions, attendance and membership had declined steadily since the 1960s. People continued to identify with religious traditions. But most appeared to be pursuing religion in a fragmented, pick and choose, à la carte fashion."[55] In 1993 he updated his findings in *Unknown Gods*, suggesting that the ongoing participation problems for the country's dominant religious groups were due in large part by the failure of these groups to respond properly to widespread interests and needs. He notes,

> The first two books were informed by and provided empirical support for the secularization thesis. Religion, by and large, I maintained, had suffered a significant lost in influence in Canada at the individual and institutional levels from the 1960s through the mid-1990s.[56]

2002 saw the release of the third (and most optimistic) book: *Restless Gods: The Renaissance of Religion in Canada*. This book drew on data suggesting that the downward slide of religious life might have leveled off, and revitalization might be in the works. Writing in 2011 however, Bibby admitted,

> To be sure, the new life was fairly modest, and I noted that it might turn out to be merely a minor blip on the secularization screen. The argument did not lack for critics both outside and inside the churches. To speak of "a renaissance" might have been to exaggerate developments a bit. Still, the available data did not support an ongoing, linear-like decline in participation similar to what occurred between 1960 and 1990.[57]

54. Generally, Bibby has focused upon Christianity and not the many other religions currently present in the Canadian context.
55. Bibby, *Beyond the Gods & Back*, 2.
56. Ibid.
57. Ibid. As we shall see, while church attendance as a measure of the health of

What of Canadian religious life today? In 2011 Bibby released the fourth book in this series, *Beyond the Gods and Back: Religion's Demise and Rise and Why it Matters*. He begins by observing just how significant Canadian church attendance was in the late 1940s to 1960s. For example, he cites a press release from the Canadian Institute of Public Opinion dated May 12, 1945, which notes that a recent Gallup poll found, "about one third of population found church absentees by poll . . . yet Canadian record better than that found in the U.S."[58] Weekly Catholic Church attendance held steady at about 85 percent through this period, while Protestant attendance remained strong at 45 percent. As Cardinal Léger would say of Montreal, "When I bow to say the evening rosary, all of Montreal bows with me."[59] In those heady days, the membership of the Anglican and United churches peaked at over one million; from the mid-40s to mid-60s the United Church alone built 1500 new churches and halls.[60] By the 1970s, however, the decline had begun, and came in earnest. As John Webster Grant noted, "Canadians were shielded from the full impact of the assault on Christendom by their lingering ruralism and isolationism, and they did not immediately recognize the signs that warned of its decline . . . Realization that Christendom was dead, even in Canada, dawned with surprising suddenness in the 1960s . . ."[61] Bowen concurs: "In short, there is general agreement that by the late 1960s at the very latest Canadian churches had come to have very little impact on the dominant secular institutions that now define our nation."[62]

Weekly church attendance, which was actually higher in Canada than the United States in the 1950s, has fallen from a high of 60 percent in 1945 to just 25 percent in 2005.[63] Bibby writes,

> Demographically, what happened was fairly straightforward. Canada's Great Religious Recession took place in large part because Protestant Mainline groups no longer knew the luxury of gushing immigration pipelines. To make matters worse, their birthrates were down and their policies and strategies for retaining their children were not always well-developed and well-executed. Their third and last numerical life-line—recruiting outsiders—was not

---

Christianity in Canada has stabilized, the numbers of those declaring they have no religious affiliation whatsoever is skyrocketing.

58. Ibid., 10.
59. Ibid., 11.
60. Ibid.
61. Grant, *The Church in the Canadian Era*, 216.
62. Bowen, *Christians in a Secular World*, 11.
63. Bibby, *Beyond the Gods & Back*, 5.

really a viable solution, given the low priority that many assigned to evangelism. The math was consequently pretty simple: by the 1970s the number of active members who were dying outnumbered the people who were taking their places.[64]

Further, Bibby notes four key trends we may observe in the Boomer[65] generation. First, they grew up in an era that saw religious dominance give way to diversity in every sphere of Canadian life. Second, whereas the generation that preceded the Boomers felt a strong sense of duty and loyalty to their denominations, Boomers tended more towards gratification: "So it is that, for some time now, the majority of us have been highly selective consumers in every area of life. Religion has not received an exemption."[66] Third, Boomers drifted from the high level of deference and respect automatically shown by their parents to institutions including schools, governments, and churches. Individual freedom became the rallying cry, resulting in the careful scrutiny of all authoritative structures. Finally, Bibby cites the doubling of women working outside the home (from 30 percent in 1960 to 60 percent in 2000) as playing a major factor in declining church attendance. Harvard sociologist Robert Putnam concurs, noting "full-time employment appears to cut home entertaining by roughly 10 percent, and church attendance by roughly 15 percent, informal visiting with friends by 25 percent, and volunteering by more than 50 percent."[67] Boomers are not necessarily negative towards traditional religion; they simply do not have the time to fit as much religious observance into their busy lives as did their parents.

Polarization

Post-boomer generations provided a small surprise to pollsters. As Bibby notes, his 1984 Project Teen Canada[68] survey showed a weekly attendance of 23 percent, which fell to 18 percent in the 1992 survey. They expected a further drop in the 2000 survey; it didn't happen. Instead, the percentage rose to 21 percent. Even in their older peers, weekly attendance has stabilized: 1990 and 1995 surveys put weekly attendance in Canada at 24 percent, which fell

---

64. Ibid., 15.

65. Baby Boomers are denoted as those born in the two decades immediately following the return of millions of fighting men from the theatres of World War II in Europe and Asia, typically dated to those born from 1946 to 1963. Chapter five will explore generational issues in greater detail.

66. Bibby, *Beyond the Gods & Back*, 21.

67. Putnam, *Bowling Alone*, 195. Cited in Bibby, *Beyond the Gods & Back*, 27.

68. Those surveyed were 15–19 years old.

to 22 percent in 2000, but rebounded to 25 percent in 2005. These numbers lead Bibby to proclaim in *Restless Gods* that something of a renaissance was taking place. As he notes in his more recent works, however, while weekly attendance as a measure of the health of Christianity was closely monitored, few noticed the trends among those declaring they never attended worship or had no religious affiliation. Those numbers are staggering: the percentage of teenagers who say they "never" attend services has almost doubled since the 1980s, from about 25 percent to 50 percent. Across Canada, the percentages of those reporting "no religion" have been consistently growing. From just 4 percent in 1971, the first year Statistics Canada included that category as an option, this number has grown to 12 percent in 1991, 16 percent by 2001, and an astonishing 24 percent in the 2001 National Household Survey.[69] By way of contrast, American numbers in 2012 stand at 20 percent in the same category, up from 15 percent just five years previous.[70] Therefore, while an overwhelming percentage of Canadians still self-declare as affiliated with a major religious group, and though attendance at weekly worship services appears to be on the rise, however slightly, we may observe in the rapidly rising percentages of those professing no religious affiliation an increasing polarization of the Canadian religious content.

Before leaving this section, we will comment briefly on the popular resurgence in atheism. Though writers such as Richard Dawkins[71] and Christopher Hitchens,[72] among others, have garnered their fair share of media, Bibby notes that Canadians who say they do not believe in God has held almost steady for the last 30 years: the figure was 6 percent in 1975, and climbed only to 7 percent in 2005. More troubling however is the movement in this area among teens, from 6 percent in 1984 to 16 percent in 2005. Bibby admits, "To the best of my knowledge, the 16 percent total for atheism among teens today is the highest level of atheism ever recorded for any age group in Canada."[73]

Secularization and Post Christendom in Canada: Summary

It would seem that the jury is still out on the full secularization of Canada even while evidence of post-Christendom abounds. While we have seen

69. "2011 National Household Survey: Data Tables."
70. "'Nones' on the Rise."
71. Dawkins, *The God Delusion*.
72. Hitchens, *God Is Not Great*.
73. Bibby, *Beyond the Gods & Back*, 48–49.

percentages of those regularly attending Sunday worship plummet, we've also noted that more than two-thirds of the country describe themselves as Christian. Simultaneously, the numbers of citizens reporting that they have no religious affiliation is rising steadily. While Christendom as defined earlier is undoubtedly on the wane, we must recognize that post-Christendom need not mean post-Christian; we will discuss this in chapter 8 as we consider appropriate Pentecostal responses to secularism and post-Christendom. Is Canada still Christian? Lori Beaman believes so: ". . . despite the inroads of secularization, and evidence crisis of religious commitment and an expanding non-European presence in its population, Canada undoubtedly remains remarkably Christian in a broad sense of that term . . ."[74] As noted, however, the foundations of Christendom—the primary influence of Christians and the Christian religion throughout the whole of the public and political sphere, has essentially come to an end. Recalling Redekop's five descriptors for our consideration of how we may consider Canada a Christian country, we have observed in the preceding pages the clear movement from category 3—*A Christian country is one in which Christianity is the dominant religion and its values are reflected in the laws of the land but the government does not use coercive power to assist religious organizations*—to category 5: *A Christian country is one in which Christianity, although mostly in a nominal form, is still the dominant religion, and its principles and ethos still impact society. However, governments, courts, media, and the schools at all levels strive to remove from the public institutions of society anything that is obviously Christian, for example, Christian celebrations of Christmas and Easter.*[75]

Is secularism still a threat? I would suggest it is, though more from within than without. That is, while churches have had their numbers whittled away by secularist forces, those still attending have exhibited increasingly secular worldviews and attitudes.[76] It is my contention that the church has been so busy "looking out the window," blaming secularization, and lamenting the demise of Christendom, that it has forgotten to "look in the mirror" and ask whether the substantial critiques lobbied against the church in recent decades are not entirely without merit.

As Barth dryly noted,

> Throughout the world, the Church is concerned today with the problem of the secularization of the modern man. It would

---

74. Beaman, *Religion and Canadian Society*, 9.

75. Redekop, "Is Canada Becoming a Post-Christian Country?"

76. As Peter Berger wrote, "American Christians [held] the same values as anyone else—only with more emphatic solemnity." Berger, *The Noise of Solemn Assemblies*. Cited in Bibby, *Beyond the Gods & Back: Religion's Demise and Rise and Why It Matters*, 35.

perhaps be more profitable if the Church were at least to begin to become concerned with the problem of its own secularization.[77]

We will seek to address this issue in chapter 9, in our discussion of *beliefs vs. values*. As we will discuss in chapter 8, however, I concur with those who view the demise of Christendom as a positive in the life of the Church, and believe the dismantling of the relationship between Christianity and Western culture can only serve to bring renewal to a Church trapped in the vestiges of Constantinianism. Further, as we shall see, Pentecostalism, by reframing what has always been the core of the movement, is still in an excellent place to bring the Gospel to those so desperately needing it—particularly those of a secular mindset, long opposed to official Christendom.

Having explored recent trends in the Canadian religious scene, we now continue our discussion of Canadian society by exploring the philosophical trends that are contributing to secularism both inside and outside the church. Due in part to space restrictions, and in part to the natural affinity between the two subjects, this study will limit its focus to postmodernism in terms of Pentecostal engagement with current trends in philosophical and cultural ideas. Missing will be substantive discussion on another key area of current thought—atheistic secularism.[78] Work remains to be done on the interaction between this other significant cultural movement and Pentecostalism. To an examination of postmodernism we now turn.

Postmodernism

Postmodernism. The very word suggests a myriad of possible definitions. Even those writers considered postmodern intone: "I have the impression that [the term Postmodernism] is applied today to anything the users of the term happen to like."[79] This should perhaps not be surprising, as it is a trend in philosophy and culture defined largely by what it is not, and what it has moved past. Postmodern ideas first appeared in the arts and architecture and has now spread to almost every sector of society, its impact growing more substantial by the day. In perhaps no area will the impact of postmodern thinking be more substantial than in Christian life and thought, particularly as it applies to the theology and methods of evangelism. This

---

77. Barth, *God in Action*, 15. Quoted in Craig A. Carter, *Rethinking Christ and Culture*, 11.

78. See for example Cimino and Smith, "The New Atheism."

79. Eco, *Postscript to the Name of the Rose*, 65.

chapter will limit itself to the discussion of postmodernity as it interacts with Christian theology in particular.

At its core postmodern thinking contains a vast array of thoughts, ideas, and concepts. Several of these are antithetical to traditional Christian thought, particularly among Western Christian groups whom the Enlightenment has profoundly impacted. In particular, the postmodern rejection of rationalism as the arbiter of truth, openness to the role of experience in determining truth, and recognition of the importance of narratives in communication, stand in stark contrast to many of the cherished values of Pentecostalism. At the same time, however, the student of postmodernity is struck by some of the more intense similarities between the postmodern way of thought and the thought patterns of the earliest Pentecostals. For the purposes of this chapter, we will explore five facets of postmodern thought, noting the themes of community and narratives, importance of experience, and rejection of rationalism as they intersect early Pentecostal thought and hermeneutics. It is to these congruencies and contradictions we now turn.

An Overview[80]

At its essence, postmodernism[81] is a worldview consisting of anti-foundationalism[82], disbelief in pure objectivity, and deconstruction of "certain" knowledge, primarily characterized by a reaction to the prevailing worldview of Modernism. It therefore behooves us to first briefly examine the chief tenets of Modernity and the current reaction to it. Although it does encapsulate some thinking of the early Greek philosophers, postmodernity[83] is not a return to the pre-modern mindset. Rather, it seeks to modify the best

---

80. This summary is abbreviated from Noel, *Pentecostal and Postmodern Hermeneutics*.

81. For a sample of sources attempting to define Postmodernity, see Finger, "Modernity, Postmodernity," 353–368; Gitlin, "The Postmodern Predicament"; Percesepe, "The Unbearable Lightness of Being Postmodern"; Gelder, "Postmodernism as an Emerging Worldview."

82. *Foundationalism* may be defined as "Philosophical or theological approaches affirming specific truths as bases and criteria for all others truths." See McKim, *Westminster Dictionary of Theological Terms*. For the Christian, the belief in the God who created humanity and the universe, and who revealed himself in Jesus Christ and through his Word, is foundational.

83. We may differentiate *Postmodernism* - a philosophical stance and presuppositions, from *postmodernity* - the outworking of postmodernism and resultant cultural shift. As Stuart Murray notes, "Whatever we think of postmodernism, we inhabit postmodernity." Murray, *Post-Christendom*, 12–13. Also see Thiselton, "Postmodernity, Postmodernism."

from the premodern mind without falling prey to the dry rationalism and restrictive epistemological foundationalism of Modernity.[84]

Modernity

The foundations of the Modern era as defined in chapter 1 may be witnessed as early as the late 1500s. Renaissance thinker Francis Bacon (1561–1626) had begun to extol the virtues of human knowledge gained through scientific experimentation. Bacon believed that expanded scientific knowledge would give humans the power they needed over the circumstances of life, altering them to our benefit.[85]

Often considered the father of Modern philosophy, René Descartes (1596–1650) attempted to devise a scientific method of investigation by which one could determine which truths could be identified as veracious. Though a skeptic in many areas, Descartes allowed that one could doubt everything except one's own existence. Borrowing from Augustine, he made popular the phrase *Cogito ergo sum*—"I think, therefore I am." Descartes' definition of the human person as a thinking substance and rational subject established the centrality of human mind in epistemology, and thus set the agenda for the next three hundred years of scientific and philosophical inquiry. Grenz notes:

> Descartes exercised immense influence on all subsequent thinking. Throughout the modern era, intellectuals in many disciplines have turned to the reasoning subject rather than divine revelation as the starting point for knowledge and reflection. Even modern theologians felt constrained to build on the foundation of rationalistic philosophy.[86]

Moral absolutes, once the purview of the deity in Christian theology, were preserved only as they served a utilitarian purpose. That which served the functioning of society was considered good, and that which hindered the growth and development of humanity was evil. Humanity, and in

---

84. "The Enlightenment project . . . took it as axiomatic that there was only one possible answer to any question. From this it followed that the world could be controlled and rationally ordered if we could only picture and represent it rightly. But this presumed that there existed a single correct mode of representation which, if we could uncover it (and this was what scientific and mathematical endeavours were all about), would provide the means to Enlightenment ends." See Harvey, *The Condition of Postmodernity*, 27.

85. See Wolterstorff, *Reason within the Bounds of Religion*, 123–24.

86. Grenz, *A Primer on Postmodernism*, 65.

particular, human individualism, became sovereign; the value of the collective was sacrificed at the altar of the individual. As Erickson notes, "In the premodern era the church's traditional authorities, the philosopher, and the Bible, had prevailed, but in the modern period, the flight from these external authorities led to a focus on the individual as the basis for authority . . . [T]he individual has priority over the collective."[87] As rationalism peaked, optimism soared in Modern thinkers who felt they could remake society into a veritable utopia, with the assumption that were reason applied properly and the principles of the universe discovered, all problems could be solved by human planning. Hence Bacon's famous dictum: "Knowledge is power."[88]

As Modernity moved from victory to victory, several smaller movements arose in reaction to it, and formed the basis for postmodernism. Early nineteenth century Romanticism reversed the cold rationalism of the Enlightenment and instead saw the universe as a living organism, with feeling at the pinnacle of our humanity. With God close at hand and intimately involved in the physical world, some taught a new Pantheism, as God became as close as the self, one with humanity and the universe, transcendent no longer. Thus, Romanticism cultivated irrationalism, encouraged introspection, and raised subjectivity and personal experience to new levels of influence.[89]

Existentialism arose in the early nineteenth century as thinkers pondered the increasing failure of both Enlightenment rationalism and romantic emotionalism to offer meaning for the individual. For the existentialist, meaning is a purely human phenomenon, discovered quite apart from the objective world. As Veith astutely observes, "While there is no ready-made meaning in life, individuals can create meaning for themselves . . . This meaning, however, has no validity for anyone else. No one can provide a meaning for someone else. Everyone must determine his or her own meaning . . ."[90] Existentialism thereby provides the rationale for contemporary relativism; religion is a personal affair, as is morality. No one can decide religious affiliation or moral belief for another—what is right for one may not be right for another. By the mid-twentieth century, the foundation was well in place for postmodern thought. Jaichandran and Madhav conclude:

> Modernity is characterized by the triumph of Enlightenment, exaltation of rights of humans, and the supremacy of reason.

---

87. Erickson, *Truth or Consequences*, 28.

88. Grenz, *A Primer on Postmodernism*, 58–59. See also Wolterstorff, *Reason with the Bounds*, 123–35.

89. Veith, *Postmodern Times*, 35–37.

90. Ibid.

Modernism assumed that human reason was the only reliable way of making sense of the universe. Anything that could not be understood in scientific terms was either not true or not worth knowing. Human beings, by means of scientific reason, could make sense of the world and even manipulate it for their own benefit with or without reference to God (who or whatever he/she/it might be) . . . this ability to understand and manipulate the natural world . . . held out the promise of unlimited progress.

As the twentieth century progressed, some of the first cracks began to appear in the modernist worldview and the myth of progress. Two world wars showed that the same scientific technological progress that promised great hope to mankind could also be used to inflict untold suffering on men, women, and children and could even destroy the whole world . . . Hope was shattered. Thus, modernism and the myth of scientific progress is dead or at least in its final stages, but there is nothing to take its place. We do not know what is coming, only that it will be the worldview that replaced modernism. Until we know exactly what form it will take, we might as well call it postmodernism for the time being.[91]

Postmodernity: The Key Tenets

There are many facets of postmodern thought, and not all erudite authors on postmodernity agree on what comprises this stimulating worldview. For the purposes of this chapter we will first provide a cursory look at five common postmodern themes: Anti-foundationalism, Deconstruction of Language, Denial of Absolute Truth, Virtual Reality, and Decimation of Individuality/Promotion of Community.[92]

The Anti-foundationalism of Postmodernism

In the postmodern mind, knowledge is uncertain. It therefore abandons foundationalism—the idea that knowledge can be built upon the basis of irrefutable first principles and basic truths which lead ultimately to God Himself, and upon which rational thought and progress can be based.[93]

---

91. Jaichandran and Madhav, "Pentecostal Spirituality," 45.

92. We are indebted in part for the breakdown of categories to Jaichandran and Madhav, "Pentecostal Spirituality," 45–49.

93. See Erickson, *Truth and Consequences*, 252–72, for an excellent discussion on

The Moderns assume that values are not merely a product of the human intellect but rather they were embedded in a reality that transcends us. This transcendent reality guarantees that truth exists; humanity does not create truth but rather discovers it through reason. Postmoderns discard the Enlightenment assumption that truth is certain and therefore entirely rational. Grenz observes, "The postmodern mind refuses to limit truth to its rational dimension and thus dethrones the human intellect as the arbiter of truth. There are other valid paths to knowledge besides reason, say the Postmoderns, including the emotions, experience, and the intuition."[94]

Deconstruction of Language

For the postmodern, metanarratives are inherently suspect. As Jaichandran and Madhav note, "This is the essence of Deconstructionism—the knocking down of would-be big stories (worldviews with universalistic pretensions), often through listening to the local understandings of truth of minority communities."[95] Overarching universal narratives that connect with all of humankind (such as the biblical story of creation) are discarded out of hand. For the supporter of deconstruction, all meaning is created by the individual; the reality of one is as real as the reality of another, for we create our own realities. Though rejecting metanarratives as the universal stories of humanity, many postmoderns accentuate the place of oral traditions, narratives, and stories within the community as essential to ongoing human communication.[96]

In terms of communication, deconstruction declares that contradictions are inherent in all discourse; the "true" meaning cannot be discovered. Readers must take an active role in determining subjective meaning. "Postmodernist theories begin with the assumption that language cannot render truths about the world in an objective way. Language, by its very

---

foundationalism, Postmodernity, and Christianity. Also see DePaul, *Resurrecting Old-Fashioned Foundationalism*.

94. Grenz, *A Primer on Postmodernism*, 7.

95. Jaichandran and Madhav, "Pentecostal Spirituality," 46. See also Grenz, *A Primer on Postmodernism*, 168, who states: "The community of participation is crucial to identity formation. A sense of personal identity develops through the telling of a personal narrative, which is always embedded in the story of the communities in which we participate."

96. Erickson, *Truth and Consequence*, 202. Another author suggests that " . . . Postmodernism [is] not a rejection of metanarrative itself, but [is] *a transitional phase rejecting the metanarratives of an integrated Western worldview for the emergence of new integrations in the global/local culture.*" See Grigg, "The Spirit of Church."

nature, shapes what we think. Since language is a cultural creation, meaning is ultimately (again) a social construction."[97]

Inherent in the practice of deconstruction is a hermeneutic of suspicion. Thomas Oden explains:

> By deconstruction, we mean the dogged application of a hermeneutic of suspicion to any given text, where one finds oneself always over against the text, always asking the sceptical question about the text, asking what self-deception or bad faith might be unconsciously motivating a particular conceptuality.[98]

The Denial of Absolute Truth: The Importance of Experience

In the Modern mind, absolute truth is simply "out there," available for discovery by the persistent truth-seeker. For the postmodern, truth does not exist outside of subjective experience; therefore, no version of truth is greater than any other. Some forms of postmodernism are inherently pluralistic—some postmodernists believe absolute truth does not exist. The postmodern mind rejects the Enlightenment notion that knowledge is objective. Grenz views postmodern reality as, "relative, indeterminate, and participatory."[99]

Virtual Reality

Reflecting on the postmodern view of human existence, Francis Schaeffer laments, "Since our existence has no meaning and we are not connected to history or its values by any binding truths, no one can be quite certain where reality and non-reality start and stop."[100] A key ingredient here is the blurring of fact with fiction, often through the participation by the individual in the virtual world via technology—all reality is virtual reality. Veith wryly observes:

> Thus the life of the mind has a new model—not Socrates searching for truth through dialogues in the marketplace, not Augustine contemplating his own life in light of Scripture, not Newton scrutinizing nature with mathematical rigor, not the scientist

---

97. Veith, *Postmodern Times*, 51. See also Adams, "A Theological Understanding."
98. Oden, *Two Worlds*, 79.
99. Grenz, *A Primer on Postmodernism*, 7.
100. Schaeffer, *The Church at the End of the Twentieth Century*, 50.

working in the lab or the historian shifting through archival evidence. The new model for intellectual achievement is a dazed couch potato watching TV.[101]

Decimation of Individuality / Promotion of Community

For Rorty in particular, the self is created by external forces such as cultural and social factors, to the extent that searching for one's inner self is pointless—it does not exist. Postmoderns have decreased the prominence of the individual in favour of the importance of community. Rorty's strong emphasis on community and society denies humanity its traditional place within Modernism as the centre of the universe.[102] Veith notes that in many cases,

> The postmodern worldview operates with a community-based understanding of truth. It affirms that whatever we accept as truth and even the way we envision truth are dependent on the community in which we participate. Further, and far more radically, the postmodern worldview affirms that this relativity extends beyond our *perceptions* of truth to its essence: there is no absolute truth; rather truth is relative to the community in which we participate.
>
> On the basis of this assumption, postmodern thinkers have given up the Enlightenment quest for any one universal, supracultural, timeless truth. They focus instead on what is held to be true within a specific community. They maintain that truth consists in the ground rules that facilitate the well-being of the community in which one participates. In keeping with this emphasis, postmodern society tends to be a communal society.[103]

As the mass culture becomes more and more impersonal, individuals lose themselves in the mass mind or in highly segmented groups. The human is lost ... The anti-humanism of the postmodernists cannot sustain any of the so-called 'human values.' Freedom, individuality, self-worth, altruism, love—these

---

101. Veith, *Postmodern Times*, 61. See also Myers, *All God's Children and Blue Suede Shoes*. Myers demonstrates the impact of television culture on all aspects of society— even academia.

102. See Rorty, *Philosophy and the Mirror of Nature*; idem, *Objectivity, Relativism, and Truth*; idem, *Consequences of Pragmatism*.

103. Grenz, *A Primer on Postmodernism*, 7–8.

are masks for oppression. The individual human being is swallowed up by culture; cultures are swallowed up by nature.[104]

With this philosophical presupposition, we may conclude that humanity becomes no more important than any other living thing—plant or animal. Naturally, the theological implications of human life without special significance are enormous.

Postmodernism and Evangelicalism: A Critique

As one might expect, Evangelicalism (including Pentecostalism) has not responded with great enthusiasm to several of the basic tenets of postmodernity.[105] At its core, postmodern thought contradicts key Evangelical beliefs at crucial points. Some postmodern individuals, for example, will likely believe that all truth is relative and subjective; the foundation of the Evangelical Gospel is that absolute truth may be found in God Himself, revealed through the life of Christ and the Scriptures. A key text here for many is John 14:6: "Jesus said, 'I am the way, the truth, and the life . . .'" The understanding of this truth as a commodity during the long reign of Christendom has immeasurably weakened our portrayal of the Gospel; perhaps an unintended consequence of the postmodern understanding of truth as relative will be the restoration of the church's commitment to the truth as embodied in the person of Christ.

On other issues, such as the rejection of rationalism, postmodern thought has something of significance to contribute to segments of Evangelicalism largely overrun with rationalist tendencies. Given the prevalence of postmodern thought within Western society and the tremendous impact of Christian values upon the same, it is inevitable that these two movements should intersect (and collide) at key junctures.

One may well ask, as Erickson has, whether postmodern influence has pervaded Evangelical thought to the extent that an evaluation of the former by the latter is necessitated or even possible.[106] Quite apart from substantial

---

104. Veith, *Postmodern Times*, 72, 79.

105. On postmodernism as a whole, some Evangelical scholars are more accepting. See, for example, Raschke, *The Next Reformation*. Raschke argues that ". . . Evangelical Christianity made its own unholy alliance with Cartesian rationalism and British evidentialism as far back as the seventeenth century, taking the wrong turn at a decisive juncture and thereby, compromising the original spirit of the Reformation . . . the postmodern turn in Western thought widens the prospects for Evangelical Christianity to flourish once again as a progressive rather than reactionary force in the present-day world," 9.

106. Erickson, *The Postmodern World*, 59.

anecdotal evidence, a variety of studies conducted by the Barna Research Group conclude that postmodern thinking has made tremendous inroads into Evangelical thought. For example, a 1991 survey in which the Barna organization presented the statement, "There is no such thing as absolute truth; different people can define truth in conflicting ways and still be correct," found that a majority of those who identified themselves as Evangelical Christians either agreed or strongly agreed with the statement. As Erickson suggests, this reveals the striking impact of postmodernity upon Evangelicalism.[107]

Postmodernism and Evangelicalism: Areas of Beneficial Interaction [108]

To be sure, the impact of postmodernity upon Evangelical Christianity is neither entirely positive nor negative. Despite calls in some Christian circles for a wholesale rejection of postmodern thought, a number of Evangelical scholars believe there is much we can learn from the Postmodern critique of the modernist thought so prevalent in much of Western Christianity. We now turn to the areas of beneficial interaction between Evangelicalism and postmodernism.

a) *The Conditioned Nature of Knowledge.* The supporters of deconstruction within postmodernity have correctly observed that time, place, culture, and past experience each influence our perception of truth and our interpretive conclusions. Many Christians, however, continue to pursue the Modern concept of truly objective knowledge. These individuals, often unaware of their own presuppositions formed by culture and experience, read into the text that which they are attempting to interpret objectively. The end result can be anything but truly objective.[109]

b) *The Limitations of Foundationalism.* Practically, postmoderns are also correct in their rejection of foundationalism as a common ground for communication about issues of faith and truth. Concepts that might be considered intuitive and self-evident by Evangelicals are in many

---

107. Ibid., 62. See Barna, *The Barna Report: What Americans*, 84–85.

108. This section is loosely based on observations by Erickson, *Truth or Consequences*.

109. On this point Erickson suggests that we should, "be willing to allow ourselves to feel the full force of the postmodernists' contention. This includes the contention that there are alternative logics." See Erickson, *Truth or Consequences*, 189.

cases no longer viewed as such by society as a whole. Christians must discover new means of finding common ground with others; natural theology based on a rational demonstration of God's existence will no longer suffice.

c) *The Necessity of a Hermeneutic of Suspicion.* Postmodernists often employ a hermeneutic of suspicion, asking whether persons have vested interest in the position they propose. Erickson suggests that in our interpretive methods we must apply a hermeneutic of suspicion to our own beliefs and doctrines, recognizing that we are far more likely to believe statements that concur with our belief systems than those that do not.[110] Postmodern thought, especially that of Derrida, is valuable as it helps us to recognize the inherent contradictions in many cherished arguments.[111] While Modernity was often content to present summaries of debated issues as if there were no possible objections, an awareness of apparent contradictions within any argument or interpretation may be viewed as healthy, particularly in terms of academic integrity.

d) *The Role of the Community.* Postmodern thought has truly made a significant contribution to Church life in particular through its emphasis on the importance of community. Reacting to the Modern exaltation of the individual, postmodernists have once again placed the individual back in significant connection with others. A writer for the *Sydney Morning Herald* describes this trend among Australian youth:

> [Today's youth] are members of a generation who spend all day together at school, then get on the bus to go home and ring each other up on the mobile phone, or send a stream of text messages to each other. 'Where are you now? Who are you with?' they inquire solicitously, while their parents pay the bill for this flow of continuous contact. Then, when they arrive home, they hop on the internet to link up again in a chat room, or via email . . . 'They are a generation that beeps and hums,' one of their fathers recently remarked, and so they are. They are the generation who, having grown up in an era of unprecedentedly rapid change, have intuitively understood that they are each other's most precious resource for coping with the inherent uncertainties of life. Their desire to connect, and to stay connected, will reshape this society. They are the harbingers of a new sense of community,

---

110. Erickson, *Truth or Consequences*, 200.
111. See Derrida, *Of Grammatology*; idem, *Margins of Philosophy*.

a new tribalism that will change everything from our old-fashioned respect for privacy to the way we conduct our relationships and build our homes. The era of individualism is not dead yet, but the intimations of its mortality are clear.[112]

Postmodernity strives to be aware of the impact of the community and our experiences with others on our own interpretation of issues and events. For the Christian, this concurs with the New Testament emphasis on the individual as a part of the body of Christ, and acknowledges the significant fact that the majority of Scripture was written not to individual believers, but to Christians who are a part of a larger body of believers.

e) *The Importance of Narratives.* For Pentecostals in particular, the Postmodern emphasis on the value of narratives rings true with what has historically been a Pentecostal focus. As Erickson notes, a majority of the world's cultures still prefer oral rather than written communication, and find it easier to remember key pieces of information in story form, rather than rational, well-argued discourse.[113] Having gleaned the "distinctive doctrines" of Subsequence and Initial Evidence from the narratives of Acts, Pentecostals as a whole will benefit from the postmodern focus upon the importance of the story.

Postmodernism and Evangelicalism: Areas of Incongruity [114]

As one might expect with a system of thought as challenging as that of postmodernity, there are numerous points of contention with traditional Evangelical thought.[115] Though the ideas presented below are seemingly contradictory to key aspects of Evangelical dogma, each presents an opportunity for a fresh Evangelical look at the concept in question.

a) *Deconstruction.* Taken to their logical conclusion, many varieties of deconstruction pose significant challenges for Christians. Based on the premise that there is contradiction inherent in each system of thought, this approach often presupposes that a logically consistent presentation of the system of truth embodied by the Christian faith

---

112. Mackay, "One for All and All for One."
113. Ibid., 202.
114. See Erickson, *Truth or Consequences*.
115. Also see Davis, "Can There Be an 'Orthodox' Postmodern Theology?," 111–23.

is impossible. Through its efforts to make the reader aware of the inherent contradictions in final and absolute statements based on rationalism, all systems of thought are thusly deconstructed, and collapse into the sum of their contradictions, rendering each meaningless. The challenge for the postmodern thinker is deconstructing the approach of deconstruction; this approach, like many others, must crumble beneath the weight of its apparent contradictions if it is believed to be credible.[116]

b) *Linguistic Challenges and Relativism.* According to McQuilkin and Mullen, postmodern thought, as it interacts with literary criticism, linguistics, and communications theory, has argued as follows:

> Language cannot accurately communicate thought to another person's mind, and with time and cultural distance the attempt becomes ever more futile . . . The inadequacy of language is not necessarily bad because meaning is constituted of a combination of what is out there (objects and events, including the words of others), and what is in here (my own subjective sense.) Though the words of others play a formative role, the controlling element is what I bring to the text. And the outcome of that mix is all the reality there is. Thus meaning is relative, particularly relative to my present subjective perceptions.[117]

Evangelicals take exception to the postmodern emphasis on the weakness of language to communicate, and the resultant rampant subjectivism. While the renewed recognition of the significant role our presuppositions play in our hermeneutics has been beneficial, many Christians are not comfortable identifying our personal version of "meaning" with reality, which we believe exists independently of our perceptions.[118] Stanley Grenz notes:

> As Christians, we can go only so far with Derrida, for example, in his unrelenting attack on the "metaphysics of

---

116. Erickson, *Truth or Consequences*, 205. Erickson insists that the approach of deconstruction should itself be subject to deconstruction. He notes that Derrida disagrees, equating deconstruction with justice, which can never be deconstructed. "Justice in itself, if such a thing exists, outside or beyond law, is not deconstructable. No more than deconstruction itself, if such a thing exists. Deconstruction is justice." See Derrida, "Force of Law," 14–15.

117. McQuilkin and Mullen, "The Impact of Postmodern Thinking on Evangelical Hermeneutics," 71.

118. Ibid.

presence" and "logocentricism." In contrast to postmodern thought, we believe that there is a unifying centre to reality. More specifically, we acknowledge that this centre has appeared in Jesus of Nazareth, who is the eternal Word present among us.

Therefore, we agree that in this world we will witness the struggle among conflicting narratives and interpretations of reality. But we add that although all interpretations are in some sense invalid, they cannot all be *equally* valid. We believe that conflicting interpretations can be evaluated according to a criterion that in some sense transcends them all.[119]

c) *Rejection of Absolute Truth.* With subjectivism raised to a new level, absolute truth is the logical casualty of the postmodern system of thinking. A solid belief in absolute truth depends, in part, upon the presupposition that objectivity is possible in determining what is true. Contrary to the Modern perception of truth as static, objective, and waiting to be discovered, in the postmodern mindset, truth is subjective. For the Evangelical, whose system of beliefs is based on the acceptance of God himself as Truth, as revealed both in Christ and through the Scriptures, the rejection of absolute truth by postmoderns could not be more significant. Without joining themselves to the subjectivity of truth promoted by those of the postmodern mindset, believers must nonetheless learn to present the absolute truth of the Gospel in a manner easily comprehended by those living with a more subjective frame of mind.

d) *Rejection of the Metanarrative.* The Bible presents the story of God and his interaction with creation and humanity. This universal story, or metanarrative, has been carefully recorded in the Bible, and is proclaimed to be relevant to all of humanity, at all times, in all locations. Evangelicals believe this story is the revelation of God himself, and he has thus inspired the writers of Scripture to record his thoughts. For Christians, there is an objective reality above all others—God himself. It is this reality, informed by the scriptural record of God's metanarrative, which informs our ethics, morality, and understanding of truth. For some postmodernists, however, no such metanarrative exists. Truth exists only as found subjectively by individuals within community. Again, the challenges of this postmodern way of thinking are significant for Evangelicals who wish to promote the Gospel

---

119. Grenz, *A Primer on Postmodernism*, 165.

in a language relevant to postmoderns, while not subscribing to all tenets of postmodern thought. For scholars such as Millard Erickson, the postmodern rejection of the Christian metanarrative is the most compelling of all reasons to view the two as incompatible.

> I would contend that the universal element in the Christian message, the claim that there is one God, one creator, one rule of the human race, is so deeply imbedded in the testimony of the biblical documents that it cannot be wrenched from Christianity without destroying the very organism. While postmodern Evangelical Christians may think the marriage with postmodernism is possible, most non-Christian postmodernists do not share that sanguine understanding of the interrelationship.[120]

Postmodernism: Summary

It has been shown that postmodernity is the natural philosophical outcome of a generation of thinkers disillusioned by the empty promises of optimistic liberalism. By carefully tracing the development of postmodern thought through Modernity into postmodernity, the philosophical underpinnings of this movement have been clearly observed.

The impact of several key philosophers on postmodern thought has been explored. Lyotard's rejection of metanarratives based on the Modern principles of rationalism has been influential,[121] just as Foucault's belief in the power of the subjective self and the impossibility of objectively discovering truth has been instrumental in shaping the postmodern mindset.[122] Derrida's objection to the use of language as has been traditionally understood, led to his promotion of deconstruction, with which all theologians must contend, specifically in the practice of hermeneutics. Rorty's insistence that truth is based simply on philosophical pragmatism, and not on any

---

120. Erickson, *The Postmodern World*, 78. I argue that postmodern thought need not be accepted as a whole; indeed many of those who consider themselves postmodern do not subscribe to the entire variety of postmodern thought as outlined herein. One may well embrace the postmodern tendency to value experience and community without surrendering the entire Christian metanarrative.

121. See in particular his work *The Postmodern Condition: A Report on Knowledge*, which was commissioned in 1979 by the government of Quebec as a report on knowledge in highly developed societies. Lyotard, *The Postmodern Condition*.

122. For a sample of his work see Foucault, *The Archeology of Knowledge and Language*.; Foucault, *Power/Knowledge*.

type of belief in absolutes, has begun to permeate western society. Christian theologians who hold to absolute truth as found in the revelation of Jesus Christ must be prepared to contend with this pragmatic theory of truth, or be deemed irrelevant to the thinking of this culture.

The key tenets of postmodernity have been delineated. These include the rejection of foundationalism, the concept that all knowledge and truth is founded upon key first principles ultimately leading to God Himself. Metanarratives are inherently suspect, though smaller stories of life within community are applauded. The concept of absolute truth as attainable has been discarded; truth is purely subjective. The exalted place of the self so prevalent within Modernity has been replaced by the devaluing of the autonomous self in favour of both the human community and biological life as a whole.

Evangelical Christians have found much to celebrate within Postmodern thought, but also have observed areas that cause grave concern. The Postmodern tendency to highly view the role of existing presuppositions in our ultimate determination of meaning is instructive for believers, as is their inherent hermeneutic of suspicion. The insistence that language cannot be used to convey truth from one to another must be resisted, for the authority of Scripture as the guide for the life and faith of the believer thus hangs in the balance. Postmoderns speak the language of anti-foundationalism; Christians must learn new approaches to find common ground with others, while still holding to the Foundation that has been laid in Jesus Christ.

The important place of community within postmodernity is a valuable reminder to Evangelicals that the individualism so rampant in western culture was never biblical; the value placed upon individual stories and narratives speak to the essential oral traditions of Christianity itself. Evangelical believers must persist in their belief in absolute truth, as found in God himself, and revealed in Christ and the Scriptures. Similarly, Christians cannot abandon their confidence in the story of God and humanity as presented in the scriptures, despite the postmodern rejection of metanarratives. It is upon the story of God and his plan for humanity that our understanding of both soteriology and eschatology rest. Holding similar core doctrinal values as Evangelicals, Pentecostals would generally agree with the above assessment. For Pentecostals however, postmodern thought presents unique challenges and opportunities; these will be delineated in chapter 8.

Conclusion

This chapter has sought to provide the necessary background for our exploration of Pentecostalism in an increasingly secular culture amidst a significant transition to post-Christendom. We have done so by first exploring whether, in fact, Canada may be considered a "Christian" country, and whether the theory of secularization may be held as true. Though discussion on this matter is ongoing, many scholars are warning of the considerable strength of secularism in our culture (and within our churches) even while challenging the assumptions of the secularization theory. I believe this approach to be meritorious. Though we are not at present witnessing the complete secularization of Canadian society, I believe that without doubt in the public sphere we may observe that *Christendom,* however pervasive it may have been in the Canadian context, should be rejected out of hand. While Canada may still be considered a Christian country by a definition that solely relies upon the self-identification of its citizens, we may conclude that in terms of the influence of the Church upon public discourse, Canada as a nation has entered post-Christendom.

We concluded this chapter by providing essential information on key tenets of postmodern thought that have permeated much of Canadian culture. The basis of those systems that so strongly challenge the Church—pluralism, relativism, and denial of absolute truth so often derived from rationalism—all may be found in postmodern thought. Without a proper understanding of postmodernism, therefore, the Church finds herself at a considerable disadvantage as she seeks to engage culture.

Chapter 4 will now explore in greater detail our representative denomination for this study, the Pentecostal Assemblies of Newfoundland and Labrador. After a brief synopsis of this small denomination in Eastern Canada, we will chart some of its efforts to arrest declining numbers and re-engage the culture. Further, we will avail of a denominational survey conducted in 2012 to assist with our understanding of how these Pentecostal believers understand their identity and strength as an organization.

Part 2

— 4 —
A Sample Pentecostal Denomination

The Pentecostal Assemblies of Newfoundland and Labrador

AT THIS POINT IN our study, we have introduced Pentecostalism and set the stage for a discussion of this revival movement vis-à-vis a post-Christendom context. We explored the history and theology of the Pentecostal movement in the West, and endeavoured to shed some light on the resultant Pentecostal subculture. In chapter 3, we brought clear evidence that Canada, in particular, is entering a post-Christendom era, and explored secularism and postmodernism as two key challenges Pentecostalism must consider as it seeks to thrive in the 21st century. In the following chapter we will investigate the impact that generational trends are having upon the Pentecostal church. Clearly understanding the role that significant generational differences have on Pentecostalism as it addresses shifts in the cultural milieu, will greatly enhance leadership's ability to navigate changing tides with discernment and boldness.

Our study will now attempt to bring further clarity to this discussion by exploring a representative Pentecostal denomination—my own tribe, the Pentecostal Assemblies of Newfoundland and Labrador (PAONL). Situated in Canada's most easterly province, the PAONL traces its roots directly back to the Azusa Street revival, and has recently celebrated its centennial. The goal of this chapter is to put "a face in the window" for our discussion of Pentecostal efforts to grow and thrive in a post-Christendom era, fraught with increasing secularism. After 70 years of significant growth that relied in part on the foundational support of Christendom, Pentecostalism in Newfoundland and Labrador now finds itself looking back on several decades of numerical decline and dozens of closed churches. While the impending death of Christendom and rampant secularism is widely lamented, it is too often poorly understood. It is my contention that until Pentecostals have a solid understanding of the cultural trends that affect the transmission and receptivity of the Gospel, our evangelistic efforts and discipleship initiatives will be hampered.

In the spirit of postmodernity therefore, this chapter will provide a narrative example to illustrate the challenges we have described. Following a brief historical background of this Pentecostal fellowship, we will explore the efforts of the PAONL to arrest the decline experienced in recent years. Further, we will explore the results of a survey administered throughout the membership of the PAONL in 2012, which sought to ascertain where, on the Life Cycle of Organizations developed by George Bullard,[1] the membership believed the PAONL to be currently placed. For a denomination in statistical decline, the state of affairs in the local church as viewed by those in the pew is terribly instructive. At issue was whether in the face of serious decline and a changing cultural landscape, the Pentecostal in the pew was able to discern the overall health and challenges to the denomination, from their vantage point in the local church. To the narrative of a small Pentecostal denomination in decline and its efforts to arrest this trend, we now turn.

A Brief History of the PAONL

As was noted in chapter 2, the Azusa Street revival from 1906–1909 effectively produced the Pentecostal movement today. Pentecostalism in Newfoundland and Labrador was birthed directly from Azusa.[2] Alice Belle Garrigus[3] (1858–1949), an unmarried public schoolteacher from Rockville, Connecticut, having received her own Baptism in the Holy Spirit through contact with Azusa participant Frank Bartleman, subsequently felt the call of God to bring the Pentecostal message to this British Dominion[4] on Canada's eastern seaboard. Garrigus reported:

> One morning a sister came in for prayer, breakfast was on the stove. She went down before the Lord and did not rise till six o'clock that night, when we had our first meal. The sister received

---

1. Bullard, "The Life Cycle and Stages of Congregational Development."

2. For a history of the Pentecostal Assemblies of Newfoundland and Labrador see Janes, *History of the Pentecostal Assemblies of Newfoundland*; Hammond, *The Joyful Sound*.

3. In her own words, see Garrigus, "Walking in the King's Highway." For further reading: Janes, *The Lady Who Came*; Janes, *The Lady Who Stayed*; Berends, *A Divided Harvest*; Berends, "Cultivating for a Harvest"; Hattie-Longmire, "Sit Down, Brother!"

4. Newfoundland entered confederation with Canada in 1949, becoming Canada's tenth province.

her baptism and went away to help others to enter in. After supper a sister, Maud Griffith by name, came toward me filled with the Spirit. I knew God had a message for me, possibly a call, and my mind flew to China. The first words she said were: "You are looking too far." Then followed a message in tongues and the word "*Newfoundland*" came forth. At that word I bounded from my chair and went leaping and dancing and praising God.[5]

The historian of the PAONL, Burton K. Janes, reports Garrigus' thoughts: "*Newfoundland?* What and where was Newfoundland? Garrigus hardly knew. Was it a country? An island? A colony? A province? Consulting a map, she located the spot."[6] When later queried by a customs official as to the purpose of entering the country, she replied, "To preach the Gospel."[7]

Garrigus arrived in Newfoundland on December 1, 1910 and, on the afternoon of Easter Sunday 1911, opened Bethesda Mission on New Gower Street in St. John's, the Newfoundland capital. Garrigus was not known for her strong organizational abilities, and the Pentecostal message did not stray far from the capital city for the first decade. The 1919 revival meetings held in a St. John's Methodist church by Victoria Booth-Clibborn Demarest (1889–1982), are widely believed to have been the spark that was fanned into the flame of Pentecost in Newfoundland. An unconfirmed report stated that 2,000 people experienced salvation during this crusade; as many as 100 of these eventually began to fellowship with Bethesda Mission.[8] Though the first Pentecostal message in Newfoundland was delivered on Easter Sunday, 1911, the Pentecostal Assemblies of Newfoundland[9] was not established until 1925.[10] From this initial effort, the Pentecostal message was carried to various parts of the island, and later to Labrador. Entire volumes can be written of the pioneers and the call to evangelize that characterized the early days of the Pentecostal Movement in Britain's oldest colony and Canada's newest province.[11]

5. Garrigus, "Walking in the King's Highway."
6. Janes, *History of the Pentecostal Assemblies of Newfoundland*, 7.
7. Janes, *The Lady Who Stayed*, 133.
8. Janes, *History of the Pentecostal Assemblies of Newfoundland*, 29.
9. Since the province of Newfoundland added "and Labrador" to its title in 2001, the Pentecostal Assemblies of Newfoundland followed suit shortly thereafter. It is abbreviated herein as PAONL.
10. Janes, *History of the Pentecostal Assemblies of Newfoundland*, 80.
11. In addition to writing the official history of the denomination, Burton K. Janes has been commissioned to write the histories of a number of PAONL assemblies. See for example, Janes, *Reflections from Ship Cove Pond to the Harbour Hills*; idem, *The Ancient Landmarks of Happy Cove*; idem, *From Hinder's Hall to Emmanuel*; idem, *The*

Though in the first several decades the movement grew slowly, it quickly caught fire. The census of 1935 recorded 3721 Pentecostals in Newfoundland, which swelled to 7558 souls by 1945, a 103 percent increase. The 1951 census reported 11,237 Pentecostals, which grew to 20,361 by 1961, and 29,000 by 1971, making Newfoundland, at the time, the most Pentecostal province in Canada, with 5 percent of the population. After the 1980s, however, growth slowed considerably, and decline began. 1981 figures put the PAONL at 36,250, which grew to 40,125 in 1991, before 2001 figures showed the first decline at 33,840, more than 2,000 fewer than 20 years earlier in 1981. The bleeding appears to have slowed in the past decade; 2011 numbers report a decline of just 2 percent from 2001, with 33,195 Pentecostals recorded.[12]

Stated another way, the trend is alarming:

- Growth from 1935–45 was *103* percent.
- 1945–51 saw an increase in numbers of *49* percent.
- The decade following World War II, 1951–61 witnessed *82* percent growth.
- 1961–71, the era of such tumultuous change, saw *42* percent growth.
- From 1971–81 the PAONL grew by *25* percent.
- By 1981–91, growth had slowed considerably to just *11* percent.

Pentecostalism's finest days in Newfoundland were during the leadership of the generation chapter 5 will label the *Seniors*; between 1935 and 1981 the PAONL experienced tremendous growth. Under the leadership of Eugene Vaters (1898–1984) for example, the number of churches increased from just a handful in 1927 to 115 in 1962, the year that A. Stanley Bursey (1906–90) became First Officer, guiding it to 156 churches by 1980.[13] The 1980s, however, were the last period of growth for the PAONL:

- The last decade of the 20th century, 1991–01, saw an alarming decline of 16 percent.
- In the first decade of the 21st century, decline by 2011 had slowed to just 2 percent.

Jug in the Window.

12. 1935–81 figures taken from Janes, *History of the Pentecostal Assemblies of Newfoundland*, 456 and 485. 1991 data is taken from Statistics Canada online data; 2001 data is from Statistics Canada 2001 census; 2011 data is from Stats Canada 2011 National Household Survey (NHS). For more information see www.statcan.gc.ca.

13. By way of comparison, the PAONL in 2015 has fewer than 120 assemblies.

Internal statistics collected annually by the PAONL tell a similar tale:

- Sunday morning attendance has declined 38 percent from 1991 to 2011.
- Although common elsewhere, it is discouraging to note that Sunday School attendance has declined 73 percent in the last two decades.[14]

Recent Decline and Mitigating Efforts

In recognition of the overall decline within its ranks, the Church Ministries department of the PAONL, led by Executive Director Dean Brenton, began in the mid-2000s to explore solutions to these challenges. I have been a part of this process from the beginning, and my experiences on this front have in part formed the impetus for this present study. In November 2012, the Discipleship Commission of the PAONL released a report summarizing the background and journey of this effort. To that report[15] we now turn.

Facing the Decline: Discipleship in the PAONL 2007–2012

The premise behind the PAONL's focus on discipleship is quite simple: *Disciples of Christ will quite naturally produce new Disciples of Christ.* As will be observed, belief in Christ is not sufficient for reproduction, nor is an understanding of oneself as a "Christian" or affirming the Pentecostal label. Discipleship is not a new concept for the Pentecostal Assemblies of Newfoundland and Labrador, although the terminology may have evolved through the years: Christian education, Bible study, equipping, training, and sanctification, are more familiar terms. The goals and intended results, however, remain the same. Past PAONL programs such as *Crusaders, Missionettes, Worker Training Courses,* and the *Mailbox Club,* focused heavily upon discipleship. In the past the PAONL invested significant discipleship

---

14. On the larger picture of members plus adherents, the internal numbers of the PAONL are smaller than those of Statistics Canada, but show a greater decline. PAONL pastors reported 31,042 members plus adherents in 1991, which declined to 23,303 in 2011—a 25 percent drop. As noted above, StatsCan numbers fell from 40,125 to 33,195 (an 18 percent drop), in the same period.

15. The following includes edited sections of the Commission's Report to the General Executive Committee of the PAONL, authored in large part by B. Dean Brenton, Executive Director of Ministry Development and Strategic Initiatives for the PAONL.

energies and resources into its own Pentecostal school system[16] and its once vibrant Sunday Schools. Past events and studies have championed this theme including the 2000 Strategic Plan "Turning Vision Into Reality," the 2006 Leadership Forums, the 2008 *State of the Fellowship* address to General Conference, and the 2010–2011 "Town Hall" meetings throughout the fellowship.

2007–2008

The 2007 Discipleship Conference initiated the PAONL's new discipleship journey. At that conference the Church Ministries Department and its leadership team introduced the theme: *Crisis in Discipleship*. The intent was far from showmanship; it was a bold statement that reflected our realities and our concerns. The evidence was overwhelming, the statistics somewhat disheartening and the path ahead daunting. Though we were in the midst of significant stagnation and decline, we felt strongly that many in our ranks had yet to acknowledge our new realities. Though some were uncomfortable with our theme, and challenged our conclusion, we wished to unequivocally state that we as Pentecostals had lost an understanding of the foundational and formational nature of discipleship; we would therefore always be in crisis. To bring a renewed focus to the task at hand, we began with the restating and reaffirming of our core beliefs and values. As the Pentecostal Assemblies of Newfoundland and Labrador:

1. We value God: His Word, His Creation, His redemptive purposes in His son, His presence through the Holy Spirit, and the imminent return of Christ.

2. We value "the lost" to whom we owe the compassion of Christ, an opportunity to receive the gospel, and entrance into Christian fellowship.

3. We value believers, their commitment to personal discipleship, their baptism in the Holy Spirit, their Christian family life, and their Christ-like example and witness.

4. We value the local assembly marked by sound doctrine, anointed proclamation, fervent prayer, divine healing, Spirit-led worship, authentic relationships, every-member ministry, Holy Spirit-empowered evangelism, and practical expression of Christian faith in the world.

---

16. For a history of the PAONL's own school system in Newfoundland see Rideout, *History of Pentecostal Schools in Newfoundland and Labrador*.

5. We value a cooperative fellowship that enhances the church's ability to fulfill its missional mandate, through servant leadership, a shared vision, positive communication, relevant ministry, and strategic mobilization of its resources.[17]

We determined that developing a strategy to address the crisis we face would require participation from all levels of leadership. A single report, curriculum, manual, or methodology will not be adequate to address the challenge before us. The discipleship crisis is not just an issue for denominational leadership, the local church, or the pastorate, but is a concern for all levels of leadership.

At the conference, Brenton argued that just as the posts of a fence must be inserted before the palings can be installed, we must identify our key "posts" to support our strategy before we add the fine detail to our plan to address discipleship. We identified the following keys to our strategy:

1. Personal discipleship
2. Intentional instruction
3. Authentic community
4. Missional church.

We felt that if these posts could be reinserted into the soil of our PAONL churches then we would move from simply diagnosing a crisis to obeying the command of discipleship.

In moving from *crisis* to *recovery* it was important to understand there were already positive trends and events in place and we would need to strengthen existing initiatives while simultaneously championing emerging opportunities. Some of the early components included:

- Provincial:
  - The launch of the Provincial Discipleship Ministry[18] under the Church Ministries Department.
  - The Provincial Directors Committee[19] discussion and implementation of discipleship strategies in their respective ministries. Some ministries began placing specific individuals in the role of discipleship coordinator. Provincial events began including strong discipleship components.

17. "Pentecostal Assemblies of Newfoundland and Labrador: We Believe."
18. I was the first Director of this ministry.
19. This includes the Directors of the Youth, Children's, Young Adults, Women's, Men's, 50 Plus, Family, and Discipleship Ministries.

- The Tyndale partnership[20] proved to be a valuable resource to the fellowship in the context of theological training. An increased focus on the importance of discipleship was built into the training program for PAONL ministerial candidates from the first semester.
- The launch of a Discipleship section on the PAONL Website.

- Local Church:
    - Revisiting the concept of an "anchor" curriculum that would be encouraged and promoted again in the fellowship.
    - Exploration of Small Group Ministry for local church implementation.
    - Endorsement/Development of a recognized new believer follow-up program
    - Promoting the PAOC[21]/PAONL Youth Leader Certification Course

- Pastoral:
    - Development of a systematic survey and evaluation tools
    - Checklist for preaching/teaching topics
    - Professional Development sessions
    - Youth Ministry Scholarship Fund
    - Tyndale ministry training

The First Survey: Teaching Essential Doctrines

At the 2007 conference I conducted the first survey of our Pastors at a provincial event on behalf of Discipleship Ministries. The goal of this survey was to determine how often Pastors were teaching core doctrines of the Christian faith such as the doctrines of Christ or Salvation, or expressions of the faith such as Water Baptism or Healing. Where Pastors had not taught on a particular topic within the last 12 months, they were asked why that was so. Further, I inquired as to whether they felt their congregations could adequately defend their beliefs, and whether the Pastor had recognized an

---

20. In 2008, after more than seven decades of partnership with a denominational Bible College, the PAONL entered into an agreement with Tyndale University College and Seminary in Toronto. Tyndale became the official training institution for PAONL ministerial candidates. I was the first Director of that program and continue in that role.

21. Pentecostal Assemblies of Canada

increased need to more thoroughly address doctrinal issues. Predictably, Pastors reported that popular Pentecostal topics such as Salvation and Prayer had been taught with great frequency, while topics such as Creation and Hermeneutics were among the most infrequent. "Too many other topics needing attention" and "I don't have time to adequately address the issues" were listed as the most common reasons for failing to teach those taught infrequently. Only 6 percent of Pastors believed their congregations could defend or share their faith "very well" and 73 percent reported recognition of the need to increase teaching in the areas of our essential doctrines.[22]

2009 Updates

By 2009 the following components were developing on a Provincial, Local, and Pastoral Level.

- A Provincial Discipleship Ministry had been launched; I was appointed Director.
- A Discipleship Conversational Team was assembled.
- Provincial Directors Committee met and discussed discipleship plans for 2009.

The summary of these meetings includes the following:

- Pastoral/Professional Development is critical to move forward.
    - Pastors must be motivated, self-learners.
    - Pastors are tired. Church structure and staffing models are often not serving us well.
    - Congregational members are often not disciples/self-feeders *because* our pastors are not disciples/self-feeders.
    - The senior pastor is the gatekeeper and has to be the primary catalyst.
- Solutions:
    - Tyndale provides us with one key solution for emerging leaders.
    - Innovative and creative programs will be necessary for existing leaders.
    - Local churches must raise the bar on membership and discipleship programming.

22. A copy of this survey and results may be found in the Appendix.

- The solution is tied to small groups and membership.
- We need a new metric, or scorecard, for ministry and spiritual growth.
- Discipleship will not happen outside of authentic community.
- We must develop a multi year systematic plan
- There must be required participation by all pastors.
- Local programs should be utilized where possible for contextualization.
- However:
  - The issues are systemic, may be found throughout our subculture, and involve all levels of leadership.
  - The issues are theological.
  - Pastoral support and participation are critical.

The Second Survey

At the May 2009 Prayer Summit[23] for PAONL pastors, I conducted a second survey[24] of our pastors to determine trends and practices within the PAONL regarding discipleship in our local assemblies. This survey concentrated more specifically on discipleship itself, asking questions such as, "How satisfied are you with the level of discipleship occurring in your local assembly?" "What is the primary source of discipleship in your local assembly?" and "Does your assembly offer an *Introduction to Membership* course?" In each instance, a number of options were provided to help focus the answers. More than half of the respondents reported "Mixed Feelings" in terms of their satisfaction on this front, with only 25 percent declaring they were "Satisfied." No Pastor reported they were "Very Satisfied." Not surprisingly, more than 50 percent indicated that preaching during Sunday services was the primary source of discipleship in their assembly. Just 15 percent offered some type of Membership course.[25] The results continued to uncover some serious weaknesses in the content and the emphasis on discipleship on a local church level.

---

23. In the off years from the biannual General Conference, a Prayer Summit for all credential holders is held in May.

24. A copy of this survey and results may be found in the Appendix.

25. As one Pastor noted, "We don't have anyone with a Doctorite [sic] degree."

At the Prayer Summit the Discipleship team noted our strategy would include four components: Provincial, Parish, Pastoral, and Personal.

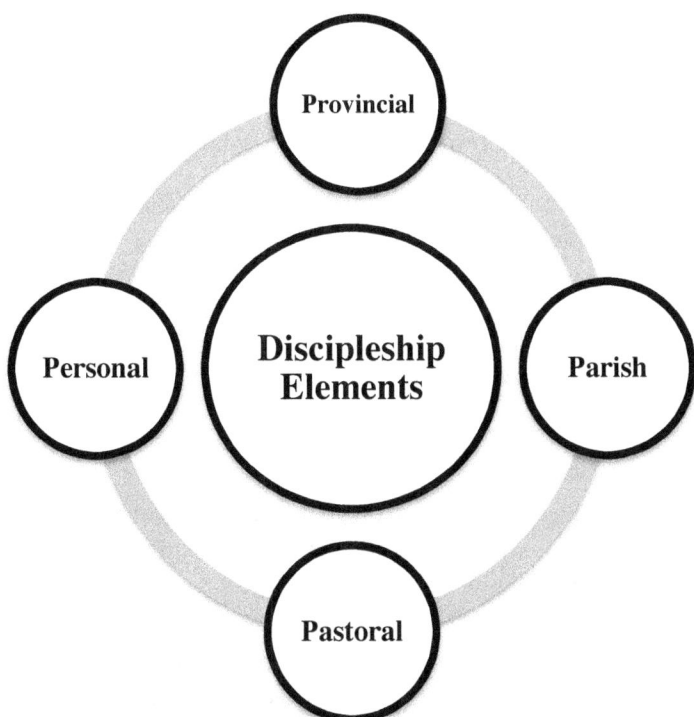

We believed that any strategy on a going forward basis must include all levels of the Fellowship. Further, the Discipleship Ministries team, functioning as a ministry of the Church Ministries department, concluded that the issues to be grappled with were too deep and pervasive to be addressed from within Church Ministries. As such, the following recommendation to the General Executive Committee[26] emerged:

> The Discipleship Ministries team requests the creation of a Commission on Discipleship through the General Executive

---

26. In the PAONL, the General Conference of all credential holders is the highest governing body. Between conferences, the General Executive Committee (GEC) is empowered to make all governance decisions. The GEC is comprised of full-time pastors that have been elected as presbyters of the twelve presbyteries in the PAONL, plus three General Executive Officers (GEO). The GEO are elected from members of General Conference, and fill the offices of General Superintendent, General Secretary-Treasurer, and the Executive Director of Church Ministries (title was changed in June 2014 to Executive Director of Ministry Development and Strategic Initiatives). They are full time employees of the PAONL.

Committee, identifying the depth of the issues and the strategies that will need to be implemented.

This development was about to bring the discipleship conversation to a whole new level.

The Commission on Discipleship

Based on the request from the Discipleship Conversational Team the General Executive Committee created the Commission on Discipleship; I was appointed co-chair, a position I held until the fall of 2013, when it was agreed the General Superintendent should serve in this role. The Commission has now met fourteen times from February 2010 to April 2015.

The Commission adopted the following Terms of Reference:

1. Re-affirm[27] the core values that would support the PAONL's vision for discipleship. (Values, Vision)

2. Identify the critical issues, arising from environmental forces and conditions that would shape the PAONL's direction in the promotion of Christian discipleship. (Internal Environment, External Environment, Critical Issues)

3. Develop a direction (i.e., sense of mission and actionable goals) to capture the PAONL's view of what discipleship should entail. (Mission, Goals)

4. Develop strategic initiatives, within a set of boundaries or parameters, to express the PAONL's view of discipleship and how it will be put in place. (Parameters, Strategies)

5. Set action plans (e.g., define responsibilities, set time lines, and determine material, financial, and human resources) needed to implement the strategic initiatives. (Action Plans, Implementation)

6. Identify how the constituency, on an on-going basis, may be made aware of the work of the Commission. (This term of reference refers to communication, which is not a step in strategic planning, but more of a process that should permeate the whole model if the target audience is going to have buy-in).

---

27. The PAONL's Core Values were revisited and approved by the GEC on Sept 22, 2009.

Definition of Discipleship

A working definition of discipleship was deemed crucial to bring clarity and cohesiveness to the discussion, and subsequent plans of action. In the November–December 2011 issue of the *Good Tidings*[28] my article entitled, "Discipleship: Helping Christ's Followers Become Christ-Like" was published.[29] It contained the following key points:

- *What is discipleship?* Discipleship is the strategic practice and intentional teachings that promote the daily lifestyle of becoming ever more like Jesus and reproducing Christ-likeness in others.
- *Why become disciples?* The chief end of salvation is formation in the image of Jesus Christ. We are saved to become disciples; it is not optional. Since discipleship is a *non-negotiable* (it is the Great Commission), discipleship must be an *intentional* focus of every believer and every ministry.
- *What are some characteristics of discipleship?*
    - Discipleship is all about *relationships:* Our personal relationship with Jesus in devotion; relationships with other believers in care and accountability; and relationships with non-believers in evangelism.
    - Discipleship is a life spent seeking Christ-likeness in the *company of other seekers*.
    - If discipleship had two bookends, they would be *transformation* and *multiplication*.
    - *Transformation* of character comes as a result of true *confession* and *repentance*.
    - *Multiplication* comes as a result of *evangelism* and *mentoring*. Disciples must produce disciples.
    - Discipleship is a *process*. We never graduate from growing more like Christ. It is a goal that should consume our attention until the day we meet Jesus face to face.
- *What are the values of a disciple?*
    - *Evangelism* (making Jesus known to others)
    - *Transformation* (being shaped into Christ's likeness)

---

28. The official publication of the PAONL
29. This was based upon the concept presented in, "Discipleship."

- *Community* (experiencing life in the fellowship of others)
- *Worship* (delighting God in all you do)
- *Service/Ministry* (investing your energies in His purposes)
- *Power* (being a dynamic presence for God in the world through the enabling of the Holy Spirit)

• What are the costs of discipleship?
- *Cross Bearing* (not our will but His)
- *Self Denial* (sacrificing for the Gospel)
- *Abiding in His Words & Teaching* (not just a hearer but a doer of the Word)
- *Love for Others* (this is how others know we are disciples)
- *Fruitfulness* (growth plus service)

The Third Survey

At the fall Discipleship Conference[30] in 2011, I presented a third survey[31] to the credential holders, this one exploring attitudes towards young adults in our assemblies, and the level of comfort our Pastors felt with the many changes occurring so rapidly in society. This time, Pastors were given pre-selected answers from which to choose. For example, I asked "How satisfied are you with the number of young adults (age 19–39) in your local assembly?" Of the 176[32] who responded, 71 percent observed they were either "dissatisfied" or "very dissatisfied." When asked whether the assembly they pastored had one or more individuals of this age group on their Deacons Board, we were pleased to note that 47 percent responded in the affirmative. When asked whether they felt competent to minister in the context of a rapidly changing culture, 34 percent felt they had a handle on societal trends, while 59 percent either responded in the negative or desired additional help in navigating these changes.

---

30. In addition to the alternating General Conferences and Prayer Summits held each May, the PAONL also has a fall conference, which is mandatory for credential holders. Even years see the General Conference in May and Leadership Conference in October. Odd years have the Prayer Summit in May and Discipleship Conference in October.

31. This survey and results may be found in the Appendix.

32. Although these surveys or questionnaires were not professionally created, they are nonetheless a reasonable source of information, and may be considered quite accurate. 176 responses out of 411 active credential holders ensure a high level of accuracy.

Finally, we asked, "Why do you think young families sometimes avoid church?" (65 percent—they prefer leisure activities to Church); "How do you think young families would answer the preceding question?" (54 percent—they'd say they are too busy); "What are your greatest frustrations with this age group?" (79 percent—they are not committed); and "What do you think young adults would list as their #1 frustration with the church?" (31 percent—Church services are irrelevant to their lives and where they are). These final questions generated a large number of useful and telling comments, quite outside of the pre-determined answers respondents were given to choose from.

2011 to Present: Life Cycles

In the course of Commission discussions, and as a part of the internal and external audits, considerable attention was given to a concept known as *Organizational Life Cycles,* based on work by George Bullard. The premise is that organizations and congregations have a Life Cycle similar to those of the people who compose them. Leaders must diagnose the congregation's place in the Life Cycle and lead accordingly. For our purposes, we sought to determine where the denomination as a whole would be placed in the Life Cycle.

Four things in congregational life determine the Life Cycle position:

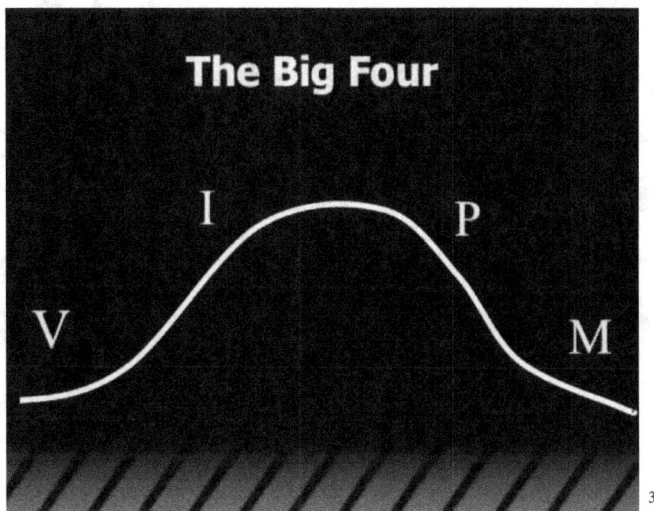

33. "Leadership in the Life Cycle" http://www.docstoc.com/docs/54004759/Leadership-in-the-Life-Cycle.

- Vision—The current understanding of God's spiritual strategic direction that is cast by leadership and owned by the people.
- Inclusion—(Relationship Experiences—Interchangeable with 'R' Relationships)—The relationship process by which people are brought to faith in God through Jesus Christ, become connected to a congregation, are assimilated into the fellowship life and care ministry of that congregation, have opportunities for spiritual growth and leadership development, and utilize their gifts and skills through Kingdom involvement.
- Program—The functional attempts to provide ministries, services, activities, and learning experiences for people connected with a congregation by membership, attendance, fellowship, or staffing.
- Management—The administration of the resources of the congregation, the decision-making structures of the congregation, the formal and informal culture of the congregation, and the openness of the congregation to transition, change, and transformation.

The Stages of Development include:

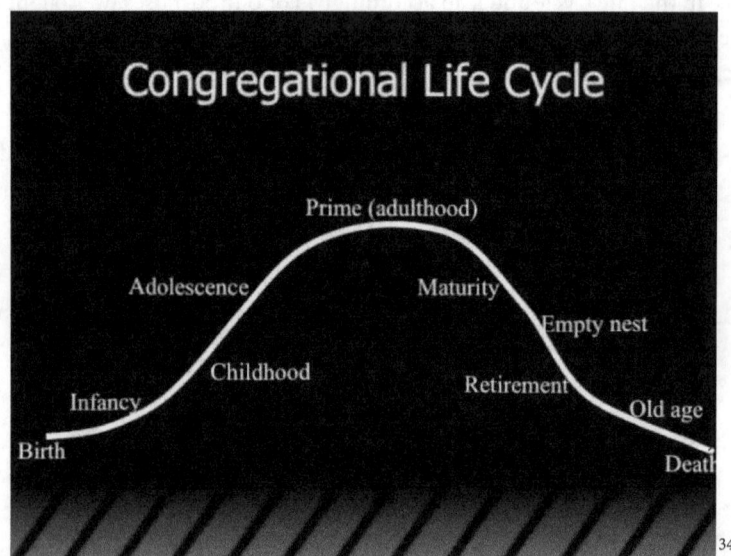

[34]

- Birth
- Infancy

34. Ibid.

- Childhood
- Adolescence
- Prime (Adulthood)
- Maturity
- Empty Nest
- Retirement
- Old Age

PAONL Provincial Discipleship Survey

In November 2011, after considerable consultation and refinement, the Commission unveiled the Discipleship Survey[35] across the fellowship. Pastors were asked to distribute these surveys following a Sunday morning service, to everyone present above the age of 14. A total of 67 questions were asked in the four key areas of Vision, Relationships, Programs, and Management. Those surveyed had to indicate their preference on a scale of 1–5, from "strongly agree" to "strongly disagree." In so doing, congregants were given opportunity to place their assembly on the Life Cycle.

For example, in Vision, we asked, "As Pentecostals, we know who we are," and "I am able to tell someone what the vision of our church is." To assess Relationships we asked "Our church is as concerned with reaching out to the community as it is with what's going on within its four walls," and "I have as many strong relationships with people outside the church as I do with people inside our church." Under programs, for example, we queried, "Our church uses programs that are creative and invigorating," and we sought to ascertain the level of Management with statements such as "Our leadership encourages lay members to develop and use their knowledge and skills in running church ministries."

Two questions in particular helped place us on the Life Cycle. "Of the four major elements - Vision, Relationships, Programs, and Management—which *one* element would you consider to be the strongest component of your local assembly?" The other listed Vision, Relationships, Programs, and Management separately, and asked respondents to rate these from 1 to 5 in terms of how strong they were perceived to be in the local assembly.

---

35. The survey is included in the Appendix.

Survey Results

Stephen Harris, Chief Technology Officer, *OnX Enterprise Solutions Ltd.* was instrumental in helping the Commission prepare the final version of the survey for distribution. After analysing the data, he prepared an Executive Summary of the findings. In part, he noted:

> In defining the sample to be measured for the survey, several key decisions were made. Specifically, it was decided to measure the attitudes of congregational attendees based on "typical" Sunday AM service attendance; in essence, the effort was designed to measure the attitudes of the "people in the pew" on a Sunday morning.
>
> The survey was conducted in the fall of 2011 and received a total of 3304 responses, which is very high[36]. This level of response results in an overall confidence level of ± 2.05 percent, 99 times out of 100.
>
> Overall the results of the survey were more positive than would have been initially expected, with respondents typically placing the church further back in the overall maturity curve away from the "retirement" position, and closer to a "late-maturity" position. Initially this was surprising, however upon further investigation against demographic results, and using advanced analysis techniques, it would appear that the congregations are accurately positioning the church on the life cycle from their position. However the congregations themselves are not necessarily reflective of the community at large. As a result, from an external vantage point, the church is moving further down the declining curve towards retirement and death, but the congregations can't see it from their vantage point. This is demonstrated by viewing the results of the survey against the demographic information contained in conversion, baptism, and infilling of the spirit data collected internally.[37]

Life Cycle Placement and Plan

There is an obvious disconnect between the "view from the pew" and the hard data of declining assembly reports. It appears we not only have a crisis

---

36. Consider that a typical national survey in Canada often includes 1,100–1,200 responses.

37. From the Executive Summary of the PAONL survey results, written by Stephen Harris for the General Executive Committee, November 2012.

in discipleship but an acknowledgement issue. Though I do not have the hard data via similar surveys of the PAOC, or Pentecostal bodies in the U.S., I expect the same is true throughout North America. To move forward as Pentecostals we will have to have honest conversations, acknowledge demanding realities, and make difficult decisions. The survey results placed the fellowship somewhere slightly above the Retirement stage. When assessed together with PAONL internal statistics over the last several decades, however, we must place ourselves somewhere in the Retirement stage or slightly further down the curve towards Old Age.

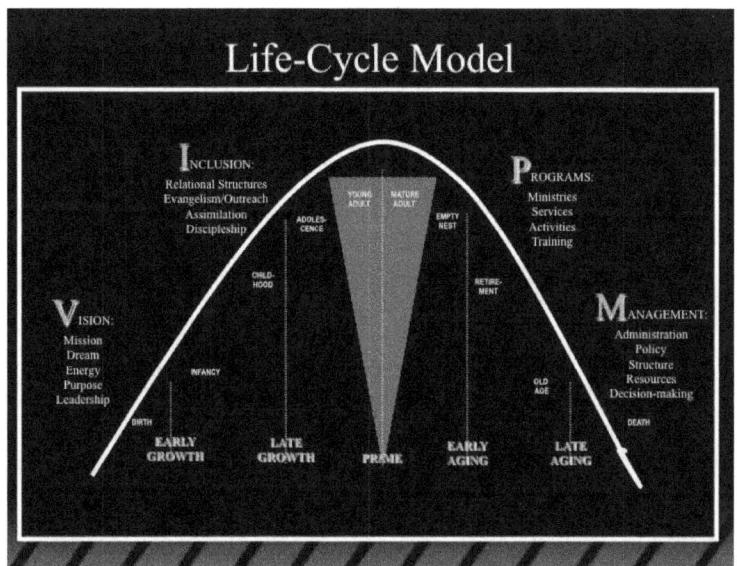

Retirement is organized around the lead roles of Programs and Management. Vision and Relationships are passive, even wounded. Bullard describes Retirement as:

> Many long-term members and attendees decided at the end of Empty Nest that this is no longer a good place to invite people to come, and be members and attendees. Simultaneously they want the congregation to be alive and vital long enough to help them with various life passages, including their own death. Existing members and attendees may feel that new people will be disappointed in the congregation. Or, new people may want to change the congregation, and if it does not work, then the congregation may be weaker than it is already. However, *existing*

38. "Leadership in the Life Cycle" http://www.docstoc.com/docs/54004759/Leadership-in-the-Life-Cycle.

members would love it if some effort were successful at again filling the sanctuary with worshipers, and restoring the congregation to past glory. Therefore, the stakeholders in the congregation who have been members or regular attendees for 20 years or more, have been professing Christians for 40 years or more, and are 60 years of age or more give permission for the newer, younger members and attendees to try new programmatic directions. At times this takes the form of an appeal made to a prospective pastor. The pastor search committee urges the new pastor to come lead them into a new era of transformation. *Change, transitions, and new ideas are said to be welcomed and supported.*

The stakeholders really do not realize what they have asked for. They want the congregation to experience qualitative and quantitative growth that is congruent with the patterns of the past. They do not realize that the necessary changes will probably result in forms and styles very different from the past. Simultaneously, the new pastor, and the newer, younger members and attendees hear what they want to hear. They seek to move forward in new programmatic directions claiming that it is the new way of doing congregational ministry for the third millennium. The stakeholders cannot usually articulate well the changes that are acceptable. They will affirm change, but they do not want to have to accept too many personal transitions, or create a congregation that is not held in high esteem in the denomination or the community. The ideal new member or regular attendee household for the stakeholders to accept would be a family with the parents in the age range 25 to 45, the father only works full-time outside the home, the wife is available during the week for volunteer activities, they have two or three children, they are hard workers who volunteer for preschool, children and/or youth leadership responsibilities, they tithe their income through the congregation, and they do not aspire to top congregational elected leadership positions.

About 18 to 24 months into the changes initiated by newer, younger leaders the stakeholders may realize that things are not working the way they thought they would. If so, they seek to stop the change efforts, and—if necessary—get rid of or discourage the leaders of the changes. Retirement congregations may actually split when this happens. Whether the stakeholders leave or the newer, younger leaders leave depends on how successful the changes have been, and for how long the change efforts have taken place[39]

---

39. Bullard, "The Life Cycle and Stages."

Although Bullard's description of the Retirement stage is set in a congregational context, it is not difficult to make the leap to denominational parallels. The similarities are evident. According to Bullard, there are a number of Leadership tasks that must occur when an organization is on the right hand side of the life cycle:

- Principle: Deal with what you lost most recently.
- Principle: Determine whether change strategies can be continuous, or must be discontinuous or even radical.
- Principle: The further down the curve, the longer it will take and less likely it will work.[40]

Once the church finds itself this far down the life cycle the goal is to redevelop those areas directly across the life cycle chart. For an organization heavily invested in Programs and Management, we must begin again to renew our Vision and focus upon Relationships.

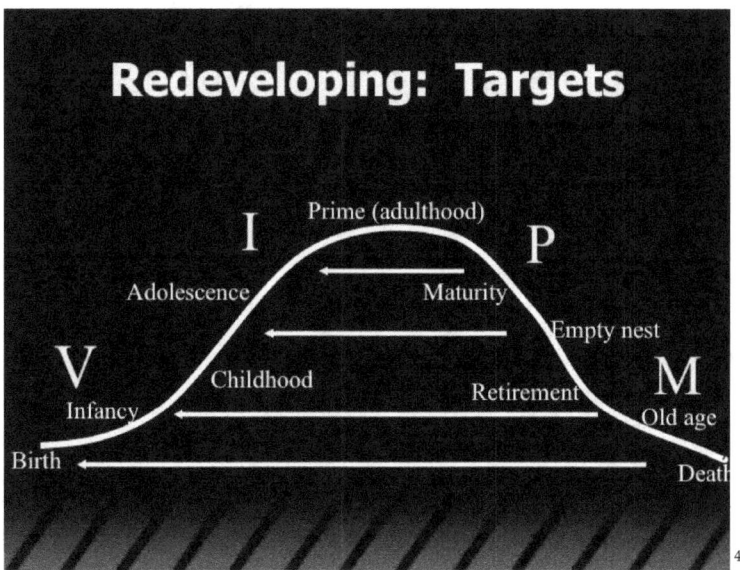

As we have considered how to concentrate once again on Vision and Relationships, we have begun to transition the work of the Commission into a new tangible and practical level. The Commission stated early in this process that although we would need to champion new proposals, we

40. Ibid.
41. "Leadership in the Life Cycle" http://www.docstoc.com/docs/54004759/Leadership-in-the-Life-Cycle.

would also need to embrace and celebrate existing initiatives. As we begin to look at "what could be," the simple discipleship model of Jesus could be translated into a simple organizational progression built on innovation and inclusion. With a focus first on individual discipleship, organizational issues will soon be cared for; as the people go, so goes the denomination.

The 2013 Discipleship Conference saw the presentation of the Commission's proposal for a four-stage, eight-year discipleship plan that will address many of the systemic issues identified by the Commission. Further, it will provide the rails upon which a renewed Vision and authentic Relationships could once again flourish. The PAONL discipleship plan will encompass the following components:

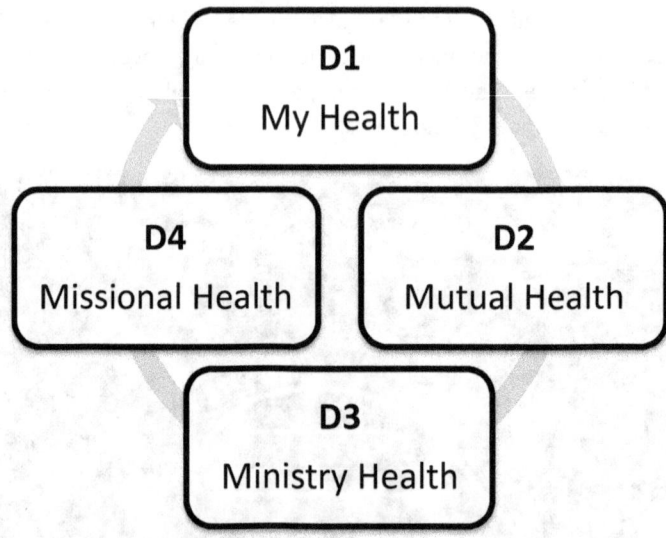

- My Health: A focus on personal discipleship and growth as well as family health.
- Mutual Health: A focus on organizational and relational health.
- Ministry Health: A focus on ministry effectiveness and expansion.
- Missional Health: A focus on community engagement and multiplication.

In essence this model could create perpetual organizational motion in producing healthy disciples who could birth healthy disciples in their homes, ministries, and communities. The PAONL Discipleship Strategy will create new action plans and activities to grow new disciples across the fellowship and at the same time expand current programs and major fellowship initiatives. The PAONL will need to revisit long-standing foundational programs, and adopt an "umbrella approach" to all future fellowship events and committee work. Each level will be marked by 24-month personal challenges, professional development, PAONL committee work, provincial events, program and curriculum development, and others as deemed necessary.

Conclusion

The goal of this chapter was to provide a snapshot of a representative classical Pentecostal denomination, struggling to adapt to changing cultural realities, and address declining numbers, without sacrificing the essence of what made Pentecostalism so effective in the first last of the last century. To this end, we introduced the PAONL in its historical context, before outlining the challenges it faces in terms of decline. We then described the efforts of the Leadership to arrest the troubling trends of the last two decades, culminating in a provincial survey that confirmed the PAONL is indeed at, or slightly past the Retirement stage on Bullard's Life Cycle. To this end, we have now introduced a multi-stage, eight-year discipleship plan which focuses first upon the individual, before moving to relationships within the Church (and community), the ministry of the local assembly, and concluding with an examination of the church's mission in the community.

As a part of this effort from the beginning, I have long sought to make a positive contribution to this ongoing conversation. Though I will continue to be involved with the development of the eight-year plan going forward, I have also desired to think more academically and theologically about the issues we as Pentecostals are facing in the 21st century. To that end, this project is offered. Having set the stage for our discussion in chapter 2 (History and Theology of Pentecostalism), and three (Post-Christendom, Secularism, and postmodernism), chapter 4 has described the very real challenges faced by one small classical denomination in particular, by way of putting "a face" as it were to these struggles.

Moving forward, I wish to offer practical and theological suggestions for Pentecostal groups facing similar struggles, which are facing tremendous societal transformation both now and in the decades to come. Our attention will now turn to our first theme—generational issues within the Church. Postmodern trends and the effects of secularism have made themselves known in a myriad of ways in the six generations now worshipping together in the Church. An understanding of the core attributes of each will further enable us to consider ways Pentecostalism may once again thrive in Western culture.

Following our discussion of the generations, the next chapter will look back at one of Pentecostalism's most successful evangelists, a pioneer who so easily flowed between the church and secular worlds that it behooves us to pause and determine what lessons might be learned from Aimee Semple McPherson. This will conclude examination of our second theme—creativity and risk. Chapter 7 will continue by addressing our third (Being Missional) and fourth (Influencing Culture) themes by first exploring the current conversation on Missional ministry today, and what Pentecostals might gain from that approach. It will then examine the conversation initiated by the Emergent Church, and seek to determine whether Pentecostalism will be well served by aligning with that movement. Chapters 8 and 9 will seek to look forward, addressing the four final themes that I believe are key for Pentecostal renewal and growth: 5) Responding as Pentecostals to Postmodern Thought and Societal Trends; 6) Embracing the Opportunities Afforded by the Collapse of Christendom; 7) A Reframing of the Pentecostal "Distinctive" of Spirit-baptism; and 8) Differentiating Between *Beliefs* and *Values*. To chapter 5, and Generational Issues, we now turn.

Part 3

— 5 —

Theme 1: Generational Issues

Introduction

TO THIS POINT WE have provided a cursory look at Pentecostalism, and have explored the significant impact of secularism and postmodernism that have helped lead Western culture into a post-Christendom era. We have examined the story of the Pentecostal Assemblies of Newfoundland and Labrador as an example of the struggle of denominations with the turn to post-Christendom. Cultural shifts such as those described in chapter 3 do not affect all age groups of society in the same ways. In that sense, generational issues may be among the least discussed but most significant challenges the Church is facing today. Further, shifting values from generation to generation represent some of the most substantial issues for Pentecostalism as it attempts to navigate the rapidly changing context of Western culture. It is one thing to come to terms with the changes secularism and postmodernism are bringing to culture; it is quite another to fully appreciate the differing ways these concepts will influence each generation. Understanding the considerable differences in worldview from older to younger generations will assist Pentecostals greatly in their quest for contextual relevance.

To be sure, differences in various generations are not new. Young adults have long wondered just how it is that age can make individuals so boring and resistant to change, while many elders look at the thinning ranks of youth and young adults in their midst and wonder how, with the lack of commitment and morality of the younger generations, the Church will survive into the future. As one elder remarked, "I see no hope for the future of our people if they are dependent on frivolous youth of today, for certainly all youth are reckless beyond words . . . When I was young, we were taught to be discreet and respectful of elders, but the present youth are exceedingly [disrespectful] and impatient of restraint." Another agreed: "The children now love luxury. They have bad manners, contempt for authority; they show disrespect to their elders.... They no longer rise when elders enter the room. They contradict their parents, chatter before company, gobble up dainties at the table, cross their legs, and are tyrants over their teachers."[1]

Hesiod and Socrates are in good company within the Church today. This chapter seeks to bridge the gap of understanding between the different generations in today's church by exploring the key attributes of the generations currently worshipping together.[2] Further, to bring some practical focus to our research, we will explore implications of generational differences for Pentecostals in Newfoundland and Labrador. To accomplish this, we will first examine the various generations, noting the key formative experiences for each, and subsequent characteristics both in terms of those common to the age, and also those of a religious nature. With the survey of Pentecostalism provided in chapter 2, and a basic understanding of the place of secularism and postmodernism in Canadian culture, we will be able to draw conclusions relative to the impact of generational differences on Pentecostalism and offer practical suggestions for dealing with the same.

Generations Within the Church Today

As one can imagine, the naming and dating of the various generations alive today is not a precise science. Scholars are typically agreed only on the dating of the Boomer generation that immediately follows World War II in 1945. For the purposes of this paper, we will use the following dates and monikers: Seniors (born before 1925); Builders (born between 1925 and 1944); Boomers (born between 1945 and 1964); Generation X (born between 1965 and 1983); Millennials (born between 1984 and 2001); and the newest (and unnamed) generation, born since 2001. Based on this dating, the median age of each generation is: Senior—100, Builder—80, Boomer—61, GenX—42, Millennials—24, with the newest generation comprised

---

1. The astute reader will recognize these quotations from much earlier than expected. The first is commonly attributed to Hesiod, 8th century BC; the second to Socrates, 2nd century BC.

2. In *One Church, Four Generations*, McIntosh lists five negative outcomes of failing to understand generational issues. 1) A slow decline for many churches and related denominations; 2) Few recruits for missions with a resulting loss of influence on unreached people; 3) Less money with which to fundraise for missions or other local church ministries; 4) A continued trend toward the liberal agenda in the United States; and 5) An inability to fulfill our God-given purpose to "make disciples of all nations." McIntosh, *One Church, Four Generations*, 22–23.

of children, the oldest of whom is just 14 years of age.³ An examination in brief of each generation will provide the necessary data to allow us to draw conclusions vis-à-vis Pentecostalism further in this paper.

Seniors and Builders—The Traditionalists

For the generations prior to the Second World War, a variety of formative events often led to similar outcomes and characteristics. For example, though my grandfather (born in 1919) experienced different things than did his father (born in 1874), their outlook on life and religious characteristics were remarkably similar. For our purposes therefore, Seniors and Builders may be explored together and referred to as "Traditionalists."⁴

The formative experiences of the oldest members of our congregations go back to the beginnings of the last century. For the most senior members of this group, the effects of World War I (1914–1918), if not the event itself, were significant, including the subsequent rebuilding of Europe, the Roaring Twenties, and sudden downturn of the world economy leading into the Great Depression (1929–1939), the impact of which is so great as to be almost impossible to measure. Also known as the *Greatest Generation*, this group includes veterans of World War II (1939–1945), and as a whole, they were deeply impacted by the war, Pearl Harbor, rationing, the absence from home of millions of young men who fought overseas—and the loss of many who never returned. The advent of the automobile and radio describes for many their total exposure to new technologies as young adults. For this age group, life was centred on three key components—family, church, and school.⁵

As a result of their formative experiences, those in this age bracket tend to be solid, loyal, and dependable individuals, who know what it is to work very hard simply to survive. These stable but very cautious individuals also tend to be somewhat intolerant of viewpoints or mentalities that have not been shaped in the crucibles of wartime and economic collapse. They are not given to flights of fancy or to being wasteful, for the experience of

---

3. As noted, there are a variety of approaches to naming and dating the generations. For example, see Carlson, "20th Century U.S. Generations"; Zemke, Filipczak and Raines, *Generations at Work*; Strauss and Howe, *Generations*; Stillman and Lynne, *When Generations Collide*; "Generational Comparisons."

4. Lancaster and Stillman note, "The Traditionalists, born between the turn of the last century and the end of World War II (1900–1945), combine two generations who tend to believe and behave similarly." Lancaster and Stillman, *When Generations Collide*, 13. Other writers name them *Veterans*, or *Elders*.

5. Adams, *Stayin' Alive*, 10.

living through the Depression is one that has shaped their entire outlook on life. From the survivalist mindset of the 1930s however, this generation (buoyed by their success during World War II) went on to generate some of the most enduring accomplishments of the century. Among G.I.s, as notes the inscription on the shrine at Iwo Jima, "uncommon valor was a common virtue."[6] Using "Veterans" for their descriptor of this generation, Zemke et al. write:

> They are the generation whose vision and hard work created the United States we know today... Viewed as a body, their accomplishments are staggering... They shook off the Great Depression and rejuvenated a failing economy. They won a world war and hammered out a lasting peace. They built a durable national infrastructure of interstate highways, bridges, and dams. They built a space program and landed a man on the moon. They created miracle vaccines, and wiped out polio, tetanus, tuberculosis, and whooping cough. Their mindset has so dominated our culture that every other set of beliefs is weighed against theirs. When people argue that we need a return to 'family values,' they mean we need to go back to the morality of the Veterans. When managers say young employees today lack a work ethic, they mean they don't have the work ethic of the Veterans."[7]

Boomers

The end of World War II in 1945 brought millions of Canadian and American men home from theatres of war in Europe and the Pacific, and the resultant reunion with their wives produced the greatest baby boom of recent history. After 200 years of population decline in the United States, in 1946 a tidal wave of babies was born across America—one every seventeen minutes for nineteen years—making them the largest American generation since the Nation's founding.[8] In general, the Boomers have been noted for bringing about a change in focus, attitude, and mindset from that of their parents. "Arriving as the inheritors of G.I. triumph, Boomers have always seen their mission not as constructing a society, but of justifying, purifying,

---

6. Strauss and Howe, *Generations*, 261–78.

7. Zemke, *Generations at Work*, 29–30. What is true for society at large is true for Pentecostalism in particular. As will be seen, this generation was the first to embrace the Pentecostal movement, and their values continue to be those against which modern Pentecostalism is measured.

8. Ibid., 64. The same holds true for Canada. See Bibby, *The Boomer Factor*, 1.

even *sanctifying* it."[9] Describing the great transition from the years of the Traditionalists to the Boomers, Michael Adams notes,

> What the Elders experienced in the 1950s as a long-awaited reward after years of sacrifice and toil, the first wave of Boomers experienced as normal, even boring. This disjunction accounts for the many novels and movies by Baby Boomers satirizing and deriding family life in the 1950s and 60s. It also accounts for the baffled irritation with which these cultural products were received by many members of the Elder generation. ("You think a suburban bungalow is no fun, try eating gruel in your teens and fighting Hitler in your twenties, you ingrate!")[10]

For Boomers, the formative decades of the 1950s and '60s brought a variety of meaningful experiences and events, from the introduction of the birth control pill to Woodstock, from the elections of John Fitzgerald Kennedy and Pierre Elliott Trudeau, to the Kent State shootings and slightly later, the FLQ crisis in Quebec. The Cold War was at its height during the teenage years of the Boomers, and the Civil Rights movement, the race to the moon and the Vietnam War rounded out their march into adulthood. Sadly, this period also witnessed the assassination of prominent leaders such as President Kennedy, Robert Kennedy, and Martin Luther King Jr. New technologies brought television into nearly every North American household, and with it, a greatly expanded view of the world.[11]

The variety of formative experiences combined with a peaceful, largely prosperous society handed to them by their parents, led the Boomers to approach life with great gusto. In contrast to that of their parents, the Boomer's evolution was marked by the accumulation of *things*, and a general optimism that comes with the sense that anything is possible. At 80 million strong, the Boomers were naturally competitive. While Traditionalists had turned their energies outward and worked together to fix a world in turmoil, Boomers looked inward and focused on fixing what was wrong at home. "Boomers have again and again been labeled the 'Me Generation,' in part because they were privileged to be able to focus on themselves and where they were going instead of needing to sublimate the needs of individuals as the Traditionalists had done."[12] Instead of the "chain of command" approach favoured by

---

9. Straus and Howe, *Generations*, 301.

10. Adams, *Stayin' Alive*, 11.

11. From 4 million television sets in the U.S. in 1952 to 50 million in 1960, the impact of television on the Boomers cannot be overstated. Lancaster and Stillman, *When Generations Collide*, 21. See also Johnson and Johnson, *Generations, Inc.*, 19.

12. Lancaster and Stillman, *When Generations Collide*, 22.

the older generations, many of whom were veterans, Boomers took more of a "change of command" view. "They saw flaws in the way the world was being managed and believed they had the idealism, education, and sheer numbers on their side to change it."[13]

Zemke et al. list six personality traits of the Boomers: 1) They believe in growth and expansion; 2) They think of themselves as stars of the show; 3) They tend to be optimistic; 4) In school and at home, Boomers learned about teamwork; 5) They have pursued their own personal gratification, uncompromisingly, and often at a high price to themselves and others; 6) They have searched their souls—repeatedly, obsessively, and recreationally; and 7) The Boomers have always been cool, which for Boomers is defined as whatever they think is in vogue at any given moment. Whereas past generations accepted that young people defined "cool," Boomers continue to believe they define cool—no matter what age they are.[14]

Generation X

At just 46 million souls,[15] the members of Generation X were born in an era where children became unfashionable. Federal approval for the birth control pill in 1960 gave couples the ability to delay having children—sometimes indefinitely. To make things worse, by the 1970s the divorce rate stood at 50 percent, meaning fully one-half of GenX watched their family life dissolve. Johnson and Johnson note, "It's hard to imagine growing up in a society that values children less without the children feeling it."[16]

---

13. Ibid.

14. Zemke et al. *Generations at Work*, 66–68. Paul Begala, advisor to the ultimate Baby Boomer, President Bill Clinton, was far less kind in his assessment: "I've spent my whole life swimming behind that garbage barge of a generation. They've ruined everything they've passed through and left me in their wake . . . At the risk of feeding their narcissism, I believe it's time someone stated the simple truth: The Baby Boomers are the most self-centered, self-seeking, self-interested, self-absorbed, self-indulgent, self-aggrandizing generation in American history. I hate the Boomers." Cravit, *The New Old*, 9. We note that at 52, Begala is himself, by most definitions, a Boomer.

15. While authors seem agreed on numbers for the Boomers, the numbers of GenX are highly debated, likely depending on the dates used. Lancaster and Stillman cite 46 million; Zemke et al. 51 million; McIntosh suggests 75 million, while Howe and Strauss suggest GenX outnumbers the Boomers, at 80 million! I prefer a post-Kennedy date for GenX, which leads to a significantly smaller demographic. In my mind, the events of the 60s and early 70s belong to the Boomers; those of the later 70s and 80s to GenX.

16. Johnson and Johnson, *Generations, Inc.* 63–65. Interestingly, the birth rate among Xers has risen dramatically, perhaps suggesting that GenX is now seeking to establish the family environment they felt was missing from their own childhoods.

GenX has often been described more in terms of what it isn't (Boomer) than what it actually is. Even the moniker "Generation X" was adopted in large part because media outlets accustomed to describing every change and whim of the Boomers, simply couldn't wrap their heads around this demographic.[17] Called "the most misunderstood generation in the workplace today,"[18] they grew up in the shadows of the Baby Boomers, and like a middle child, passively resisted anything the elder sibling embraced.[19] In many ways, the GenX temperament is simply anti-Boomer.

Seminal events in the lives of GenX include: terrorism at the Munich Olympics, the Watergate scandal, the beginning of the Energy Crisis, massive layoffs and downsizing of Western corporations, the stock market crash of 1987, the hostage-taking of Americans in Iran, the Challenger disaster, the bombing of Flight 103 over Lockerbie, the televangelist scandals, and the fall of the Berlin Wall.[20] Overall, many of their memories from youth are not encouraging. "If the mantra of Baby Boomers is 'We are all brothers and sisters on one big happy team,' the mantra of Generation X is 'Take care of yourself because no one else will.'"[21]

Lancaster and Stillman note:

> While Traditionalists were characterized as being extremely *loyal* and Boomers *optimistic*, Xers have been marked by *skepticism*. They grew up seeing every major American institution called into question. From the presidency to the military to organized religion to corporate America, you name the institution and Xers can name the crime. Combine that with a U.S. divorce rate that *tripled* during the birth years of Generation X and you have a generation that distrusts the permanence of institutional and personal relationships. As a result, Xers tend to put more faith in themselves as individuals and less faith in the institutions that seem to have failed them time and again.[22]

The following personality traits of GenX are instructive, and demonstrate the anti-Boomer mentality of this generation: 1) They are self-reliant, many having been raised by divorced parents who each worked full time; 2) They are therefore seeking a sense of family, now having more children

---

17. In their book on GenX, Howe and Strauss titled their first chapter, "We don't even have a name." in *13th Gen*.
18. Lancaster and Stillman, *When Generations Collide*, 24.
19. Zemke et al. *Generations at Work*, 93.
20. McIntosh, *Four Generations*, 124–31.
21. Johnson and Johnson, *Generations, Inc.*, 67.
22. Lancaster and Stillman, *When Generations Collide*, 24.

than did their parents; 3) They want balance between work and life, having watched Boomers pay far too high a price for success; 4) They have a non-traditional orientation about time and space, believing that getting the job is more important than working particular hours—if the job gets done at home, via laptop or smartphone, then that is *their* business; 5) They like informality, having grown up in a very formal world with the workplace (and church) tenor set years ago by Traditionalists; 6) Their approach to authority is casual, though they aren't as much anti-authority as they are unimpressed by it; 7) They are sceptical, having been paid lip service only by everyone from their parents, to marketers and national leadership—words that often did not match actions; 8) They are attracted to the edge, expressing a sense of risk and adventure that typically occurs outside the workplace; and 9) They are technologically savvy, having a natural affinity for the technology that has been a part of their lives since birth.[23]

Though inherently suspicious of institutions, and typically sceptical about life in general, the direst of predictions concerning GenX have not in fact come to pass. According to "The Generation X Report," which surveyed 4,000 GenXers over a 20 year period as part of the *Longitudinal Study of American Youth*, Generation X are hardworking, family-oriented individuals, who on the whole lead well-balanced and happy lives.[24]

Millennials

The final group to be explored (those born since 2001 are not old enough to be defined by generational tendencies at this point)[25], the Millennials are the teenagers and young adults of today's church. Born since 1983, the Millennials are now of an age where sociologists are able to discern trends and attitudes. Formative events for Millennials include: the first laptop, *Exxon Valdez* spill, Gulf War, Rodney King beating, Oklahoma City bombing, acquittal of O.J. Simpson, the Clinton-Lewinsky scandal, Columbine Massacre, 9/11, explosion of the *Columbia*, invasion of Iraq, advent of social networking, and introduction of new technologies such as the iPod, smartphone, and tablet computer.[26]

With changes in society coming at an ever-increasing pace, it may well be that the traditional 20-year term for a generation is too long. We may see

---

23. Zemke et al., *Generations at Work*, 98–102.
24. Miller, *Active, Balanced, and Happy*.
25. This article does make the effort. Benhamou, "Everything You Need to Know About Generation Z."
26. Johnson and Johnson, *Generations, Inc.*, 101–102.

significant differences in the oldest and youngest Millennials, for example, in a way not observed in the oldest and youngest Boomers. Further, as Reginald Bibby notes about Canada, "Never in our 150-year-old history have we had an emerging generation that has been exposed to such an explosion of change and choice. We don't really know what to expect; we really don't know how they will 'turn out.'"[27]

Despite having faced similar deleterious events on the world stage, as did GenX before them, scholars are generally agreed[28] that the Millennials carry little of the cynicism and negativity of the Xers.[29] For one, many Millennials are being raised by young Boomer and GenX parents who are intent on reversing the parenting mistakes of the past. Sometimes referred to as "helicopter parents," they hover over their children's every move, catering to them in any way they can—unlike the parents of GenX who often left their children to fend for themselves.[30] Millennials are the pride and joy of their parents, and it shows in their young attitudes. Howe and Strauss note that rather than being another "lost" generation, Millennials have been born in an era when America began expressing more positive attitudes about children. "During the GenX child era, planned parenting almost always meant contraceptives or abortions; during the Millennial childhood, it more often means visits to the fertility clinic."[31] Lancaster and Stillman note, "It's as if the Traditionalists have given the Millennials a dose of their *loyalty* and faith in institutions, Boomers have given them confidence to be *optimistic* about their ability to make things happen, and Xers have given them just enough *scepticism* to be cautious. As a result, the pragmatic Millennials have combined these traits into their own identity."[32]

Markedly different than their predecessors, Millennials may be associated with the following characteristics: 1) They are optimists, and are upbeat about the world, with 90 percent describing themselves as "happy," "confident," and "positive;" 2) They are not self-absorbed, but like to be team players. They overwhelmingly see "selfishness" as the cause of most major

---

27. *The Emerging Millennials*, 3.

28. Of course, there are always exceptions. See for example Twenge, *Generation Me: Why Today's Young Americans Are More Confident, Assertive, Entitled - and More Miserable Than Ever Before*; Bauerlein, *The Dumbest Generation: How the Digital Age Stupefies Young Americans and Jeopardizes Our Future*. The titles really say it all.

29. For example see, Rainer and Rainer, *The Millennials*. Although the book is somewhat dated now as this discussion is so time sensitive, the title of Howe and Strauss' book on the Millennials is also instructive: *Millennials Rising*.

30. Johnson and Johnson, *Generations, Inc.*, 103.

31. Howe and Strauss, *Millennials Rising*, 1.

32. Lancaster and Stillman, *When Generations Collide*, 29–20.

societal problems; 3) They accept authority—a majority report feeling close to their parents and identifying with their parents' values; 4) They tend to follow the rules, stymying some experts as rates of homicide, violent crime, abortion, and pregnancy are falling; 5) They are the most watched-over generation in history, doted upon by parents dedicated to giving their children every possible advantage; 6) They are smarter than most people think; and 7) They believe in the future and see themselves as cutting edge, mastering new technologies with aplomb, and dedicating themselves to progress.[33]

Finally, a word about postmodernism is in order. Despite heavy debate in some circles as to the longevity of this philosophical adjustment, it is clear to many that the impact of postmodern thought is now widely felt in the younger generations. Beginning with GenX, but most assuredly in the Millennials, postmodern modes of thinking are well in vogue.[34] Although space and the focus of this paper will not permit a detailed exploration, three foci in particular are relevant. First, postmodern thought eschews the traditional role of rationalism as a determinant of truth and instead is quite open to the role of experience and intuition in the process. Second, postmoderns often reject the concept of absolute truth, preferring instead a more pluralistic approach. Finally, in many cases individuality—so prized by the Boomers—has given way to the priority of community, mirroring in many ways the mentality of the Traditionalists.

Reflections on Pentecostalism and Generations

To return to our sample denomination, we observe that Pentecostalism's finest days in Newfoundland and Labrador were during the leadership of the Traditionalists. As noted above, between 1935 and 1981 the PAONL experienced tremendous growth. Under the leadership of Eugene Vaters (1898–1984) for example, the number of churches increased from just a handful in 1927 to 115 in 1962, the year that A. Stanley Bursey (1906–90) became First Officer, guiding it to 156 churches by 1980[35].

When one listens to Newfoundland Pentecostals speak with longing about times past and attitudes now uncommon, appreciation for the spirit and mentality of the Traditionalists is unmistakeable. Early Pentecostals indelibly placed their stamp upon the movement, to such an extent that the self-sacrificing, hard-working, "my word is my bond," and "if God said it,

33. Ibid., 7–10.
34. McIntosh, *Four Generations*, 164–65.
35. By way of comparison, the PAONL in 2015 has fewer than 120 assemblies.

then I believe it, and that settles it," attitude of the Traditionalists remains the lofty goal of Pentecostals even today. Pentecostals remember local "revivals" with great fondness, and almost without exception these occurred during the leadership of individuals who are either now deceased, or in their most senior years. Interestingly, the acceptance of the Pentecostal message and worldview for Traditionalists often meant that it ran counter to the prevailing epistemological attitudes of their day. At a time when reason was highly valued, early Pentecostals accepted the movement's emphasis on the present work of the Holy Spirit and the miraculous entirely, as it were, by faith. The task of spreading this "new" Pentecostal message, which seemed so foreign and undignified to the many established churches of the era, was well suited to the Traditionalists' generation, accustomed as they were to a difficult life full of hard work with little praise.

Pentecostalism in Newfoundland has reached a critical point, in part[36] because of change in leadership and membership from the Traditionalists to the Boomers, and the resultant change in mindset. Our forebears were no-nonsense folks, fiercely dedicated to the Christian gospel, who consistently placed the needs of the Church and Pentecostal movement above their own. Worship times were far less about pleasing the worshippers and focused instead on pleasing the One worshiped. Outreach consisted largely of passionate worship services, to which the "lost" were invited, with the prayer they would be convicted of sin and find themselves at the altar. Giving, which has always been substantial in this age group, continues to occur sacrificially and not out of surplus. Though legalism[37] had been inherited from holiness movements such as Methodism, early Pentecostals bore the restrictions with a grace typical of their age.

When Boomers came of leadership age in the 1970s and '80s however, Pentecostalism changed with the times. As in other areas of society, Boomers determined what did not suit them about Pentecostalism and began to effect change. While legalism was justifiably jettisoned, the spiritual passion that accompanied the Traditionalists' willingness to follow the "rules" was sometimes lost. Sunday services were increasingly focused on the seeker, and many "worship wars" ensued as a "me first" attitude crept through the church. Giving continued to be high, but more often occurred

---

36. We should not suggest that the decline in the PAONL is due entirely to generational shifts. There are many more issues at play. The generational piece is, however, a key factor worth considering carefully.

37. As described in chapter one, this denotes the tendency in the PAONL to have focused on extremes of the holiness movement, such as prohibiting women from the wearing of makeup, jewelry, or men's clothing (pants), and the forbidding of any kind of work on Sunday.

out of abundance. The high price of success paid so readily throughout the Boomer world also affected the Pentecostal church, as two-income families had less time to disciple their children, and less energy with which to volunteer for church ministry.[38] Attitudes toward outreach continued to be attractional, however, as Boomers sustained "the community will come to us" mentality of their forebears.

By the time GenX came of age in the 1980s and early 1990s, they found a Pentecostal church established and funded by the Traditionalists that met the needs of the Boomers. Church leadership, typically occupied by younger Traditionalists and older Boomers, was not always appreciative of the new attitudes and ideas espoused by the more cynical and mistrustful Xers. Though some Pentecostals born in the Baby Boom years rejected the faith of their parents, many others stayed and found leadership roles within the movement. With their natural antagonism towards Boomer values, however, large numbers of GenX did not remain with the church during their young adult years, feeling their mindset, and that of the Boomers' Pentecostal church, were incompatible.[39] With GenX focused more upon encountered needs rather than giving to a church that gave them little say about how finances were spent, receiptable giving among the younger generations pales in comparison to that of their parents and grandparents.[40] Young Pentecostals of the 1980s and early '90s began to strongly sense the need to be missional, desiring to bring the Gospel into the community rather than waiting for the community to "come to church." This was often met with scepticism within the attractional model that many considered a key tenet of traditional Pentecostalism.[41]

With the advent of the Millennials, however, Pentecostalism in Canada and elsewhere may once again thrive. Their positive attitudes, willingness to get involved, and tremendous optimism may allow Millennials to lead

---

38. "Most Builders were raised during the one-breadwinner system. When the mother did not work outside the home, there was more time for church participation and volunteerism. It was not unusual for the family to spend several evenings a week at church activities. A strong commitment to Christ was, and is, played out in a strong commitment to church attendance. Most Boomers, Busters, and Bridgers are part of a dual-income or single-parent family. The pressure of both parents working outside the home leaves much less time to go to church. They will often be too tired to attend church in the evening and will decide to stay home and spend time together. Their strong commitment to Christ is played out in commitment to their relationships and community." McIntosh, *Four Generations*, 206.

39. See Dyck, "The Leavers."

40. McIntosh, *Four Generations*, 22.

41. How often I have heard this statement: "We just need to have powerful services like we did in times past, and the lost will once again come to our church!"

classical Pentecostalism to new heights. With the Pentecostal message no longer antithetical to their own worldviews, these postmoderns quite easily believe the distinctives for which Pentecostalism was so often ridiculed in decades past. Older Boomers are now passing from the scene of leadership, with younger Boomers and GenX realizing the need to grapple with the significant mindset shift occurring in young adults. Millennials are being welcomed into Pentecostalism at a time when the leadership is calling for a return to the values, ethics, and sacrificial mindset of the Traditionalists—all contextualized for the current ministry situation of the Millennial world.[42]

Practical Suggestions and a Few Caveats

The Differences are Vast

The success of Pentecostal groups in the future may well depend on how seriously they acknowledge the significant differences in the thought patterns of the Millennials versus the Boomers. It is easy for older church members to recall their own young adult years, and to believe that their memories of thinking differently than their grandparents accurately mirror the differences between an average 20-year-old and their 70-year-old counterpart today. That assumption, however, would be a colossal error. If sociologists and statisticians are correct, the change of mindset since the 1980s is incredibly significant, and will continue to diverge from that of the current leadership in most churches.

Congregations that wish to grow again will need to be in continuous dialogue with the younger generations, sometimes with persons in the room who are able to translate the values of the young adults to the leadership.[43] The importance of authenticity (even when not always personally practiced), value placed on relationships, dislike of formal situations (including Sunday morning worship), low regard for denominations versus high regard for the Church universal, and passion for social justice—all expressed with a missional mindset—mark the Millennial contribution to Church life.[44] Current leadership should be warned, however, that making the shift

---

42. Although this is speculation on my part, I suspect in some contexts, significant leadership will pass from the young Boomers directly to the older Millennials, bypassing GenX completely.

43. There are a number of excellent resources available to help the Church leader desiring to more fully understand and integrate Millennials into church life. See Burstein, *Fast Future*; Dyck, *Generation Ex-Christian*; Smith, *Souls in Transition*; Wuthnow, *After the Baby Boomers*; Sawler, *Goodbye Generation*.

44. Curiously, when considering the Millennial attitude toward church life, one

from Church life as created by the Traditionalists, and now managed by the Boomers, to something easily embraced by the Millennials, will not be easy—but the future of Pentecostal denominations may depend on it.[45]

The Opportunities are Endless

Those who are willing to listen to and learn from all other generations, however, will find that the possibilities for growth are considerable. Quite apart from the importance of older leadership learning to speak the language of the Millennials, young adults must recognize the valuable lessons that can be acquired from their elders. Though space will not permit a thorough evaluation of each of the ideas presented, the following areas are presented as a sample of those from which the generations may learn from each other. These seven subjects are offered in brief with hopes that these would form the basis for extensive conversation within Pentecostalism going forward.

Missional vs. Attractional

Pentecostal leadership must continue to recognize that the natural tendency in GenX and the Millennials towards missional living is in fact, biblical. Sunday services were never intended to be the sole means of outreach; the Church was called to go into the community. The oldest Pentecostals understood this,[46] and Pentecostal groups should allow the younger generations to revitalize this biblical concept. Chapter 7 will take a closer look at the Missional conversation and the significant opportunities it presents for North American Pentecostalism.

---

is struck by how dissimilar it is in many ways to current practice, and yet remarkably similar to another model of church life—one recorded in the New Testament.

45. If, as some scientists believe, the Millennial brain is actually being rewired due to excessive exposure to digital information networks, and is "always on" in terms of the internet, this challenge may be greater than heretofore recognized. See "What Is the Likely Future of Generation AO in 2020?"

46. In his research, Shane Simms has discovered that older Pentecostals do not resonate with missional language—until they are asked to share their stories of the growth of Pentecostalism in the early years. Suddenly, he notes, they come alive as they tell their stories of God's leading into the community, and of sharing the gospel on wharves, near woodpiles, and in homes—all at the leading of the Holy Spirit—and all before talk of being "missional" was in vogue. Simms, "Moving Forward in Mission."

Formal vs. Informal

In terms of the dislike of formality in GenX and Millennials, older and younger have something both to learn and to teach. Assemblies would do well to recognize the significant aversion to formal situations among young adults.[47] In general, individuals under 40 rarely dress in their "Sunday best" anymore (few even own formal attire), and many avoid reserved settings as best they can. Sadly, a formal Sunday service has often been considered the gateway to the Christian faith; young adults may be absent from the Church (and the faith) simply because the worship setting is now uncomfortable for them. Conversely however, informality can bring with it a loss of reverence for God's presence that older believers know well.[48] While young adults can help congregations become families where relationships happen more naturally, and where unneeded formalism is eliminated, elders can help teach a sense of reverence to those who may have never known it.[49]

Technology

While everyone may not be thrilled, technology is here to stay, and again, learning can occur in both directions. Traditionalists were raised in an era when the radio was the most advanced means of entertainment available, and whole families learned the art of sitting together and quietly listening to a three-hour hockey game! Older Pentecostals therefore, often have no trouble listening to a 60-minute sermon without the aid of visuals. In what may be regarded as an understatement, Millennials are not given to listening to an hour of anything—including music—without visual assistance. Congregations would be well served to include technology in both their worship and propagation of the Gospel, for ours is an increasingly technological society.[50] Traditionalists may, however, remind youth periodically

---

47. Students of culture will notice that even the most sacred of occasions—weddings and funerals among them—have become far less formal, as Millennials shatter long-held perceptions of what may be considered appropriate. See for example, "JK Wedding Entrance Dance" posted on YouTube, which has now been viewed more than 88,000,000 times.

48. I personally witnessed this recently when I took a group of Pentecostal students to a local Roman Catholic Church to join the congregation in the celebration of Mass. I was shocked to observe my students laughing and telling jokes—in the middle of the Mass itself—seemingly oblivious to the tremendous reverence accorded the sacrament by the congregation.

49. McIntosh, *Four Generations*, 203.

50. Ibid., 208.

that technology is neither a substitute for preparation, nor a replacement for anointed ministry.

Community vs. Individual

Both Millennials and Traditionalists can remind Pentecostals of the importance of focus upon the community over that of the individual. From the Boomers' natural focus on the advancement of self, to the predilection of GenX towards self-preservation, individuality is far too prevalent in Pentecostal assemblies. As Millennials lead the way, with Traditionalists lending support, Pentecostals can once again value the community over the self, and focus upon the needs of others over their own. The Emergent church has consistently highlighted the importance of community within the church. Chapter 7 will seek to ascertain the lessons Pentecostals may learn from this 21st century movement.

Self-Education

Another area of convergence between young and old may be in the area of self-learning. Older Pentecostals knew what it was to educate themselves, both biblically and doctrinally. Often with limited formal education, Traditionalists took their faith so seriously as to dig deeply and read carefully, relying on more than the twice-weekly sermons at church for personal education and discipleship.[51] The middle generations—the Boomers and GenX—seem to have lost this ability, relying instead on "professional" pastoral staff for their spiritual growth, and that often just once per week. Millennials may be reversing this trend, more often researching their own faith and using technology to bring clarification to their many spiritual questions. Clearly, with the fall of Christendom and increase in secularism, believers will need to care for their own spiritual growth, even while doing so in a committed community of other believers.

---

51. By way of a personal example, I well remember visiting my paternal grandmother the year she turned 80; I was in seminary at the time. She sat me down and announced that she was going to lead me through the "70 weeks" of Daniel 9, the Olivet Discourse of Matthew 24, and relevant portions of Revelation, to ensure that I fully understood how God had prophesied the seven years of tribulation yet to come. She had a grade seven education.

Social Justice

Pentecostals would do well to follow the Millennials' lead as they passionately concern themselves with social justice. Some Classical Pentecostals have tended to view all of social justice through the lens of the so-called "social gospel," understood to be devoid of an explicit call for salvation. This reflects a poor understanding of the New Testament call to care for the poor and oppressed, while still proclaiming the saving message of Christ. The Millennial concern for justice should bring Pentecostals into a greater balance than ever, as they recognize that Christ's gospel is a social gospel. Bifurcating concern for social justice with salvation of the soul is a false dichotomy that must be abandoned. On the other hand, older Pentecostals must bring balance to the Millennial worldview, reminding their younger counterparts that social justice without a concern for the eternal soul is not the gospel of Christ either.

The Story

Finally, all Pentecostals should embrace a return to the power of narratives. Early Pentecostals were known as much for their testimonials as they were for almost any other aspect of their worship. The declining use of testimonies and narratives within Classical Pentecostalism has meant that youth no longer hear the stories and, therefore, worldview of the elders. Clearly, something important has thus been lost. Happily, the younger generations naturally gravitate toward personal narratives even while eschewing grand meta-narratives; it is a hallmark of postmodernity.[52] The opportunity is present to unite all generations, as youth readily accept that which has been a part of Pentecostalism from the beginning. All Pentecostals—from Traditionalists to Millennials—must once again tell their story. The results may be surprising.

Conclusion

This chapter has explored key attributes of the various generations worshipping together each Sunday in Pentecostal assemblies throughout North America: the Traditionalists, Boomers, Generation X, and the Millennials. For each, we have noted the key formative experiences for their demographic, and have observed essential generational characteristics, before

---

52. McIntosh, *Four Generations*, 188.

concluding with some observations relative to the functioning of these generations within the PAONL today. Finally, practical suggestions were offered as Pentecostalism seeks to move forward with the evangelism and discipleship of its youngest generations. While societal changes are significant, and though the Church is not immune to these changes, continuing conversation between the generations may in fact bring Pentecostals back to a balanced approach that will facilitate great discipleship and growth in the years to come. From my perspective, no denomination that fails to understand the significant changes within each generation, particularly the youngest, will successfully navigate the incredible changes occurring within Western society and culture.

We now wish to better understand the attitudes and methods of a pioneer in engaging modern culture, by way of Aimee Semple McPherson's example. Although more than ninety years have passed since she began her ministry, Pentecostals today may learn numerous lessons from her approach.

— 6 —

Theme 2: Creativity and Risk

Ministry Lessons from the Life of Aimee Semple McPherson

Someone must have seen her marching up Main Street from the direction of the bank and the barbershop, a very young woman in a white dress, carrying a chair.

Her auburn hair was swept up from her temples into a loose chignon, revealing the cameo perfection of her profile. She had set the chair down firmly against the curb on the street corner and jumped up upon it as though she were about to sing or give a speech to no one in particular; at that hour of the evening in Mount Forest, Ontario there were few people around—some after-dinner strollers, an occasional carriage or automobile, a kid on his bicycle.

Standing on the chair, she raised her long hands toward heaven as if calling for help in whatever it was she had undertaken to do. And then she did nothing. Given her unconcealable nervous energy, this was probably harder for the young woman than anything. She closed her large, wide-set eyes and just stood there with her arms straight up, like a statue of marble invisibly vibrating.

That had been quite a while ago. A man stopped to admire her, and another. A little boy was tempted to toss a pebble at her to make sure she was alive, but his mother caught his wrist. Once people saw her, they could not pull their eyes away, partly because she was so beautiful in the intensity of her concentration, partly because they had gathered to see if she would move.

Now the crowd that gathered around the shapely young woman began arguing over how long she had been standing there, on the chair, at the corner of Main Street in Mount

Forest, Ontario, with her hands up. Some said it was no more than twenty minutes. But one old farmer claimed he had been watching her when the sun was above the pines. That had to be an hour past, because now it was well on toward dusk. And still he could scarcely detect the rise and fall of her breast as she breathed in and out.

It was not hard to draw a crowd in Mount Forest, in 1915. A new motorcar or a dogfight would do it. But this was probably the only time a person ever drew a crowd there, and held it, just by standing still in silence.

They fell to speculating and arguing over what could be the matter with the little woman on the chair—whether she was crazy, possessed by the devil, or catatonic. She certainly was not a native of Mount Forest. Someone in the crowd said he had just seen this young woman at Victory Mission just up the street. Someone else offered the information that the rigid Madonna on the chair above them was Sister Aimee Semple McPherson.[1]

Introduction and Biography

The story of Aimee Semple McPherson has captured the imagination of ecclesiastical scholars and historians in the decades since her death.[2] That this girl from small town Ontario was able to build one of the largest religious organizations of her time remains a fascinating tale of perseverance

---

1. Epstein, *Sister Aimee*, 3–4. See also Robinson, *Working Miracles*. Robinson notes that: "When she was sure a large enough crowd had gathered, she yelled 'Follow me!' Then she ran as fast as she could back toward the mission. The crowd followed wondering what this crazed woman was going to do . . . When she reached Victory Hall the crowd followed her in like rats led by a pied piper—and once they were all inside—she slammed the door shut and locked it. She made no attempt to unlock the door again until she had finished speaking. But instead of complaining, the crowd was mesmerized. Aimee was entertaining. She was funny. She was colourful. This woman was a born storyteller, who could speak the language of the common people, and Aimee convinced people that God loved them. The next night the crowd was much bigger. They loved this positive style of preaching. Most of the evangelical Christians in southern Ontario were used to hearing about hellfire and damnation, and about a frightening vengeful God" (30–32).

2. A key biographer, Edith Blumhofer, has noted, however, that in the decades immediately following her death, she attracted little notice in the academy, in no small part due to the disdain it has shown for popular religion, among which Pentecostalism is chief. As focus narrowed in recent years on the role of women in American Christianity, however, interest in her life story—female preacher with enormous popular appeal; founder of a denomination; social worker; editor; pioneer broadcaster and author—has steadily increased. See Blumhofer, "Reflections on the Source", 21.

and a finely-tuned sense of how to communicate the gospel to the culture of her times. This chapter will explore the life and times of McPherson, noting both her unparalleled success in ministry and the many controversies that are undeniably part of her story. We will then seek to determine what lessons from her tremendous success in the culture of the day that might be applied to North American Pentecostals as they seek to navigate rapidly changing societal trends.

Aimee Semple McPherson is considered by some to be the most recognizable Pentecostal preacher of the early twentieth century, and was certainly one of its most colourful and creative.[3] Pentecostal historian Vinson Synan has noted, "[she] holds a prominent rank among all religious leaders of the twentieth century, regardless of their sex, and may well be the most important ordained woman minister in the history of Christianity."[4] While the proceeding may be overstated and reflect Pentecostal historiography's tendency to focus primarily on the last century, McPherson was undoubtedly a key religious figure of the first half of the twentieth century. During a time when women were not often permitted to ordination and works of ministerial service such as preaching, McPherson built her own 5300-seat auditorium. Alexander paints a striking portrait:

> In the midst of the rigid personal asceticism that characterized early Holiness-Pentecostalism, when most adherents and leaders denounced stylish attire as "worldly" and most Pentecostal women could be best described as plain and unadorned, McPherson—petite, stylishly coiffed, and fashionably dressed—as physically attractive and striking in appearance. Some described her as looking more like a flapper than a Pentecostal preacher. At a time when most Pentecostals preached separation from "worldly" alliances, including those with the rich and powerful, her friends included politicians and movie stars . . .[5]

According to Edith Blumhofer, during the heyday of McPherson's ministry in the 1920s she made the front page of America's biggest newspapers at least three times a week on average.[6] Except for a very brief period in the late 1980s during the fall of the televangelists, perhaps no religious leader can claim such national exposure. A brief look at the background and early life of McPherson will enable us to better explore this significant figure in religious history.

3. Alexander, *Limited Liberty*, 89.
4. Synan, *The Twentieth Century Pentecostal*, 100.
5. Alexander, *Limited Liberty*, 89.
6. Blumhofer, "Sister."

Early Life

Born in a farmhouse near Salford, Ontario, on October 9, 1890, Aimee Elizabeth Kennedy was the only child of the unlikely marriage between James Morgan Kennedy and his young housekeeper, Mildred "Minnie" Pearce, thirty-five years his junior. Minnie had been brought into the Kennedy home at a young age to care for James' dying wife, Elizabeth. Upon the death of his wife, however, James continued to find her indispensible, and despite much talk of the arrangement from the neighbours, James and Minnie were wed when he was fifty, and she just fifteen.[7] So it was that even before she was born, young Aimee's[8] world had already known controversy.[9]

In the culture of the time, the various Protestant groups of southern Ontario were remarkably intertwined, and were noted for their unity in working towards the same task of infusing the culture with Christian values and sustaining the social fabric, viewing themselves not as rivals but partners. At the time of Aimee's birth, a relative newcomer to the scene—the Salvation Army—was making significant waves as it took "the war against sin" enthusiastically to the towns nearby her home. Though the core of their theological message was the standardized Wesleyan fare on sin, holiness, and free grace, this new movement excelled at attracting the attention of the masses:

> . . . Army officers packaged that message in startling ways calculated to gain attention. They cheerfully agreed with critics who complained that there was no religion in much of what they did to announce Army offensives. Rather, religion was the overriding intention of noisy, attention-getting pageantry and entertainment. It was the result, not the substance, and the end justified the means. From the bass drums . . . to the testimony shirts . . . from the setting of religious lyrics to show tunes to parades with banners and brass bands; from the red, blue, and gold flags . . . everything about the Army was calculated to attract and arouse curiosity.[10]

Throughout Aimee's childhood years, Minnie maintained a very close involvement with the Salvation Army, which impacted Aimee directly.

---

7. Understandably self-conscious about the age difference, he listed his age as 42, and hers as 22. Blumhofer, *Aimee Semple McPherson*, 33.

8. Though customary to refer to a biographical subject by surname only, almost all academic works on McPherson regularly refer to her as "Aimee" or "Sister" as she was known throughout her ministry. This chapter will follow suit.

9. Epstein, *Sister Aimee*, 5–6.

10. Blumhofer, *Everybody's Sister*, 34.

Blumhofer notes, "The Army barracks was the focus of much of Aimee Kennedy's young life."[11] This involvement undoubtedly taught the young woman a great deal about the power of music, drama, and enthusiasm to draw a crowd to the preaching of the Gospel. Further, given the important role of Catherine Booth as co-founder of the Army, Aimee was also exposed to equality of the genders in ministry in ways she would not have witnessed elsewhere. These were lessons that she would not forget as she began public ministry of her own.

Conversion, Marriage, Tragedy and Divorce

Aimee was converted in 1907, at the age of seventeen, at a Pentecostal revival meeting under the preaching of Robert Semple, a young evangelist from Ireland. Shortly thereafter, as she reports in her autobiography, while seeking God for direction, she records "It was as though a great voice had spoken in trumpet tones. 'Now that you, yourself, have been saved—go, help rescue others!'"[12]

Following her call, Aimee began to seek the Pentecostal Spirit-baptism, and soon received the experience she sought, just one year after the Azusa Street outpouring began in 1906.[13] It would appear that Aimee found the preacher as attractive as his message, for Robert Semple and Aimee Kennedy were married just eight months after her conversion. A local newspaper described the "very popular" bride as "a gold medalist in elocution," who "has always been a cheerful contributor at local entertainments."[14]

The newlyweds first went to Chicago in 1909 to work in William Durham's Pentecostal Mission. Her first Canadian trip shortly thereafter saw the couple preach in Berlin (now Kitchener), and London, helping to establish what is now London Gospel Temple, before enjoying ten final days at the Hebden Mission in downtown Toronto. The move of the Holy Spirit there was experienced through "a wave of baptisms" and those present noted Robert to be particularly "led of the Spirit" while they delighted in "Sister

---

11. Ibid., 46.

12. McPherson, *The Story of My Life*, 25. Originally published in 1951 by Echo Park Evangelistic Association, Los Angeles.

13. McPherson, *This Is That*, 50.

14. "Semple-Kennedy," 10.

Semple's gift of interpretation."[15] She spoke "the very words in given tongues that . . . made the presence of God very manifest to all."[16]

In 1910, the couple set out as missionaries to Hong Kong, where they were engaged in evangelistic work. Tragedy struck when both contracted Malaria and though Aimee recovered, Robert died in Hong Kong after just two years of marriage. Pregnant at the time of Robert's death, Aimee returned to the United States where she lived with her mother and daughter Roberta in New York, until she married Harold McPherson, a wholesale grocer from Rhode Island. In the next years Aimee struggled with the intensified call to preach, falling ill in 1915, though convinced that if she obeyed her calling, she would be healed. According to her own word, she finally gave in and accepted her call, and within two weeks was completely well.[17] From this point forward, Aimee began a series of campaigns throughout the United States and Canada, and never faltered for a lack of preaching engagements.

In 1917 Aimee began *The Bridal Call*, a monthly magazine associated with her ministry. She noted:

> [The Lord] showed me his exact plan for the Bridal Call; that its message was not to be one of controversy, fighting, great wisdom or eloquence, but simply what its name implied—a call to the bride to prepare for her heavenly Bridegroom. So whatever reports, testimonies, or other matter may be in the paper, we endeavour to have one article making plain the way of salvation, one on the baptism of the Holy Ghost, and one on the coming of the Lord and the preparation to meet Him.[18]

Though initially supportive of his wife's itinerant ministry, McPherson eventually tired of life on the road and demanded that Aimee settle down into a more traditional lifestyle. It was not to be, and, having separated in 1919, the couple finally divorced in 1921.[19]

---

15. McPherson noted that it was during their time with Durham in Chicago that God, "gave me the gift of interpretation." *This is That*, 68.

16. Blumhofer, *Everybody's Sister*, 86.

17. McPherson, *This is That*, 93–106. McPherson relates, in characteristic Pentecostal frankness, that God had given her a choice of going on the mission field, or being taken by death to heaven to be with Him (102).

18. Ibid., 141–42.

19. Epstein, *Sister Aimee*, 218. Epstein notes that Harold originally filed for divorce in 1919, citing desertion.

THEME 2: CREATIVITY AND RISK

From the very beginning, and perhaps due to her Salvation Army roots, Aimee was a show woman who used a variety of unconventional tactics to draw and hold crowds for her revival meetings. These included,

> ... standing in the middle of a busy town square and pretending she was a statue, going into saloons and dance halls and taking the stage to announce that her revival meeting was in town, and dropping tracts from an airplane in a community where one of her meetings was to be held . . . She travelled throughout the country in an automobile on which she had plastered Bible verses and evangelistic slogans such as "Jesus Saves," "Jesus is Coming Soon," and "Do You Know Where You'll Spend Eternity?"[20]

In the five years following her move to California in 1918, Aimee made nine trips across the United States, holding meetings both in large cities and small towns. Her first international campaign, in 1922, saw her preach to increasing crowds over a five-month period, taking her to New Zealand, England, and numerous times, to Canada.[21]

It is hard to overestimate the strength of her appeal. In 1921, for example, healing meetings held at Balboa Park in San Diego drew the cooperation of almost all of the city's Protestant churches, with police estimating that a full fifty percent of San Diego had attended.[22] Aimee recounted, "Squadrons of police and a detachment of Marines from the Naval Base had been detailed to handle the multitudes at the entrance of the pavilion. Otherwise I am sure we ourselves would scarcely have gotten in. As it was, it took a Marine on each running-board and an advance guard of police to make a way for the car . . ."[23] One cannot imagine what kind of religious gathering today in a large American city would attract one-half of its citizens.

The Church of the Foursquare Gospel and Angelus Temple

Despite her extensive and sometimes worldwide travel, Aimee always returned to her base in Los Angeles, where in 1922 she set up the Echo Park Evangelistic Association to help consolidate the variety of ministry expressions into a cohesive form. Using her campaigns and magazine as tools with which to promote her vision and seek financial help, on New Year's Day, in

---

20. Alexander, *Limited Liberty*, 94. It is widely believed that Aimee was the first woman to drive across the United States without a male accompanying her.
21. Ibid., 96.
22. Blumhofer, "Reflections," 23.
23. McPherson, *In the Service of the King*, 223.

1923, Aimee dedicated the 5300-seat Angelus Temple in Los Angeles, completely free of debt.[24] To draw attention to the grand opening, Aimee had entered a replica of Angelus Temple, decorated with thousands of pink roses and white carnations, in the Pasadena *Tournament of Roses* parade. The float did as was intended, for thousands awaited outside Angelus Temple for its opening at 2 p.m. that afternoon. After Sister Aimee led the crowd outside in singing "All Hail the Power of Jesus' Name" and in the Act of Dedication, she stepped inside, the doors opened, and the 5300 seats were filled in a matter of minutes.[25] "It was here that 'Sister'—as she was known by admirers—dressed in the white nurse-like uniform and blue cape adapted from her earlier Salvation Army days preached every single night and two times on Sunday for three years . . . People stood in line for hours to gain entry to each service which, at least in the early years, was full to overflowing."[26]

As Aimee reported:

> From the moment the Temple was opened, on January 1, 1923, the crowds came. In spite of its 5,300 seats, the great auditorium was taxed to capacity nightly. Revival spirit ran quite high, the altars were filled, and 12,000 were converted the first year. Miracles of healing, so real and so evident even to the unbelievers, brought a thoughtful world to our doors and to our altars.
>
> Hundreds were filled with the Holy Spirit, and students came from far and near to study at our Bible School. Thousands were prayed for by our workers in the Prayer Tower, who ministered 24-hours-a-day, and were also ministered to through our commissary which provided the food and clothing.
>
> During the first five years more than 1,200 have joined the Temple annually, more than 10,000 each year have wept their way to the altar and more than 3,000 have been baptized in water.[27] A special siding was built by the electric railroad company near the church and special trains, many cars long, were run to every service. During the big meetings on weeknights and three

---

24. Blumhofer, *Everybody's Sister*, 246.
25. Douglas Rudd, *Aimee Semple McPherson*, 91–92.
26. Alexander, *Limited Liberty*, 96.

27. A more objective report from Blumhofer concurs: "In the first six months, some 8,000 professed conversion, and 1,500 were immersed in the Temple's baptistery." Though Aimee had intended to have the Temple open just four days a week, Blumhofer notes that people would come and camp out by the Temple's doors whenever it was closed, waiting for it to open, and that it often accommodated up to 7,500 people, far more than the 5,300 it was designed for. While churches today would struggle to gain a congregation for a 1 p.m. service, some 88,356 people attended the 1 p.m. service at the Temple, *in 1924 alone. Everybody's Sister*, 247–48.

times on Sunday, that siding is jammed with cars waiting to take the multitudes.[28]

In the coming years, Aimee busily set about building a radio station (1924), a Bible College (1925), a social service ministry, the Angelus Temple Commissary (1927), and in 1929 her first sacred opera, "O Worship the King," was performed, each of which she launched with typical fanfare.[29] Throughout these years, her ministry continued to thrive. Her 1922 decision to cease her affiliation with the Assemblies of God (USA), the predominant Pentecostal denomination of her time, led many to conclude that Sister's theology was drifting from her Pentecostal roots. As will be discussed below, her personal theology remained very much Pentecostal; she did, after all, name her denomination the International Church of the Foursquare Gospel, emphasizing Jesus as Saviour, Healer, Spirit-Baptizer, and Coming King.[30] Despite this however, she was very careful to craft her services in a more generic sense. Though she shunned the Pentecostal title,[31] no doubt due to her keen sense of what was palatable to the public and church world of that era, her theology maintained a distinctly Pentecostal flair, while she insisted that her services were more "middle of the road" during which "Bible Christianity" was preached rather than Pentecostal doctrine.[32]

The star of her services, if not God himself, was certainly Aimee. Her audience, proclaimed Vanity Fair, worshipped "under the spell of the greatest showman of our times . . ." which listed McPherson as one of the most influential individuals of the post-Civil war era, including—and her company here is instructive—Harry Houdini and P.T. Barnum.[33] A reporter noted that "her showmanship was superb; her timing matchless; her dramatic instinct uncanny . . . As a director she is incomparable . . . at the first sign of restlessness she steps forward . . . with that swift, uncanny perception of hers . . . always, in emergency, she lifts those pink palms, flashes her infectious

---

28. Rudd, *Aimee Semple McPherson*, 95. Rudd lists the source as a quote from *The Personal Testimony of Aimee Semple McPherson*.

29. Alexander, *Limited Liberty*, 99–102.

30. The denomination was founded almost five years after the 1923 opening of Angelus Temple, on August 15, 1927. Barfoot believes that following the debacle of her kidnapping, "It was a denomination created for her survival as much as anything else." Barfoot, *Aimee Semple*, 474.

31. Ibid., 384. Barfoot notes that her early ads in the *Los Angeles Times* were devoid of any mention of Pentecostalism, focusing instead on health, happiness, heaven, and holiness as key words, and were usually placed under the "undenominational" section of church ads.

32. Alexander, *Limited Liberty*, 97.

33. Sutton, *Resurrection of Christian America*, 74.

smile, and breaks into a hymn, catching back her hearers before they notice they are slipping . . ."[34] "In this show-devouring city, no entertainment compares in popularity with that of Angelus Temple; the audience, whether devout or otherwise, concede it the best for the money (or for no money) in town."[35]

Controversy and Decline

The most controversial episode of McPherson's life involved a three-week disappearance in May 1926, and the criminal charges associated with it. Although the exact details are disputed, McPherson disappeared while sunbathing with her secretary on a local beach. She was presumed drowned by her followers; her mother announced in that evening's service that "Sister is gone; we know she is with Jesus."[36] For days, Los Angeles was obsessed with Aimee; some twenty-five thousand showed up at the beach on Memorial Day alone.[37] Rumours swirled that she was not in fact dead, but was either kidnapped or on a romantic tryst. Though Minnie Kennedy had hoped that memorial services for Aimee on June 20 would quell the public's insatiable interest in the story, within three days, on June 23, Aimee appeared in Mexico, the victim, she said, of a kidnapping, from which she had managed to escape.[38] On June 25 she arrived back in Los Angeles to more than 50,000 followers who stood waiting at the train station, sang hymns of praise, and boisterously welcomed her back from the dead. Blumhofer notes:

> The crowd at the station was the largest that had ever gathered to welcome anyone arriving in Los Angeles—president, politician, sports figure, or movie star. It was the third time that year McPherson had broken her own record for such a crowd. The throng stretched from the station as far as the eye could see. Police estimated that over 100,000 more lined to the route to Aimee Semple McPherson's home beside her church . . . watching the parade that escorted Sister home. A white-robed band from the

---

34. Ibid., 75
35. Ibid.
36. Blumhofer, *Everybody's Sister*, 282.
37. Ibid., 283.
38. The entire episode is recounted in Aimee's 1927 publication, *In the Service of the King*. In fact, the story of her escape from the kidnappers is featured prominently as the first three chapters, before she returns to her childhood in the fourth chapter.

Temple led twenty cowboys, a squad of motorcycle policemen, and a procession of cheering thousands through the streets.[39]

Despite her popular return, enough suspicion was raised in the minds of the public that a grand jury was convened to consider charges of perjury. In the end, however, the district attorney did not have enough evidence against McPherson, and the charges were dropped. This episode, however, changed the minds of many about Aimee, and the press began to take a more suspicious attitude towards her and her antics.[40]

Tensions that had simmered below the surface for years between Aimee and Minnie finally boiled over in 1927 as Aimee asked for her mother's resignation from her significant role at Angelus Temple. Again, as with the kidnapping, the press had a field day, and Aimee's image was further tarnished.[41] Trouble continued for McPherson in 1930 when she suffered what was characterized as a nervous breakdown, due in part to the strain of the perjury charge and investigation. Her 1931 marriage to Temple choir member David Hutton, which ended in divorce just over three years later, further contributed to her loss of credibility, as detractors quickly pointed out the Pentecostal prohibition against remarriage for those divorced.[42]

Though she continued both her nation-wide campaigns and weekly ministry at Angelus Temple, Aimee's star never again shone as brightly as it did in the early 1920s. Her final controversial moment came appropriately enough, at death. In Oakland for a campaign in the fall of 1944, Aimee had retired for the evening and had taken some sedatives to help her sleep. She never awakened, and was pronounced dead on the morning of September 27, 1944, at just fifty-three years of age. Though rumours of a suicide long lingered, the official corner's report indicated death by accidental overdose.[43] Her body was flown back to Los Angeles where she lay in state at Angelus Temple for three days, while 60,000 people passed by her casket. Aimee was buried on October 9, 1944, with 3,700 in attendance.[44]

39. Blumhofer, *Everybody's Sister*, 2.
40. Alexander, *Limited Liberty*, 103–4.
41. Blumhofer, *Everybody's Sister*, 305–10.
42. Ibid., 104.
43. Epstein, *Sister Aimee*, 438–40.
44. Ibid., 439.

Lessons Learned from Aimee

Despite the many controversies surrounding her in later life, all agree that Aimee managed to connect the presentation of the Gospel with the masses in an extraordinary manner. Through the celebrity and the scandal, we pause now to ask what lessons from the life of this early Pentecostal leader might be applicable today, as North American Pentecostals seek also to connect the Gospel message with society at large. Although this list will by no means be exhaustive, the following are instructive.

Into *All* the World

First, we note that Aimee was often willing to go where other clergy would dare not tread. While some restricted (and today restrict) their ministries to their own congregations and ventured little into the community (expect perhaps among those similar in status to their own middle and upper class folk), Aimee regularly ventured into the shadier areas of town to engage those that the church—and even society—often found beneath their attention. Further, unlike the fundamentalists of her day (and too often Pentecostals of today), Aimee was a full participant in the effort to improve lives around her. Sutton states:

> From the evangelist's earliest days in Los Angeles, she and her congregation contributed to the city's powerful Progressive-Era tradition of social and moral reform work. By fighting vice in the forms of prostitution, gambling, drinking, smoking, and dancing, she helped make Los Angeles one of the "cleanest" cities in the West. A popular speaker at local women's groups, veteran's meetings, chamber of commerce conventions, and temperance organizations, the evangelist championed quite a number of causes.[45]

Further, Blumhofer notes that Aimee often ministered personally to those who had been broken down through life's experiences.

---

45. Sutton, *Resurrection of Christian America*, 61. The author also notes that Aimee had a special place in her heart for unwed mothers, whom society regularly shunned at that time. Often disowned by their families, Aimee would seek these girls out after her services, invite them to the parsonage for dinner, and, more often than not, have them stay with her throughout their pregnancy. Once their babies were born, if she could not mediate reconciliation with the girl's family, she would pair them up with a lonely widow, who would care for the infants while the mother worked. Sutton, *Resurrection of Christian America*, 63.

Her visits to the "dives" and dance halls in Winnipeg, her foray into San Diego's boxing arena, the late-night hours she spent in the red light districts of Denver all became part of the McPherson legend. These visits were much more than publicity gimmicks; they expressed part of McPherson's personality. When she made a midnight visit to Denver's vice district in 1921, for example, *The Denver Post* noted with approval that she did not condemn people, or even speak about sin. Rather, "to this congregation of the abandoned, Aimee McPherson sang songs of hope in which they joined, and gave to them the promise of new life if they would be true to themselves."[46]

Today's Pentecostals can learn much from Aimee in this regard. Though Pentecostals could often be found among the lower classes of society, the movement today, at least in the West, thrives among the middle and upper middle classes of society. Forays into red lights districts are far less common, and I am personally struck by how much value a secular newspaper placed on the fact that this Pentecostal minister did not judge or condemn those most familiar with vice and sin, but instead offered hope. For a movement known today as much for its legalism, judgment, and condemnation of sin (and sadly, sinners), Aimee offers a wonderful example of how the Gospel might again be first and foremost, *good news*. Further, in parting ways with the fundamentalists of her time, she did not withdraw from society as a whole, but rather passionately engaged it with the Gospel. Though Pentecostalism is now realizing that its strict interpretation of "come out from among them and be ye separate"[47] does not mean the withdrawal from the world that was thought, there is still much to learn from McPherson's participation in society and her work towards overcoming its ills.

Media in all Forms

Second, we observe how Aimee used the media of the times to communicate the Gospel message, including extraordinary drama, costumes, and illustrated sermons. By all accounts, Aimee used the lessons she learned as a child, watching the Salvation Army draw attention to its message and gatherings, to great effect in her own ministry. Considering for a moment that Angelus Temple was based in Los Angeles, a city dedicated almost entirely to entertainment and the arts, it is incredible to conclude that this minister

---

46. Blumhofer, "Reflections," 24. She is quoting Frances Wayne, "Healer Visits Denver Underworld."

47. 2 Corinthians 6:17, KJV

of Pentecostal persuasion regularly outdid the secular world in terms of the pageantry and showmanship offered. Writing for *Harper's Monthly*, a decidedly non-Christian publication, Sarah Comstock described what she observed during a 1927 visit:

> Aimee Semple McPherson is staging month after month and even year after year the most perennially successful show in the United States . . . As a show-producer with unflagging power to draw she knows no equal. She is playwright, producer, director and star performer all in one . . . she plays her own role with an abandon that sweeps her hearers by hundreds to the altar.
>
> Illustrated sermons are her master effort, a novel and highly original use that she makes of properties, lights, stage noises, and mechanical devices to point her message. Heaven and Hell, sinner and saint, Satan, the fleshpots of Egypt, angels of Paradise, and temptations of a bejazzed world are made visual by actors, costumes, and theatrical tricks of any and every sort that may occur to her ingenious mind . . . [48]

A near crash-landing in 1925 by an airplane carrying McPherson, and the resulting front-page coverage was capitalized upon as Aimee preached a new, heavily advertised sermon, "The Heavenly Aeroplane." Sutton's description is worth reading at length; the reader may keep in mind that this was in 1925.

> She found that mixing her real-life adventures with drama, spectacle, and scripture could transform the simple gospel of personal salvation into a spellbinding epic. Such innovations allowed her to compete with Hollywood for the attraction of the masses . . . "The Heavenly Aeroplane" . . . drew crowds of people to the Temple, many scrambling for seats, hiding in stairwells, and storming emergency escape routes. Thousands were turned away. Those who made it into the church witnessed an impressive scene. The stage was set up as a grassy field with mountains in the background. Two miniature planes occupied the foreground, and suspended above the stage hung a model

---

48. Quoted in Blumhofer, *Everybody's Sister*, 260. All of life was material for a dramatic sermon: a speeding ticket one day with her daughter caught Aimee's attention. In one of her best-remembered sermons, she appeared that Sunday, in police uniform, on stage with a police motorcycle, bringing a sermon entitled, "Stop! You're Under Arrest," the context of which was that many of her hearers were speeding down the wrong avenues of life. Later embellishments in popular memory had Sister speeding up and down the isles of the Temple on her motorcycle, preaching as she did. Blumhofer, *Everybody's Sister*, 261.

"Holy City" . . . McPherson preached in her leather flight hat, goggles, and pilot's coat.

In a rousing sermon she carefully described each of the planes beside her. The first had the devil for a pilot, sin as its engine, temptation as its propeller, and self-righteousness and disobedience as its wings. This plane called to the audience, "Right this way! Step up ladies and gentlemen! All aboard for the theatre, the dance hall, card parties, for riches and popularity." With a cry of "contact," McPherson released the plane's propeller. It rolled from one side of the stage to the other, where it dramatically crashed. She then turned to the other plane, piloted by Jesus. This plane, she explained, would shuttle to the Holy City all who accepted Christ as Savior. The engine was the Holy Spirit, the propeller faith, and the wings obedience and love. At McPherson's cry of "contact!" the plane took off across a runway, then lifted off the ground, flying above the evangelist's head. It continued upward over the choir lofts, then turned and headed straight for the Heavenly City. The sermon ended with an old-fashioned altar call admonishing listeners to take a flight on God's plane.[49]

Aimee was aware that not all believers would find her methods orthodox; the same is likely true today, some 90 years later. Many outspoken opponents, typically other pastors, lambasted her "worldly" methods. Early in her ministry, however, she realized that "the methods so often used to impart religion were too archaic, too sedate, and too lifeless ever to capture the interest of the throngs." She would be different. "I developed methods," she explained in 1927, "which have brought hundreds of thousands to meetings who otherwise would never have come . . . Religion, to thrive in the present day, must utilize present-day methods. The methods change with the years, but the religion always remains the same." She instructed her students to do the same. "Remember you have competition . . . there are movies and the boxing-galleries and the bowling allies. Students, beat the old devil at his game . . . using every means you can at your disposal to get the message over."[50]

49. Sutton, *Resurrection of Christian America*, 68–69.

50. Quoted from various sources in Sutton, *Resurrection of Christian America*, 76–77. See also Barfoot, *Making of Modern Pentecostalism*, 434.

Cutting Edge Technology

Third, Aimee used the cutting edge technology of her day to win an audience. In 1924 she constructed her own state-of-the-art broadcasting station and recording studio on the third floor of Angeles Temple. In February, Radio KFSG (Kall Four Square Gospel) began its premiere broadcast with the hymn "Give the Winds a Mighty Voice, Jesus Saves." Aimee's was the first religious broadcasting station; her commercial license to operate was the first license granted to any woman by the FCC. She broadcasted to an estimated 200,000 receiving sets within a couple of hundred miles,[51] and immediately began a daily sunrise broadcast called "The Sunshine Hour."[52] So few radio stations at the time competed for use of the airwaves that broadcasts could be heard for thousands of miles; Aimee's voice soon became one of the most recognizable in all of the United States.[53]

Again, there are solid lessons to be learned. We note first that Aimee used all available tools to spread the Gospel message, no matter how new. Radio of her time may be likened to social networking of ours. Not only did Aimee use what was available, she was the very first Christian minister to use these tools in many cases. We may often witness churches today so far behind the times in terms of methodology for attracting individuals to the Gospel message that by the time they get on board with the newest instrument available, society has moved in to something else. Further, whereas many churches are content with an attractional model of church growth, whereby they hold service after service, waiting for the unsaved to miraculously attend, Aimee's approach was Missional—a buzzword in this decade—that she employed successfully 90 years earlier. She did not simply hold services in Angelus Temple waiting for the crowds to join her. She went out in the city, and through whatever means were available, *compelled* individuals to come and hear the Gospel presentation.

Kingdom vs. Denomination

Finally, we note that Aimee was more concerned with the promotion of the Gospel than the promotion of one denomination in particular, which in her case was the Assemblies of God. In 1922, after considerable debate, Aimee

---

51. Other estimates put the number at 1,000,000 listeners in 250,000 homes. See Barfoot, *Making of Modern Pentecostalism*, 417.

52. Epstein, *Sister Aimee*, 264.

53. Blumhofer, *Everybody's Sister*, 266–67. Blumhofer notes that in January 1923, for example, *The New York Times* advertised on a station broadcasting out of Havana, Cuba, as well as one out of Los Angeles.

had returned her AG credentials, prompting an article in the *Pentecostal Evangel*, the official publication of the AG, entitled "Is Mrs. McPherson Pentecostal?" The article concluded she was not, and urged readers to pray for her restoration. She responded with passion, noting that most Pentecostals failed to understand Pentecostalism biblically, and confused it with "giving way to fleshly emotions and doing all manner of ludicrous things."[54] She wrote:

> To be Spirit filled is the grandest, proudest tribute of sobriety and piety one can possess. The Holy Spirit is not marked by wildness, hysteria, screaming, or unseemly manifestations, but by deep, holy, sober, godly, reverent, prayerful exaltation of the gentle Christ of Galilee, an earnest passion for souls, a biblical and scriptural Holy Ghost boldness, and wisdom that will be the means of leading men and women to the Cross in which we glory.[55]

Though she believed in the "initial evidence" of Holy Spirit baptism, healing was often the prime focus of her services[56]—a fact that Aimee appears to have resisted.[57] For Aimee, it was all about souls:[58] "In our meetings, all else is subservient to, and directed toward, a decision to follow in the footsteps of Christ."[59] Some authors have suggested that in her attempt to appeal to a broader range of folk than did classical Pentecostalism, ". . . she demanded a type of control that excluded the 'emotional excesses' of many Pentecostal meetings, but that her detractors termed the 'free flow of the Holy Spirit'. She limited demonstrations such as shouting (or dancing), injections of 'hallelujahs' and 'amens' or outbursts of glossolalia that permeated most Pentecostal meetings."[60] Other writers, however, noting that McPherson indeed promoted the same experiential faith to which she herself subscribed, state that "Worship in McPherson's meetings was demonstrative, and the audience felt free to shout. In several instances, those who

54. Blumhofer, *Everybody's Sister*, 185.

55. Ibid., 185–86.

56. D.E. Ray notes that Aimee rejected the theology of those who suggested the sick must submit to the will of God, for it was His will that they suffer. She believed one must actively pursue divine healing. She wrote, "Do not say, 'Well, if it is the Lord's will to heal me, I will be healed, and, if not, I won't.' You will never get your healing that way." Ray, "Aimee Semple McPherson and Her Seriously Exciting Gospel," 161.

57. See Giacomo, "Aimee Semple Mcpherson", 162.

58. When questioned, Aimee told one reporter, "My meetings are ninety-nine percent *soul*-saving and *one* percent healing. God heals the sick that they may go out and save others . . . The central thought when they come to me is first and last and all the time—save their souls." Epstein, *Sister Aimee*, 220.

59. McPherson, *In the Service of the King*, 231.

60. Alexander, *Limited Liberty*, 99.

were supernaturally healed released shouts of joy. At other times, miracles led the crowds to burst out in spontaneous praise to God."[61] Blumhofer is perhaps the most balanced at this point, suggesting, "She was determined to discourage pointless hubbub but still encourage emotional and verbal responsiveness."[62] Sutton notes,

> . . . she never compromised her Pentecostal theological beliefs but rather inserted them into the context of American revivalism. Rather than separate from the nation's historic denominations, she hoped to reform them from the inside out. At heart, McPherson was never anything but a Pentecostal. Like many of her modern day counterparts, however, she downplayed the controversial elements of the movement and instead took a moderate position that facilitated broad alliances.[63]

Again, the lesson here for Pentecostals is clear. At a time when Pentecostals are struggling with their identity, Aimee's ability to incorporate what was best about Pentecostal teaching, while not alienating the masses by including the most extreme forms of Pentecostal praxis, is instructive. She was able to create an identity of New Testament pneumatological Christianity without reducing the focus of her services, and message, to a narrow denominational emphasis. Pentecostals today, caught as they are between those who would become a bland type of Evangelical and those who would withdraw back into the excesses of Pentecostal practice, could learn much about balance from this pioneer.

Conclusion

Through our exploration of Aimee Semple McPherson's early life and ministry, tremendous success, and controversial methods and occurrences, we have nonetheless observed an early pioneer of Pentecostal ministry who did as much to advance the Kingdom of God, status of women, and charismatic practice as almost anyone to date. Her life and ministry remain an inspiring witness as to what one individual can accomplish when faith in God and vision are joined with courage and confidence to try creative new ideas that many would consider risky.

61. Michel, "Aimee Semple McPherson", 177.
62. Blumhofer, *Everybody's Sister*, 147.
63. Sutton, *Resurrection of Christian America*, 43. While Sutton may be correct for North American Pentecostalism as a whole, the same would not be true for Newfoundland Pentecostals, who are only now engaging questions of alliances with other Christian bodies, and the threat to identity that this can pose.

Unfortunately, however, this passionate pioneer has not enjoyed honorific status as a central founder of classical Pentecostalism such has been assigned to others. Outside of her own denomination, Aimee's work remains surprisingly unknown. Very likely, as the years have passed, stories of affairs and divorce, kidnapping, court cases, and power struggles, have overshadowed the extraordinary accomplishments of a woman who was far ahead of her time.

Pentecostals today, and all ministers of the Gospel, owe much to this courageous innovator. In sum, Ray maintains:

> Given the explosive growth of Pentecostalism in the last hundred years, both in the US and around the world, McPherson's success—at least in terms of numbers—is instructive. She embodied many of the elements that define the movement as a whole: simplicity, accessibility, optimism, energy, media savvy, relevance, and cultural flexibility that yet had clearly defined limits. Even more important, she showed how Pentecostalism could give people a sense of power, vitality, and self-worth. She was a remarkable purveyor of those qualities. Most of all, McPherson offered serious excitement to every follower, in every aspect of her teaching and preaching. She did this, not as it has often been supposed, by hood-winking the public or simply putting on a good show—though she did put on a good show. She had earnest intent and real substance. Her message was exciting, not at the expense of theology, but because of it. The Gospel she presented was thus irresistible to thousands of people, each of whom could feel like a special person in God's kingdom . . . [64]

Would to God that Pentecostals once again discover the *seriously exciting Gospel!* In so doing, we may once again discover the value of community involvement. Further, as Aimee so aptly demonstrated, there is great reward in allowing the Holy Spirit to birth creative ideas for ministry within us, and being willing to take the risks necessary to try out new and untested ideas in cultural engagement. Indeed, in addition to acceptance of the other lessons learned from the ministry of McPherson, the shift from an inward (attractive) to an outward (missional) model will be key for Pentecostals in the immediate future. Additionally, Pentecostals must be willing to learn from newer movements that take seriously the challenges of secularism and post-Christendom. Therefore, an exploration of the Missional and Emergent movements vis-à-vis Pentecostalism is the subject of chapter 7.

---

64. Ray, "Exciting Gospel," 168–69.

— 7 —
Themes 3 & 4: Being Missional and Influencing Culture

Pentecostalism and the Missional Church / Emergent Church Movements

WE NOW WISH TO explore two recent conversations occurring within Christian circles, both of which recognize the challenges and opportunities arising from the shift to post-Christendom and secularism. Each seeks to make inroads relative to the propagation of the gospel within contemporary culture, but take slightly different approaches. In the first half of this chapter we will explore the Missional conversation of the last decade; in the second the Emergent Church will be our focus. Following a summary of their distinguishing marks and key foci, we will evaluate what Pentecostals may learn from their varying approaches, and what directions should be avoided.

Introduction: The Missional Conversation

Despite its having appeared on the scene just less than two decades ago with the publication of *Missional Church: A Vision for the Sending of the Church in North America*,[1] the word "missional" is now ubiquitous in book titles, church growth articles, blogs, and denominational literature.[2] Representing a significant change in thinking about the church and its local context, "missional" language has come to represent a powerful new way of reflecting on the nature of the church and her purpose in the rapidly changing world of the twenty-first century.

1. Guder, *Missional Church*.
2. For an excellent (though slightly dated) survey of material on the missional church, see MacIlvaine III, "What Is the Missional Church Movement?," 101.

As will be demonstrated below, the notion of the "missional church" has undergone considerable debate in its short lifespan, with strident proponents often disagreeing on key concepts. At its core, however, "missional" simply means an approach to evangelism and discipleship whereby one seeks to partner with God who is already at work in the community, as opposed to waiting for the lost to "come to church" and therein, find salvation. Though largely promoted and championed by seasoned leaders, the missional approach has been welcomed eagerly by younger believers, many of whom have a more natural affinity for community involvement than do their elders.

Notwithstanding its remarkable success described above, North American Pentecostalism is now at a crossroads of sorts. Tremendous societal shifts have meant that the church is no longer the centre of the community. Pentecostal churches that once grew on the basis of their weekly services and altar calls for salvation, now find that unbelievers rarely attend Sunday gatherings or special evangelistic services. In many cases growth has been replaced by decline.

With their robust Pneumatology, Pentecostalism would seem a natural fit with the missional focus on God the Holy Spirit already at work in communities. Strangely, however, Pentecostalism in the West has been very attractional in emphasis, and slow to embrace the tenets of missional thought and practice. This chapter will seek to bring the missional church discussion to Pentecostalism,[3] evaluating key missional concepts in terms of Pentecostal theology and practice. To accomplish this, we will first briefly explore the missional conversation, noting points of convergence among the key proponents, and will conclude with an evaluation of the missional conversation in terms of Pentecostal belief and practice, with an eye towards a praxeological assist for a Pentecostal church navigating 21st century culture.

A Brief Synopsis: The Missional Movement

"The word 'missional' seems to have travelled the remarkable path of going from obscurity to banality in only one decade."[4] This lament from Alan Roxburgh, a key writer and thinker in the missional conversation, is significant. Since 1998, the volume of books, articles, blogs, and conferences that are addressing the concepts of the missional church, has exploded. As often happens however, and as Roxburgh has noted, overuse can result

---

3. We note that MacIlvaine's survey cites missional works written from almost every major denomination viewpoint—except Pentecostalism.
4. Van Gelder and Dwight, *The Missional Church in Perspective*, 1.

in a word that actually has reduced meaning or impact. The search for a definition of "missional" is further hindered when authors resist providing a solid description in favour of the ever-popular "conversation" about trends, concepts, and practice. Roxburgh and Boren note that their intentionally vague description of missional concepts might "feel about as solid as Jell-O."[5] Other authors maintain that the concept of missional church struck such a chord with readers that the word soon became used in a variety of ways, depending on the local context of the advocate. According to Van Gelder and Zscheile, "missional" therefore displays an inherent elasticity that allows various faith traditions to express an understanding of mission from their own biblical and theological perspectives.[6]

Despite this elasticity, Van Gelder and Zscheile point to Darrell Guder's definition as one widely quoted: "The ecclesiocentric understanding of mission has been replaced during this century by a profoundly theocentric reconceptualization of Christian mission. We have come to see that mission is not merely an activity of the church. Rather, mission is the result of God's initiative, rooted in God's purposes to restore and heal creation."[7] More to the point, W. Rodman MacIlvaine writes, "A missional church is a unified body of believers, intent on being God's missionary presence to the indigenous community that surrounds them, recognizing that God is already at work. Taking seriously the fact that they have been sent by the risen Christ to be agents of God's pre-existing mission, missional churches embrace a distinctly countercultural mindset."[8]

Van Gelder and Roxburgh have identified four common themes in North American missional literature.

1. *God is a missionary God who sends the church into the world.* This understanding shifts the agency of mission from the church to God. It is God's mission that has a church rather than a church that has a mission.

2. *God's mission in the world is related to the reign (kingdom) of God.* This understanding makes the work of God in the world larger than the

---

5. Roxburgh and Boren, *Introducing the Missional Church*, 25.

6. *Missional Church in Perspective*, 2–3.

7. Guder, *Missional Church*, 4, quoted in Van Gelder and Roxburgh, *Missional Church in Perspective*, 3. David Bosch is also quoted regularly on this point: "The classical doctrine of the *missio Dei* as God the Father sending the Son, and God the Father and Son sending the Spirit, [is] expanded to include yet another "movement": Father, Son, and Holy Spirit sending the church into the world." *Transforming Mission*, 390.

8. MacIlvaine, "What is the Missional Church Movement?," 91.

mission of the church, although the church is directly involved in the reign (kingdom) of God.

3. *The missional church is an incarnational (versus an attractional) ministry sent to engage a postmodern, post-Christendom, globalized context.* This understanding requires every congregation to take on a missionary posture for engaging its local context, with this missionary engagement shaping everything a congregation does.

4. *The internal life of the missional church focuses on every believer living as a disciple engaging in mission.* This understanding makes every member a minister, with the spiritual growth of every disciple becoming the primary focus as the body is built up to participate more fully in God's mission in the world.[9]

These four themes will serve this chapter as rails upon which to explore the interaction between missional ideas and Pentecostalism. The time would seem right for Pentecostals to thoroughly evaluate the missional approach, for missional concepts seem to have engaged the imagination of a younger generation of believers, who best understand the changes in a society now profoundly impacted by postmodernity.

A Pentecostal Assessment of the Missional Church

As noted above, to assist in our discussion of Pentecostalism and the missional church, we will explore the four themes posited by Van Gelder and Roxburgh as representing the majority of missional conversation.

1. God as Missionary

God is a missionary God who sends the church into the world. On this point, it is fair to say that Pentecostals have had it right, at least in the sense that God's sending was equated with "missions" overseas.[10] Viewed as something conducted "over there" rather than "here at home" Pentecostals clearly understood that it was God's mission to reach all nations, and it was the church's duty to participate.[11] From the earliest days of the Azusa Street

---

9. Van Gelder and Roxburgh, *Missional Church in Perspective*, 4.

10. "Sending" in terms of the home community was largely misunderstood, as we will note shortly.

11. Eleonora Scott provides a solid corrective to those who emphasize mission at home to the neglect of missions abroad. Speaking of the Emergent Church, she writes, "EM can have merit only if the whole world is kept at the forefront of our understanding

revival, adherents were concerned to spread the Pentecostal message (which they equated with the full gospel), to the ends of the earth. Without doubt, the belief of early Pentecostals that they were living the last of the last days[12] made a significant contribution to their overwhelming recognition of the importance of missions. Influenced by the rise of premillennialism in the late nineteenth century, Pentecostals were convinced that civilization would only get worse before it improved. With the constant rumblings of Zionism and the possibilities of international war, they became convinced that the end was near. The stage was set for those who wished to help usher in Christ's kingdom—every nation on earth must be evangelized.[13]

Though this perception was not unique to Pentecostals—shared as it was by many premillennialists—they seized upon the notion that they could have a role in quickening the Second Coming, and worked solidly to this end.[14] So convinced were they of the imminent return of Christ, that most were unwilling to build or rent permanent places of worship, believing in the futility of such efforts when faced with the shortness of time.[15] Following Azusa Street, participants were placed in every corner of the world, with little or no preparatory training. "This early evangelistic zeal was characterized by a spontaneity in sending forth personnel without prearranged financial help. Missionaries went strictly 'by faith.'"[16]

Allan Anderson notes, "Pentecostal churches were missionary by their very nature and the dichotomy between 'church' and 'mission' that for so long plagued other Christian churches did not exist. This central

---

of 'missional'. It is good to encourage cooperation with local initiatives and avoid being 'an extension of colonialism', but we must not forget that there are still places in the world with little or no Christian witness and insufficient resources for evangelism. If by 'missional' we neglect the church's responsibility to other nations, then we introduce a new kind of imperialism—deciding that our culture's spiritual needs are more important (or just as important) than that of other nations. While everything is mission and everyone should be a missionary, this must not marginalize the needs in other countries, or the needs of those who join God's mission to those in other countries. Scott, "A Theological Critique of the Emerging," 345.

12. See Hollenweger, *The Pentecostals*. 413–21.

13. Dempster, Klaus, and Petersen, *Called and Empowered*, 207. Their literal reading of Matthew 24:14 reinforced their urgency: "This gospel of the kingdom shall be preached in all the world for a witness unto all nations; and then shall the end come" (AV).

14. McGee, "Assemblies of God Mission Theology," 166.

15. Anderson, *Vision of the Disinherited*, 77. Indeed, Anderson believes that it was their urgent eschatology, not their pneumatology, which were the key elements of Pentecostal belief. "In the early years at least, speaking in tongues and healing were subordinate elements in what was first and foremost a millenarian movement" (80).

16. McClung, "Explosion, Motivation, and Consolidation," 163.

missiological thrust was clearly a strong point in Pentecostalism and fundamental to its existence."[17] True to missional teaching today, they did not view this as their mission, or even the mission of the Church. This was the mission of God, and they were commanded to go and participate. They were possessed with a passion to go to the ends of the earth for their Lord, and no sacrifice seemed too great to them that the gospel might be proclaimed and the coming of the Lord hastened.[18] Unfortunately, as we will see below however, this understanding of "sending" did not extend to the home communities of Pentecostals.

2. God's Mission and Reign

God's mission in the world is related to the reign (kingdom) of God. Craig Van Gelder, in *The Essence of the Church: A Community Created by the Spirit*, has provided an excellent discussion on the relationship of God's kingdom to the missional church. He notes, "The field of biblical studies over the past half century has seen an emerging consensus that an understanding of the church must start with an understanding of the kingdom of God. More specifically, it must start with the announcement of the inauguration of God's redemptive reign in the person and presence of Jesus."[19] As with other key concepts, however, Van Gelder also observes the variety of definitions assigned to the kingdom of God, including: ". . . Christ's rule in the hearts of people; the presence of the institutional church; a thousand-year reign of Christ yet to be fulfilled; the providential care of God to sustain his creation; and the ideal moral life modeled in the example of Jesus."[20]

In addition to these voices, Van Gelder defines the kingdom of God as the idea that:

> God in Jesus powerfully entered human history with a reign that re-established life on the basis of redemptive power. This reign of God looks toward the sovereign rule of God as creator and sustainer of all life—God's providence. But this reign of God is about the dynamic presence of God's redemptive power confronting

---

17. Anderson, *An Introduction to Pentecostalism*, 215.

18. McClung, "Explosion," 163. This passion for missions continues today in classical Pentecostalism. In terms of financial giving alone, we note that the Pentecostal Assemblies of Newfoundland and Labrador, with less than 120 churches, gave over $2.5 million to missions work in 2011. The Pentecostal church in Springdale, NL, a rural town of less than 3000, gave approximately $250,000 to missions in 2010.

19. Van Gelder, *The Essence of the Church*, 74.

20. Ibid.

the forces of evil and restoring life to its fullness—God's redemptive work. This fullness of life looks back to the intent of creation design and forward to the promises associated with the new heavens and new earth. This redemptive reign has two dimensions: it is already present, but also future in some aspects.[21]

Without a proper understanding of God's kingdom, missional leaders argue, we will fail to address many of the challenges that currently exist in church life.[22] I fully agree, and lament the fact that if there is a significant weakness currently in Pentecostal theology and lay understanding, it is in the area of the kingdom of God / ecclesiology. To be fair, Pentecostalism is young as denominations go, and the last few years have seen two books on Pentecostal ecclesiology, both of which are endeavouring to contribute to the missional conversation from a Pentecostal viewpoint.[23] To my knowledge, however, these are the first and only books to address ecclesiology from a Pentecostal perspective.

Participation in the kingdom of God for Pentecostals has largely been a result of their strong eschatological focus.[24] Pentecostals went into the world evangelistically, to get souls ready for the soon return of Jesus Christ. In other words, Pentecostals participated in God's mission because the kingdom was soon to come—not so much because it was already here. In the West, Pentecostalism struggles to grow, in part, because diminishing focus upon eschatological realities has immediately and negatively impacted growth. As the world below looked increasingly prosperous and palatable to successive generations of Pentecostals, apocalyptic fervour and urgency declined.[25] A proper understanding of the kingdom of God should therefore assist with a renewed focus on evangelism as Pentecostals seek to partner with God's mission in the "here and now", even while they seek renewed emphasis on the necessity of getting souls ready for the "sweet by and by."

---

21. Ibid., 75.

22. For more on the connection between mission and ecclesiology, see Bliese, "The Mission Matrix," 237–48.

23. See Chan, *Pentecostal Ecclesiology*; Thomas, *Toward a Pentecostal Ecclesiology*.

24. "There has . . . always existed in Pentecostal thought a close relationship between the Church and eschatology or the reality of the Kingdom of God." Macchia, "The Church of the Latter Rain," 249.

25. Anderson, *An Introduction to Pentecostalism*, 219.

3. Incarnational vs. Attractional

The missional church is an incarnational (versus an attractional) ministry sent to engage a postmodern, post-Christendom, globalized context. Pentecostalism is ideally suited to fulfill this mandate on several fronts, but has had limited success. To begin, we have previously noted that despite what is a native connection to incarnational ministry on many levels, Pentecostalism had, in the West, become increasingly attractional. Focusing in particular on my own denomination, the PAONL, our unwritten motto for church growth was, for many years, "If you light a big enough fire in the church, the whole town will come to watch it burn." The key idea being that, if revival is happening in the Sunday (or weekday) services, the town will automatically attend out of curiosity. Unfortunately for Pentecostals today, the only revival of souls many can remember happened a generation ago, and was achieved using the method described above. A special speaker would be invited, perhaps for a week or more, "revival" would break out, and many souls would come to Christ. While younger generations are pushing for a missional approach, it is untried and unknown. What is known is that the last time God moved, it was via the attractional model.

Pentecostalism is therefore struggling, in a number of contexts, with the concept of post-Christendom. As noted above, the church had been the centre of the community for so long, those congregations finally recognizing this is no longer the case have little idea as to how they should proceed. Lesslie Newbigin, a key voice in the conversation on gospel and post-church culture, noted that the Protestant church in the West increasingly surrendered the public sphere to control by Enlightenment assumptions and survived by retreating into its own private world.[26] In the Pentecostal context as discussed in chapter 1, the "surrender" often happened quite willingly, as the "doctrine of separation"—a misinterpretation of 2 Corinthians 6:17[27]—was woven intrinsically into the classical Pentecostal mindset. As Alice B. Garrigus, the foundress of the PAONL, said during a 1926 sermon entitled *Separation*, ". . . if you let down the wall which God has put up between the church and the world, the offense of the cross will cease."[28] As has been noted, women's clothing was of considerable concern. Referring to the shortening of hemlines in popular styles, Garrigus observed, "We have had many plagues, but the plague of legs is the worst of all!" After considerable discussion, minute #27 of the 1927 General Conference read,

---

26. Newbigin, *The Other Side of 1984*, 22.

27. Therefore come out from them and be separate, says the Lord. Touch no unclean thing, and I will receive you. (NIV 1984)

28. Milley, *Message of Separation*, 10.

"Move that this conference now in session of the Pentecostal Assemblies of N.F.L.D. place on record as standing against picnics."[29] Worldliness knew no bounds.

This past separation now causes a core dilemma for the church. In one generation we have moved therefore from a church that believed the community was no place for a believer to be found, to one that hears constantly from its younger pastors that unless we are involved in the community, we will die.[30] Newbigin notes, "The church has lived so long as a permitted and even privileged minority, accepting relegation to the private sphere in a culture whose public life is controlled by a totally different vision of reality, that it has almost lost the power to address a radical change to that vision and therefore to modern western civilization as a whole."[31]

Though many Pentecostals churches have rejected sustained emphasis on socio-economic justice as too closely resembling the "social gospel," Melvyn Ming believes that such a focus could allow Pentecostals to once again engage their culture. ". . . If leaders in the Pentecostal churches could facilitate the intentional action of missional congregants toward addressing the real needs within their local community, there is great opportunity for these efforts to resonate with the very culture they are attempting to reach."[32] At the very least, following Jesus' many commandments to love and serve those around us, including our enemies, will open community doors that for too long have remained closed. Perhaps, cooking lessons for unwed mothers, and after school sports programs for junior high students, will facilitate the spread of gospel in this hour in ways that traditional revival meetings no longer can.

---

29. Ibid., 11, 19.

30. MacIlvaine believes that the move towards missional church has been resisted in some circles for two reasons. First, the term *Missio Dei* had often been hijacked by proponents of Process theology and had come to mean little more than a social gospel committed to meeting needs but failing to stress personal salvation. Second, from the 1920s through to the 40s, many North American evangelicals, Pentecostals included, when confronted with denominational liberalism, the fundamentalist-modernist controversy, and Scopes Trial, retreated into a shell of legalism and cultural isolationism that can persist to this day. "During this time in some traditions, radical separation from culture was seen as evidence of Christian spirituality." *What is the Missional Church Movement?*, 97–98.

31. Newbigin, *The Other Side of 1984*, 23.

32. Rush, "The Impact of Postmodernism on Pentecostal Churches," 22–23.

4. Every Believer Engaged in Mission

The internal life of the missional church focuses on every believer living as a disciple engaging in mission. As with several of the other key foci in the missional conversation, classical Pentecostalism naturally shares an affinity with this concept. Cecil M. Robeck, Jr., perhaps the leading Pentecostal historian of our time, supports the notion that Pentecostals placed tremendous importance on the role of individuals in building the community of faith. Concerning the Azusa Street revival, he notes, "[Seymour] had created a climate in which anyone able to lead in a prayer, give a personal testimony, sing a song, manifest some *charism*, or exhort the saints was allowed to do so."[33] Frank Bartleman, a participant in the Azusa Street revival, wrote, "No subjects or sermons were announced ahead of time, and no special speakers for such an hour. No one knew what might be coming, what God would do. All was spontaneous, ordered by the Spirit. We wanted to hear from God, through whomever He might speak . . ."[34]

With the Bible in one hand, and their "Baptism in the Holy Spirit" in the other, the earliest Pentecostals set out to win others for Christ. Key to this process was the Pentecostal story on the individual level—the sharing of God's work in the lives of individual believers was an integral component of almost every early Pentecostal gathering. Pentecostals instinctively recognized the power of the individual story as a means of connecting communities and communicating truth, much as postmoderns today value the same. For Pentecostals, however, the truth communicated was that of their place within the larger narrative of God's redemptive plan. Steven Jack Land notes, "Thus, the point of Pentecostal spirituality . . . was to experience life as part of a biblical drama of participation in God's history . . . Whether it was couched in terms of biblical dispensations, discrete personal experiences, or missionary travels, all of this language was meant to speak of the mighty acts of God's story of redemption in Scripture, in their lives and in the world . . . The narrative of salvation provided the structure for formation within the missionary movement."[35] Allan Anderson agrees, and observes:

> Most forms of Pentecostalism teach that every member is a minister and should be involved in mission and evangelism wherever they find themselves. Although increasing institutionalization

---

33. Robeck, *The Azusa Street Mission and Revival*, 115.

34. Bartleman, *Another Wave of Revival*, 59. See also Stronstad, *The Prophethood of All Believers*. Stronstad, in a clear reference to Luther's commitment to a priesthood of all believers, argues that with Pentecost, every believer ought to be charismatically empowered for kingdom service.

35. Land, *Pentecostal Spirituality*, 62.

> often causes a reappearance of the clergy/laity divide, the mass involvement of the 'laity' in the Pentecostal movement was one of the reasons for its success. A theologically articulate clergy was not the priority, because cerebral and clerical Christianity had in the minds of many people already failed them. What was needed was a demonstration of power by people to whom ordinary people could easily relate. This was the democratization of Christianity, for henceforth the mystery of the gospel would no longer be reserved for a select privileged and educated few, but would be revealed to whoever was willing to receive it and pass it on.[36]

Many missional writers have noted the importance of the Holy Spirit's direction and empowerment in the missional church. Van Gelder and Zscheile write, "Participatory leadership for the missional church is grounded in the premise that the church finds its identity in participation in God's mission in the world, and that it is primarily the Holy Spirit who leads Christian communities . . . Participatory leadership assumes that authority is distributed among the community by God, both in the form of spiritual gifts and in the presence of the Spirit."[37] Pentecostals, with their inherent focus on the person and work of the Holy Spirit in their midst, should have therefore been natural leaders in the missional movement. As Roxburgh and Boren note, however, Pentecostal focus on all things pneumatological did not always translate into a missional application:

> A basic conviction of the Pentecostal and charismatic movements of the twentieth century was that Christians are people who are shaped by the life and work of the Spirit among us. This insight was a gift to the church. But our sense is that this reenergizing of the church affected its inner life without really influencing the ways in which the Spirit shapes the church for a missional life. Structures and programs remained essentially untouched, and a fundamentally attractional model of the church went unchallenged in most cases.[38]

---

36. Anderson, *An Introduction to Pentecostalism*, 216–17.
37. Van Gelder and Zscheile, *The Missional Church in Perspective*, 155.
38. Roxburgh and Boren, *Introducing the Missional Church*, 120.

Summary: The Missional Conversation

This chapter has explored our third theme by surveying the missional conversation of the last decade. Using the four themes proposed by Van Gelder and Roxburgh to summarize the consistent motifs of the sometimes varied missional movement, we have described both the natural affinity to, and struggle inherent within Pentecostalism's efforts to move from a largely attractional past, to a future with a missional 'raison d'etre'.

I believe that if Pentecostalism is to flourish in its second century as it did in its first, the time is ripe for a fresh evaluation of its ecclesiology, particularly in terms of its praxis. In advancing towards a missional understanding of church life and evangelism, we have noted that Pentecostalism already stands in solidarity with several of the key concepts expounded in the missional conversation. With a renewed focus on ecclesiology, a better understanding of the kingdom of God, and continued emphasis on the Spirit's role in the life and practice of both believer and congregation, Pentecostalism in the West may well change the course of its current decline, and witness revival fires burning brightly once again—even without a "week of special meetings."

As the leaders of the Emergent Church proclaim their ability to engage and influence culture, we do well to consider whether the Emergent approach might assist Pentecostalism in similar efforts. Continuing this conversation, we will now address a number of other prominent theological and practical concerns arising from the interaction of Pentecostalism with the Emergent Church movement.

Introduction: The Emergent Conversation

Pentecostalism and the Emergent Church: the former, begun just over one hundred years ago, now numbers more than 500 million adherents. The latter, a phenomena of the late twentieth century, has not yet had its influence properly measured. Classical Pentecostalism, though varied worldwide, is reasonably consistent in the West; the Emerging/Emergent[39] movement

---

39. There are those who maintain a strict differentiation between the Emerging and Emergent movements. At its most basic, *Emerging* is used for those who are simply trying to contextualize the Gospel for postmoderns, and *Emergent* referring to the organization once headed up by Tony Jones and associated especially with Doug Pagitt and Brian McLaren. See DeYoung and Kluck, *Why We're Not Emergent*, 16. Though the official Emergent network, *Emergent Village*, no longer exists, (www.emergentvillage.org now takes the viewer to a home improvement site), this study will use the terms distinctly, for though the official Emergent network ceases to exist, the influence of its

however, despite some general trends within its advocates and practitioners, remains a nebulous force, difficult to grasp at times even for those known to be key supporters.

We have previously noted that North American Pentecostalism is showing signs of struggle as it endeavours to evangelize its youngest generations. As scholars consider the incredible appeal of the Emergent Church in this very demographic, Pentecostals must consider potential lessons to be learned from this young movement. As Pentecostalism seeks to understand and evangelize the younger generations of society—GenX and the Millennials—it will need to become conversant with, and clearly assess, the tenets of the Emergent Church movement, for its influence over the thought and theology of the youngest generations is significant. Some Pentecostals may argue that with the Emergent success in engaging culture, and Pentecostal difficulty with the same, Emergents have much to teach Pentecostalism. The question asked therefore, in light of our third theme, is an important one: should the Pentecostal movement align itself with some of the doctrines and practices observed in Emergent circles? Will an embracing of Emergent philosophy realign Pentecostal beliefs and values to the point where Pentecostalism once again sees the success of its first decades?

With a foundational understanding of Pentecostalism in hand, we will first provide a brief synopsis of the Emergent Church movement. The similarities and differences between what was the primary Christian movement of the early twentieth century and what may be the primary Christian movement of the twenty-first will be explored. We will conclude with an assessment of the Emergent Church in terms of the possibility of its contribution to Pentecostal rejuvenation.

A Brief Synopsis: The Emergent Church

Unlike Pentecostalism, which though varied can still be reasonably viewed as a movement with cohesive doctrine, a key challenge with the Emerging/Emergent church movement is in obtaining a definition that will encompass the tremendous variety therein. To a large extent, the basis of the movement is the very popular books penned by self-identified Emergent authors[40], who in many cases are pastoring flagship Emergent churches. As Kevin

---

key authors and churches continues.

40. Some of the best known Emergent works include: McLaren, *A Generous Orthodoxy* idem, *A New Kind of Christianity*; Jones, *The New Christians*; Kimball, *The Emerging Church*; Pagitt and Jones, *An Emergent Manifesto of Hope*; Ward, *Liquid Church*; Rollins, *How (Not) to Speak of God*.

DeYoung suggests, with no governing body or denominational ties, defining the Emerging Church is "like nailing Jell-O to the wall."[41] DeYoung also notes, however:

> ... the Jell-O like nature of the emerging church is also intentional. It is, after all, a "conversation." Emergent authors, bloggers, and pastors do not see themselves as leaders or authoritative theologians, but as talkers. This is one of the most admirable and frustrating parts about the emerging church. It's admirable because emerging Christians admit that their ideas are only exploration and experimentation, and not definitive in any way. That's refreshingly honest and self-effacing. It's frustrating because the "we're just in conversation" mantra can become a shtick whereby emergent leaders are easy to listen to and impossible to pin down.[42]

Essentially, Emergent seems to be a reaction to the larger, consumerist mega-churches where relationships are not the chief concern. In some cases, the high value placed on relationships leads to a low appreciation of formal doctrinal statements, for these are seen as divisive and contrary to relational growth. Other emerging leaders will desire relevance but not at the expense of doctrines traditionally understood as orthodox and foundational.[43]

Eddie Gibbs and Ryan Bolger, in their book, *Emerging Churches: Creating Christian Community in Postmodern Cultures,* note "Emerging churches are communities that practice the way of Jesus within postmodern cultures. This definition encompasses nine practices. Emerging churches (1) identify with the life of Jesus, (2) transform the secular realm, and (3) live highly communal lives. Because of these three activities, they (4) welcome the stranger, (5) serve with generosity, (6) participate as producers, (7) create as created beings, (8) lead as a body, and (9) take part in spiritual activities."[44]

Scot McKnight has written extensively on the emerging/emergent church for lay readers. In 2007 he cautioned, "Emerging is the wider, informal, global, ecclesial (church-centered) focus of the movement, while Emergent is an official organization in the U.S. and the U.K. While Emergent is the intellectual and philosophical network of the emerging movement,

---

41. Interestingly, this was the same metaphor used earlier in this chapter to describe the Missional conversation.
42. DeYoung and Kluck, *Why We're Not Emergent,* 17.
43. Piper, "What Is the Emerging Church?."
44. Gibbs and Bolger, *Emerging Churches.* Cited in Scot McKnight, "Five Streams of the Emerging Church."

it is a mistake to narrow all of emerging to the Emergent Village."[45] For the purposes of this work, therefore, we will focus on the continuing influence of the Emergent Church[46] in particular. The rationale for this decision rests largely on the significant influence that Emergent writers have among young adults, including Pentecostals. Even those generally unfamiliar with theological discussions are familiar with names like Brian McLaren, and the Universalist themes of books such as Rob Bell's, *Love Wins*.[47]

However loosely defined the movement may be, there are still characteristics that may be observed as common to most writers within this vein. D.A. Carson describes the Emergent church as a protest movement: a protest against traditional evangelicalism, a protest against modernity, and a protest against seeker-sensitive mega-churches.[48] Within this protest, a great deal of re-thinking traditional Christianity is taking place. Since those involved are typically adverse to self-definition, this list of eleven common characteristics within the Emergent movement by Doug Pagitt, one of its more influential leaders, is instructive.

1. A Kingdom of God focus—join the Kingdom of God wherever it finds it.
2. Pursue faithfulness to God through new practices, structures and understandings.
3. Tend to have a hopeful and positive view of God's engagement in the world—we should find the activity of God in the world and join it.
4. Committed to loving God and loving neighbor and loving enemy in real ways in this world.
5. Deeply connected to the story of God and the Bible.
6. Living with the guidance of the Holy Spirit—not culture or understandings.
7. Theologically active—thinking deeply about these practices.
8. Openness to the "other"—outsider, foreigner, doesn't get freaked out.
9. Want the good news of God to change the world and be the good news for all creation.

---

45. McKnight, "Five Streams." As we noted above, this official network no longer exists.

46. The interested reader can find a more detailed description of the origins of the Emergent Church from the perspective of Dan Kimball, a founding member as it were. See Kimball, "Origin of the Terms 'Emerging' and 'Emergent' Church - Part 1."

47. Bell, *Love Wins*.

48. Carson, *Becoming Conversant with the Emerging Church*, 11–44.

10. We understand community to be an essential part of the Christian life.
11. We are interested in the future more than fighting the battles of the past—we are people who are trying to live the story of Jesus in our world in ways consistent to where we have come from.[49]

Many Christians are troubled by how these foci actually work out into Christian practice and doctrine. With a more pejorative tone, apologist Matt Slick has noted twelve common characteristics within the Emergent movement, ranging from the well-acknowledged desire to reach postmoderns, to "an emphasis on experience and feelings over absolutes" and "concentration on relationship-building over proclamation of the gospel."[50]

The Emergent Movement and Pentecostalism

As a protest movement itself, Pentecostalism can find much to empathize with in the various items noted above.[51] Pentecostal and Emergent authors are sometimes in the same place—attempting to bring about the same changes. In others, the Emergents speak a word of correction to Pentecostalism that is sorely needed, for in some cases early Pentecostalism embodied the change Emergents are now looking for—though having drifted from their roots, Pentecostals are now a part of the target. Finally, however, there are trends within the Emergent church that Pentecostalism will—and must—reject.

A. Areas of Compatibility and Challenge

In general, the Emergent push towards a focus on the Kingdom of God, and their desire for a deep connection with the story of God[52] sits well with Pentecostals. Pentecostalism has long celebrated "other-worldliness" and recognized the fact that "this world is not my home." Though differing slightly in meaning, Pentecostals have valued God's Kingdom highly, and have understood that God's Spirit was working to build his Kingdom on

---

49. Jones, "11 Common Characteristics of the Church Emerging."
50. Slick, "What Is the Emerging Church?"
51. Though there are multiple lists of such characteristics, the eleven points, given by one of Emergent's founders, and twelve given by an evangelical critic, encapsulates well the general drift of both the movement, and its detractors, and will therefore be considered satisfactory for the purposes of interaction with Pentecostalism.
52. See for example Pagitt, "The Emerging Church and Embodied Theology," 117–58.

earth, even as the enemy was seeking to destroy it. Further, Pentecostals have acknowledged the importance of the narrative and have long been accused of building their most distinctive doctrines from the stories Luke records in the book of Acts. Seeking to avoid stale traditionalism in worship and practice, Pentecostals were known in their earliest days as a powerful reaction to the stagnant liberalism and dry rationalism of the late 18th century. With Pentecostalism having surpassed its centennial, many observers have noted the institutionalization, and stringent form characteristic of older denominations, can now be found in Pentecostalism also.[53] In this, the Emergent push for fresh and vibrant worship might speak a much-needed word of correction to their older sibling.

2010 marked an interesting occurrence, as Tony Jones, theologian-in-residence at Solomon's Porch fellowship in Minneapolis, and key Emergent author, was the invited keynote speaker at *The Society for Pentecostal Studies* annual meeting. Jones noted a variety of areas in which Pentecostals and Emergents could learn from each other. On the one hand, Emergent believers can learn how to speak of the Holy Spirit from Pentecostals. While Emergents are strong believers in the Spirit, Jones observed, they do not always have the language to articulate how important theologically and practically the Holy Spirit is for the believer today. Further, from Pentecostals Emergents can learn how to properly discern the Spirit's leading and work.[54]

On the other hand, Jones suggested that Emergents excel at engaging the community and listening to God in corporate environments, regardless of one's ecclesiastical credentials. In this area, Jones rightly observed that Emergents are succeeding in contrast to today's Pentecostals—and it is a sign of drift in Pentecostalism from its roots. Further, Jones challenged Pentecostals to return to their roots and revive an eagerness to help the poor and downcast, even as they spread the Gospel. With success has come wealth, and with wealth has come an ability to forget those less fortunate. Pentecostals were admonished to remember what it was like to be outsiders, and Jones noted that respectability in later years has placed Pentecostalism in the same position of "gatekeeper" as were those diametrically opposed to Pentecostalism several generations earlier.[55] Finally, in a challenge directed

---

53. See, for example, Vondey, *Beyond Pentecostalism*, 182–91.

54. Jones' address was posted verbatim on his website; this section is taken from his comments. See Jones, "What Pentecostals Have to Learn from Emergents."

55. The *Society for Pentecostal Studies* annual meeting in 2010 was an unfortunate example of exactly that. The conference was to be held on the campus of one of the Assemblies of God universities. When word reached AG headquarters that Jones was invited as keynote, the denomination forbade SPS from having Jones on their grounds, observing that his belief in equal rights for homosexual couples (not support of gay

to this body of Pentecostal academics that would hearken back to their roots, Jones intoned:

> My challenge to you is to learn from the mistakes of your Presbyterian, Episcopalian, and Methodist forbears: Don't let your theology migrate north—and by "north," I mean up, from the heart to the head, from the streets to the ivory tower. Forget about trying to impress the Ivy Leaguers—they're the past, not the future. And forget about "trickle-down" modes of theological education, where the smartest person in the room teaches the next one down, and so on and so on. That, too, is the past. Instead, learn how to blog. Tweet your theology. Write popular books instead of monographs. In other words, teach everyday people how to think theologically.[56]

B. Areas of Critique and Concern

For all of their success in challenging the worst in Modernistic evangelicalism, in which Pentecostalism is a full partner, the Emergent movement has not always demonstrated the same critical approach toward the tenets of postmodernism upon which they've based their critique. Postmodern thought regularly eschews belief in objective truth or metanarratives, for example, both of which are key components of traditional Christian orthodoxy. Further, the postmodern focus on experience as the primary source of epistemology challenges the traditional Christian belief in Scripture's ability to communicate truths to the reader via propositions. Finally, having acquiesced to a weak understanding of objective truth and the ability of the Scripture to provide much beyond inspirational stories that motivate the community, some Emergent thinkers are falling prey to doctrinal ambiguity and relativism as they seek to engage their culture.

1. Absolutely Denying Absolutes

For example, in his opening chapter of *Becoming Conversant with the Emerging Church*, D.A. Carson focuses on a workshop led by Brian McLaren at a conference for Emerging Church leaders. A number of questions were raised in the Q&A that followed, including one on homosexuality. McLaren noted

---

marriage itself) was unacceptable.

56 Jones, *What Pentecostals Have to Learn from Emergents*, Retrieved from www.patheos.com.

that there is no one satisfactory position on homosexuality, because all positions hurt someone, and that is always bad. Further, since we cannot be 100 percent sure what the Bible means when it appears to condemn homosexual practice, we cannot use the Bible to make propositional statements about homosexual practice today. If McLaren accepted a number of positions, he could be accused of relativism, a common outflow of postmodern thought. Instead, he refrains from offering any position at all, believing this avoids both modernistic certainty and postmodern pluralism.[57] Albert Mohler Jr. notes, ". . . McLaren's carefully nuanced non-answer to the question is illustrative of the Emerging Church movement's failure to render clear answers in the aftermath of a rejection of absolute truth."[58] Carson concludes, "In short, emergent writers do not handle the truth claims of Christianity very well. While formally repudiating the hard forms of postmodernism, when it comes to their actual arguments they either cave in to these hard forms or, to say the least, never provide any hint of how Christians informed by postmodern insights can speak about truth in the ways that Scripture does . . ."[59]

2. Use of the Bible

Further to the Emergent tendency to sidestep questions of absolute truth are questions surrounding their use and view of the Bible. The naïve acceptance of postmodern virtues so often displayed poses a challenge for Emergent thinkers when it comes time to explore the various propositional statements (read absolute truths) recorded in the Scriptures. Emergents typically complain that Modern evangelicals read the Bible as a textbook. Brian McLaren argues,

> When we theological conservatives seek to understand the Bible, we generally analyze it. We break it down into chapters, paragraphs, verses, sentences, clauses, phrases, words, prefixes, roots, suffixes, jots and tittles. Now we understand it, we tell ourselves. Now we have conquered the text, captured the meaning, removed all mystery, stuffed it and preserved it for posterity, like a taxidermist with a deer head.[60]

---

57. Carson, *Becoming Conversant with the Emerging Church*, 34–45.
58. Mohler, "What Should We Think." As Kevin DeYoung notes, "Never has ambivalence sounded so courageous." *Why We're Not Emergent*, 46.
59. Carson, *Becoming Conversant with the Emerging Church*, 131–32.
60. McLaren and Campolo, *Adventures in Missing the Point*, 79.

Point well taken. To be sure, Modernism has influenced Western evangelicalism to the point where the Bible can be read as a scientific textbook. But the correction deemed necessary by McLaren and other Emergent writers is to swing to the other extreme of biblical interpretation, where there really is no objective truth to be found in the Scriptures, where authorial intent is not nearly as important as what the Scriptures say to the individual on the day of their reading, where propositional truths are neglected in favour of the experiences told via stories and poetry. McLaren states, "Our sermons tend to exegete texts in such a way that stories, poetry, and biography (among other features of the Bible)—the 'chaff'—were sifted out, while the 'wheat' of doctrines and principles were saved. Modern Western people love that approach; meanwhile, however, people of a postmodern bent . . . find the doctrines and principles as interesting as grass clippings."[61]

3. Exclusivity of Christ

For Pentecostals, the Emergent tendency to "engage culture" by oftentimes becoming indistinguishable from the culture, is disconcerting. Western culture has so embraced relativism, for example, that traditional Evangelical understandings of the exclusivity of Christ now seem archaic and ignorant. Representative of many Emergent writers, McLaren proclaims,

> . . . *If the Christian religion were ever to be recast to fit within the Greco-Roman mind, it could become something very different from what Jesus intended, and something very dangerous* . . . this is precisely what has happened. Christianity has a persistent problem with pluralism not because of Jesus or his Jewish roots, but because of its Greco-Roman captivity.
>
> If we could break free from the Greco-Roman soul-sort narrative, think of what could change. We Christians could offer Jesus (not Christianity) as a gift to the world, and we would no longer consider it a requirement of faithfulness to insult other religions and call their founders demonic. We would no longer

---

61. Ibid., 77. In one of his newer works, McLaren goes even further, suggesting that our entire understanding of the Bible has come from the time since Jesus, and is totally infected by a Greco-Roman worldview. We do not understand Jesus and the plan of God from the time of creation forward; we understand him from the present time backward. It is Greco-Roman philosophy, McLaren argues, that has framed God as one so upset with sin that He sent an atoning sacrifice, and as one who will eternally punish those who refuse to accept Christ's offer of grace. We can again discover the true God of the Bible, if we were to liberate the Scriptures from the scourge of Greco-Roman thinking, and from concepts such as original sin, total depravity, 'the Fall', and eternal conscious torment in hell. See *A New Kind of Christianity*, 33–45.

envision a day when all other religions would be abolished and only our own would remain. We would no longer consider ourselves as normative and others as "other." We would stop seeing the line that separates good and evil running between our religion and all others. We would be freed from the tendency to always think "insider/outsider" and "us/them." We would learn to discover God in the other, and we would discover a bigger "us," in which people of all faiths could be included.[62]

4. Eternal Punishment

Another doctrine to take a hit in the Emergent discussion of theology is belief in a place of eternal punishment. Hell, it seems, is no longer fashionable. This notion has appeared in a number of Emergent writings, but none as popular (or garnered as much media attention) as a recent offering from Rob Bell, *Love Wins: A Book About Heaven, Hell, and the Fate of Every Person who has Ever Lived*. In it, Bell challenges the traditional Christian understanding of Heaven and Hell, and the idea that those who've accepted Christ as Saviour will be eternally separated from those who do not. Instead, though avoiding labels, as Emergents are wont to do, Bell proposes a type of Universalism, in which God's love does win, and wins over everybody's heart in the end. Though overstating the accuracy of this historical point, Bell declares, "At the center of the Christian tradition since the first church have been a number who insist that history is not tragic, hell is not forever, and love, in the end, wins and all will be reconciled to God."[63] For Bell, and contra traditional Protestant dogma, Hell is not an actual place of physical torment, but rather a metaphor of the consequences for those who reject Christ's superior way of life. Punishment is not forever, and even in "hell" however defined, God's love consistently plies the hearts of those who've insisted on going their own way, and eventually prevails. As one can imagine, Hell so defined is much more palatable to the postmodern psyche.[64]

5. The Atonement

Quite apart from sending the unrepentant to Hell, historical Christian understandings of Christ's substitutionary atonement and necessity of Christ's

---

62. McLaren, *A New Kind of Christianity*, 214–15. Italics from the author.
63. Bell, *Love Wins*, 109.
64. For a popular review of this work, see Galli, "Rob Bell's Bridge Too Far."

death are similarly uncomfortable for many Emergent writers. British theologians Steve Chalke and Alan Mann in their book, *The Lost Message of Jesus*[65] (for which Brian McLaren wrote the forward), contend that penal substitutionary atonement is akin to "divine child abuse," a phrase oft repeated by Emergent writers. In his critique of Emergent writers on this point, Robert Sagers notes:

> Others within the emerging church movement, such as Spencer Burker and Barry Taylor, write that it was not Jesus' intention to die as a propitiation of God's wrath for the sins of the world. Instead, Jesus died because He threatened the religious community by breaking their rules, which He did out of His sacrificial love for others. Christians, then, need to balance penal substitution—which can "reinforce a caricature of a God who is angry, bloodthirsty, and judgmental"—with good works done in love. After all, they assert, "[w]hat counts is not a belief system but a holistic approach of following what you feel, experience, discover, and believe; it is a willingness to join Jesus in his vision for a transformed humanity."[66]

Summary: The Emergent Conversation

With an understanding of Pentecostalism already in hand, this chapter has given a brief synopsis of the Emergent Church, noting their shared reaction to the epistemological assumptions of Modernity that have found their ways into the doctrines and practice of the current Evangelical church. We have noted mutually beneficial foci and areas of similarity between the two movements. Unfortunately, however, many of the Emergent writers seem increasingly willing to jettison traditional doctrines of Christian orthodoxy. To be sure, Pentecostalism has, more than most other Evangelical groups in the 20th century, focused upon one's feelings and experiences. Unlike some of their Emergent friends, however, they have not done this at the expense of Biblical truth or traditional Christian orthodoxy. Perhaps the key difference in the two movements can be found in their attitudes towards culture: Pentecostals saw themselves as aliens and strangers in contemporary society, and sought a stance of separation. Emergents try to accommodate themselves to culture, in their sincere efforts to free the message of Jesus from the strictures of Evangelical Christianity. While they are to be

---

65. Chalke and Mann, *The Lost Message of Jesus*, 182.

66. Sagers, "The Emerging Church and Salvation," in *Evangelicals Engaging Emergent*, 196–97.

applauded for this mindset and their efforts, removing the core of that same Gospel, in terms of the necessity of atonement, authority of the Scriptures, and uniqueness of Jesus Christ, will not, in the long run, serve their cause well. As Emergents challenge Pentecostalism to remain free from the negative assumptions of Modernity that have hampered the Western Church, Pentecostals must work with Emergents to ensure that their zealous accommodation of culture does not leave them with an impoverished Gospel.

Conclusion

The challenge therefore remains: how does a religious movement already more than a century old preserve what is best about its foundational beliefs and practices, while embracing new ideas and concepts designed to better communicate timeless truths to a generation already locked in the aftermath of postmodern philosophy? Our final chapters will offer a collection of personal insights and proposals on issues that Pentecostalism must seriously consider in the coming years via focus on our remaining four themes. While surely not exhaustive, these represent my own examples of areas needing attention.

— 8 —

Themes 5 & 6: Reclaiming Our Supernatural Heritage and Embracing Post Christendom

Pentecostal Appraisals of Postmodernity and Post Christendom

PICKING UP FROM OUR introduction to postmodernism in chapter 3, this chapter will examine a pneumatological approach to recent postmodern thought so prevalent in Western culture, impacting especially the youngest generations. It may well be that Pentecostals have already in their narratives and subculture the perfect tools for reaching those now in the sway of postmodernity. We will then discuss the many issues arising out of changing societal values around faith and religion, focusing in particular on the tremendous challenge secularism and the turn to post-Christendom is proving to be for Pentecostalism.

Postmodernism and Opportunities for Pentecostalism

In chapter 3 we observed that within postmodern thought is a worldview consisting of anti-foundationalism, disbelief in pure objectivity, and deconstruction of "certain" knowledge, primarily characterized by a reaction to the prevailing worldview of Modernism. As will be demonstrated more thoroughly in the next few pages, it is clear that these philosophical trends have had an impact on today's youth. Although the significance or permanence of "postmodernity" may well be debated, it seems clear that certain of its presuppositions are making inroads into the thinking of the post-Boomer generations. In terms of the rejection of the rationalism often espoused by organized religion, and importance of experience in particular, today's students and young adults are approaching the Christian faith, and our attempts to propagate the Gospel, in ways not seen since pre-Enlightenment times.

Postmodern Trends and Young Adults[1]

In his excellent work, *The Younger Evangelicals*, Robert E. Webber draws a number of conclusions regarding the differences between the youngest Evangelicals in North America, and the generations preceding them. Foremost on Webber's list is the fact that today's youth are fully aware that they are maturing in a postmodern world. As such, they themselves have a much broader concept of what constitutes "reason" for they acknowledge that all rationality, scientific and otherwise, has some measure of faith inherent within.[2]

Tony Jones believes strongly in the impact of postmodernity upon present and future generations. He notes that in general, the Boomers studied under Modern professors, fully appreciative of the Enlightenment. Generation X studied during the transitional phase. "But the Millennials are getting full-blown, no-holds-barred Postmodern thought."[3] Little wonder then that the industries based directly on selling to youth, such as those of music, cinema, and advertising, are embracing the postmodern ethos. Further, for those working with today's youth, it is important to recognize that they were born into a culture of transition; those born today are entering a world thoroughly familiar with postmodern tenets.[4]

---

1. Portions of this segment are abbreviated from Noel, *Pentecostal and Postmodern*, specifically the fifth chapter.

2. Webber, *The Younger Evangelicals*, 47–48.

3. Jones, *Postmodern Youth Ministry*, 29. I think Jones overstates the case here. While this is certainly true in terms of marketing and advertising, or in the case of the multiplicity of entertainment available, it would not be consistently accurate in the public universities of North America. While specific disciplines may be incorporating aspects of postmodern thought, the university system as a whole has not fully transitioned to a postmodern approach. D.A. Carson believes postmodernism is increasingly a non-issue, having already lost its status as a vibrant intellectual tradition. In terms of the university, he notes, " . . . even when aging and inflexible professors cherish the postmodern training they received when they were graduate students and still try to pass it on, they are receiving increasing push back from the current generation of graduate students." He suggests that while postmodernism may no longer be considered cutting edge, its influence is still being widely felt, not so much from its authority, but from its legacy of indecision, in the assumption that all religions, and all cultures, say the same thing and at the very least, have equal value. As was the case with Jones, I believe Carson also protests too much. See Carson, *Christ and Culture Revisited*, vi.

4. Jones, *Postmodern Youth Ministry*, 29.

Other authors take this concept even further, acknowledging that what is learned from ministry to young adults will soon have to be applied throughout culture. Brad Cecil challenges those who suggest that postmodernity is simply another trend on the conference circuit, arguing instead that it is the most important cultural shift of the last 500 years. "It's not a generation issue exclusive to GenX or Millennials. In fact, it's fast becoming the adopted epistemology of all adults. Everyone in ministry—not just youth and young adult pastors—will have to wrestle with this phenomenon."[5]

Anti-Religious but Pro-Spiritual

In *Virtual Faith: The Irreverent Spiritual Quest of Generation X*, author Tom Beaudoin suggests four themes inherent in GenX spirituality. First, this generation is inherently suspicious of Christianity as has been presented by organized religious institutions. Further, Xers wish to emphasize the sacred nature of their shared experiences, communal in nature, and lived daily in human existence. Third, today's youth identify with the scriptural theme of the suffering servant. Finally, Generation X seeks unique ways of being religious and expressing their faith. Students of postmodernity will observe its impact on this generation throughout these themes.[6] Christians need not fear these themes, for in many ways they look back to Christian themes of the premodern era. As Robert Webber asks, "Where do we go to find a Christianity that speaks meaningfully to a Postmodern world? . . . [O]ur challenge is not to reinvent Christianity, but to restore and then adapt classical Christianity to the Postmodern cultural situation."[7]

Organized religion and religious groups have fallen into some disfavour with those most impacted by postmodernity, and precisely for the reasons mentioned above.[8] Many churches have watched the great decline in church attendance among all ages with alarm (and many appear not to have noticed), with teenagers and young adults leading the way.[9] In his book *Canada's Teens: Yesterday, Today, and Tomorrow*, Bibby reveals the results of two national surveys completed in 2000. The dichotomy between identity and practice is readily apparent: among Canadian teens, a full 75 percent

---

5. Cecil, quoted in Jones, *Postmodern Youth Ministry*, preface.
6. Beaudoin, *Virtual Faith*, 26, 41–42.
7. Webber, *Ancient-Future Faith*, 24.
8. Bibby and Posterski, *Teen Trends*, 50–51.
9. As noted in chapter three, weekly church attendance in Canada by all ages declined from 61 percent in 1956, to 35 percent in 1985, according to *Gallup Canada*, one of the country's largest polling organizations. Quoted in Bibby, *Restless Gods*, 12–13.

identify with some religious group, while only 22 percent attend weekly services. As many youth and young adults continue to avoid traditional denominations in particular, and organized Christianity in general, observers often inquire as to where, if anywhere, they are headed. In an interview in *The Twentysomething American Dream*, a typical GenX attitude is observed: "What the hell's going to church for? These days you've got to take religion into your own hands."[10]

Bibby and Posterski note that paradoxically, youth are having difficulty relating to organized relationship precisely as they exhibit a strong interest in the things that religion has traditionally focused upon—the supernatural, spirituality, ethics, morality, and meaning. 46 percent rate *the quest for truth* as "very important" and 24 percent rate *spirituality* the same. Only 10 percent of teens, however, rate *religious involvement* as very important. "Time and again, young people express an openness to things spiritual, and disinterest in things organizational."[11]

Tony Jones believes that postmodern thought may well be a positive force in the Church, and challenges those who would suggest that new modes of thinking are in some way inherently evil. For Jones, many of the postmodern critiques of Modernism should be welcomed by the Church. "No longer are we beholden to the scientific proof model of evangelism—everything does not need to be explained and rationalized. This should come as a relief to Christian youth workers who have been attempting to *explain* great mysteries like the incarnation, the resurrection, and the Lord's Supper.[12]

Pentecostalism and the Postmodern

Scholars have long noted the inherent emotionalism in Pentecostalism, and their typical openness to experience and the supernatural. An article for *The Economist* notes the experiential dimension of this movement, suggesting that the most remarkable religious success story of the past century has been "the least intellectual (and most emotive)" religious movement of all. Though founded by a "one-eyed black preacher" who was convinced that God would send revival if people prayed hard enough, there are now hundreds of millions of adherents worldwide. According to the Pew Forum on

---

10. Cohen, *The Twenty-Something American Dream*, 183.
11. Bibby and Posterski, *Teen Trends*, 53.
12. Jones, *Postmodern Youth Ministry*, 39.

Religion, many of these have witnessed healings and/or exorcisms, and have "received direct revelation from God."[13]

As has been established, many youth today are bypassing the Christian church, the appointed herald of the only supernatural God, for cheap and deadly imitations elsewhere. Pentecostalism must take up this challenge, for its own sons and daughters are among this generation of Postmodern youth. This challenge is not new: more than 20 years ago Posterski and Bibby proclaimed that any attempt to present the Gospel to the minds of Postmodern youth will have to:

> ... carefully explore the realm of the supernatural. Young people do not have God grudges on their shoulders. They are not antireligious. Rather, out of the legacy of their heritage and the input of their world, they are supernaturalists ... Young people are predisposed to the supernatural, and although they don't intend to turn to organized religion to actively pursue their interest, they are not negative about spiritual realities.[14]

Beaudoin agrees: "The turn to experience in GenX pop culture encompasses not only personal and communal religious experience but also an emerging sensual spirituality, an experience of living faith in the world, and a desire for an encounter of the human and 'divine.'"[15]

In his PhD dissertation for the University of Auckland, Viv Grigg argues that Pentecostalism is stylistically well suited to reach a postmodern generation. First, charismatic and Pentecostal theology as expressed in transformational conversations fits well with the multiple stories of postmodernism, just as Evangelical theology is often heavily entwined with Modernist rationalism. Second, the experiential nature of Pentecostalism connects well with those seeking a spiritual experience. Third, holism in Pentecostal circles is expressed by narratives rather than following logical progressions towards universal truth.[16]

Grigg goes even further, arguing that Pentecostals are essentially "postmodern phenomena," for they've moved from integrating the voices of Western power centres to "listening to the multiple voices of the peoples." He suggests, "Pentecostals have rejected the language, the theology, and the style of Christianity of the 'official,' 'powerful,' churches."[17] There can be no

---

13. "O Come All Ye Faithful."
14. Bibby and Posterski, *Teen Trends*, 261.
15. Beaudoin, *The Irreverent Spiritual Quest of Generation X*, 165.
16. Grigg, "The Spirit of Church and the Postmodern City."
17. Ibid. I would suggest that while this was true in early Pentecostalism, the contemporary Pentecostal church, at least in North America, has simply created its own

doubt as to the appeal of this type of Christian denomination for today's postmodern youth. Bibby agrees, noting "This is a generation of young people whose current involvement in religion is appreciable. In light of their widespread interest in meaning and mystery, the supernatural and the spiritual, religious groups who have something to bring need to bring it—and, to put it bluntly, stop complaining about the apathy of youth."[18]

Neil Hudson concurs, suggesting that the emphasis on experience at the heart of Pentecostalism may well strategically place the movement to reach the youngest generations. At the heart of Pentecostalism, according to Hudson, is an emphasis on a God who does intervene and do surprising things among his people, a God who is to be encountered, who performs miracles both as a sign to his own people and a cause of wonder for non-believers. Worship for Pentecostals is, therefore, "where one experiences something" as opposed to where one is taught something.[19]

If the classical format of the Evangelical service brings the didactic elements to the fore, including the centrality of the Scriptures, for contemporary Pentecostalism the worship band and display of worship songs are more central. As noted above, the goal and desire of Pentecostal services is that the God of the Bible might be experienced—not just appreciated intellectually. While this experience can occur during sermons, it more likely and more often occurs during sung worship or in a ministry time following the sermon where individuals receive prayer. Hudson concludes: "For some, grappling with evangelizing amongst the sensory nature of a postmodern generation, this emphasis on experience resonates with the desires expressed in society. It is no surprise that there is a growing feeling that Pentecostalism might succeed in evangelizing a postmodern generation more effectively than they ever did in the rationalistic modernist era.[20]

As Rodney Stark notes, "In an endless cycle, faith is revived and new faiths born to take the places of those withered denominations *that lost their sense of the supernatural.*"[21] In the words of one young lady,

> All I want is reality. Show me God. Tell me what He is really like. Help me to understand why life is the way it is, and how I can experience it more fully and with greater joy. I don't want the

---

version of "official" Christianity.

18. Bibby, *Canada's Teens*, 131–32.
19. Hudson, "British Pentecostal's Past Development."
20. Ibid.
21. Stark and Bainbridge, *The Future of Religion*, 529–30. Italics by the author.

THEMES 5 & 6: RECLAIMING OUR SUPERNATURAL HERITAGE

> empty promises. I want the real thing. And I'll go wherever I find that truth system.[22]

For Pentecostals, therefore, the opportunity has never been greater, as they are now faced with a generation of society seeking the same existential approach to God that they have held so dearly for almost a century. Tony Jones notes, "One of the most noteworthy characteristics of the Postmodern/post-Christian world is the dramatic rise of spirituality. Propositional truth is out and mysticism is in. People are not necessarily put off by a religion that does not 'make sense'—they are more concerned with whether a religion can bring them into contact with God."[23] In an age of increasing secularism combined with the influence of postmodern thought, Pentecostals must once again unashamedly bring inquirers into contact with a supernatural God who does supernatural things in the lives of his creation, and often in unexpected ways.

Postmodern thought therefore presents an incredible opportunity for Pentecostal churches to engage culture.[24] Though the postmodern rejection of objective and absolute truth will challenge Pentecostalism to rethink its approach to evangelism, the rejection of rationalism in the postmodern mind will serve Pentecostalism well. Ivan Satyavrata, President of Southern Asia Bible College, states:

> The postmodernist's emphasis on experience represents the greatest opportunity for Pentecostals to communicate the truth of the gospel—perhaps since the New Testament—but certainly since John Wesley and the Methodist revival. In the 21st century we are witnessing a legitimization of what Pentecostals already believe in terms of the plausibility structure of what people are willing to believe. This is one of the reasons the church is exploding in Africa, Latin America, and Asia where, under the influence of Pentecostal missionaries, there is an openness to, and an affirmation of, experience that more rationalistic Western cultures are reluctant to open themselves to.[25]

---

22. Anonymous teenager quoted in Barna, *Baby Busters*, 144.

23. Jones, *Postmodern Youth Ministry*, 63.

24. Johns, "Pentecostalism and the Postmodern Worldview," 73–96; Jaichandran and Madhav, "Pentecostal Spirituality in a Postmodern World," 39–61; Del Colle, "Postmodernism and the Pentecostal-Charismatic Experience," 97–116.

25. Young, "Pentecostal Ministry in a Postmodern Culture."

Christ and Culture: Niebuhr's Five Options

In chapter 3, we explored the turn to post-Christendom in the Western world, and noted in particular the rise of secularism as both a cause and effect of the demise of Christendom. Just as we examined how Pentecostals might respond appropriately to postmodern thought and evidence of postmodernity in our context, we now wish to offer suggestions for a Pentecostal appropriation of the possibilities and opportunities inherent within an increasingly secular and post-Christendom context.

Our discussion will be well served to first consider the five options presented by Niebuhr in his 1951 classic *Christ and Culture*.[26] Writing more than 60 years ago, Niebuhr offers five perspectives on the Christian response to contemporary culture; his work has long been considered the foundational work on this subject. Beginning with definitions of Christ (acknowledging that our descriptions will always be incomplete) and culture ("the total process of human activity") Niebuhr seeks to then summarize the possible approaches to the Christ vs. culture debate.

The first, termed *Christ Against Culture*, emphasizes the opposition between Christ and culture. "Whatever may be the customs of the society in which the Christian lives, and whatever the human achievement it conserves, Christ is seen as opposed to them, so that he confronts men with the challenge of an 'either-or' decision."[27] This view uncompromisingly affirms the Lordship of Christ and his authority over the Christian, and rejects absolutely any claims of loyalty by contemporary culture. For one to be completely loyal to Christ, one draws a clear line of separation from the world. On the opposite end of the spectrum, with option two, *The Christ of Culture*, proponents seek to ". . . hail Jesus as the Messiah of their society, the fulfiller of its hopes and aspirations, the perfecter of its true faith, the source of its holiest spirit."[28] There is no inherent tension between the Church and contemporary culture, the social laws and the Gospel, or the workings of divine grace and human effort. Culture is interpreted through an understanding of Christ, and perhaps more troubling, Christ is understood as his teachings and actions match what is best about civilization.

Third, Niebuhr notes the vast majority of Christianity has refused to side with the "anti-cultural radicals" or the "accommodators," but have sought a different approach, termed *Christ Above Culture*. In this view, the

26. Niebuhr, *Christ and Culture*. For a helpful summary, see "'Christ and Culture' by Richard Niebuhr: Book Summary," in *Regeneration*. Also Carson, *Christ and Culture Revisited*, 9–65.

27. Niebuhr, *Christ and Culture*, 40.

28. Ibid., 83.

tension is not between Christ and culture, but between God and humanity. As God stands above culture, it is neither inherently good nor evil, but as a human sphere may exhibit both extremes. As humanity functions in the social realm it does so in the cultural realm, and thus culture is a tool in the hand of God. Carson notes, "Synthesists seek a 'both-and' solution. They maintain the gap between Christ and culture that the cultural Christian never takes seriously and that the radical does not even try to breech—yet they insist that Christ is as sovereign over the culture as over the church."[29]

Similar to this is the *Christ and Culture in Paradox* understanding, which seeks to clarify that viewing Christ as above culture may be desirable, but is ultimately very challenging due to the sin within culture. Like the "Christ Against Culture" position, these dualists see a clear distinction between Christ and sinful humanity, but in contrast place themselves fully in the sinful category with the rest of humanity who do not follow Christ. Finally, Niebuhr posits the *Christ as the Transformer of Culture* position. Those who hold this position "hold fast to the radical distinction between God's work in Christ and man's work on culture" but reject the road of isolationism from culture that has plagued exclusivist Christianity. While not seeking to modify Christ's judgment of sin as found in culture, they also believe that "such culture is under God's sovereign rule, and that the Christian must carry on cultural work in obedience to the Lord." We may distinguish the approach of these "conversionists" from their "dualist" compatriots by their more "positive and helpful attitude toward culture."[30] Although Niebuhr did not embrace either of his five options explicitly, only the last option of the five received no negative criticism whatsoever; many scholars have interpreted this as his tacit approval.[31]

Classical Pentecostalism's emphasis on "separation" from the world as evidence of commitment to Christ, as described above, clearly places it I believe in Niebuhr's first category, *Christ Against Culture*. Culture, and its institutions were inherently evil, a part as they were of a fallen, sinful world. The Christian task was to introduce humanity to Christ, so others might also enjoy similar separation from the culture and its negative influence. This understanding, of course, does not fit well with Christ's own description of believers as *in*, but not *of*, the world. Further, this separation from culture, at least on the surface, was far easier in a society structured by Christendom. Pentecostals could assume a posture of antagonism vis-à-vis culture, and feel secure in their "withdrawal" from the world, because Christendom

---

29. Carson, *Christ and Culture Revisited*, 21.
30. Niebuhr, *Christ and Culture*, 191.
31. Carson, *Christ and Culture Revisited*, 29.

supported all of the major societal structures around them. We could afford the luxury of posturing against "worldly endeavours" because many of these structures were, in the broad strokes at least, supportive of the Christendom narrative.

Further, and less pejoratively, Pentecostals were loath to embrace any task that detracted them from their core focus of winning souls before the soon return of Christ. Kent Duncan notes that J. Roswell Flower, first General Secretary of the Assemblies of God (USA), declared in 1920 that institutional ventures (such as orphanages and schools) were "clearly out of bounds for Pentecostal missionaries serving in 'the last days.'" Pentecostal missionaries, he wrote, ". . . cannot follow the methods laid down by those who have gone before them, neither can they bend their energies in building up charitable institutions, hospitals, and schools as do the denominational societies. The Pentecostal commission is to witness, *witness*, WITNESS . . . It is so easy to be turned aside to do work which is very good in itself, but which is short of the Pentecostal standard. Our missionaries are in danger of this."[32] Though this strident attitude did not prevail over the course of the decades that followed, it still appears from time to time as Pentecostals grapple with the balance between the proclamation of the Gospel and the desire to meet the real needs of hunger, housing, and medicine.[33]

With the support of Christendom, early Pentecostals were therefore able to more easily maintain a policy of separation. But as we have observed, times have changed. Should Pentecostals therefore seek to embrace one of Niebuhr's remaining approaches? We note first that a challenge with Niebuhr's work is that it was written from within Christendom, and assumed its perspective. As Craig Carter notes, ". . . once one rejects the Christendom assumptions behind Niebuhr's book, the whole typology becomes suspect . . . It is taken for granted by Niebuhr that, since Western culture is Christian, Christians therefore have a responsibility for culture . . . Christendom is presupposed, and the problem is how to relate Christ to it."[34] If this understanding is true, is there then any value in Niebuhr's typology for our post-Christendom context?

---

32. Flower, "Pentecostal Commission," 12. Quoted in Duncan, "Emerging Engagement."

33. Even since my ordination with the PAONL in 2000, I have heard the argument presented that Pentecostal missionaries must not stray from the task of proclamation in order to become involved in social needs.

34. Carter, *Rethinking Christ and Culture*, 15, 17. Carter endeavours to engage Niebuhr's work via a post-Christendom perspective, and offers a new typology of understanding Christ and culture.

I believe so. Without entangling ourselves in substantial debate relative to the details of Niebuhr's work, such as his particular understanding of "culture" or the placing of certain historical figures into specific categories of his five options, we may nonetheless observe significant value in considering the broad strokes of his proposal. Though the concerns raised by Carter and others are not without merit, the five categories suggested by Niebuhr serve our purposes quite well as they guide our understanding of the possible approaches Christians may take when engaging culture, even if culture is defined differently than Niebuhr suggested.

We recognize that Christ did not come to establish Christendom, but rather the kingdom of God in the hearts of his followers. In this sense we do not wish to speak of "culture" as in any way suggesting "Christian culture" or assuming the Christendom mentality. Rather, when speaking of culture we wish to consider simply how believers in Christ can first engage their own neighbours—the men and women of their communities—with the Good News of Christ. In this way, through our influence of the individuals around us, we wish to effect change in culture, devoid of any assumptions that "culture" is in any way "Christian"—nor should it be. From this perspective Niebuhr's categories—with the above proviso—may serve us well. First, however, let us present a few considerations for Pentecostals seeking to move forward. In so doing, we will explore more deeply the merits and drawbacks of Niebuhr's categories.

Pentecostalism and Post Christendom

1. Embracing Post Christendom

By way of reminder, we define Christendom as ". . . the concept of Western civilization as having a religious arm (the church) and a secular arm (civil government), both of which are united in their adherence to the Christian faith . . . the essence of the idea is the assertion that Western civilization is Christian."[35] I stand with others who celebrate the collapse of Christendom, and welcome its demise. The goal of the Incarnation was never to establish Christian governments or an officially Christian society, but to establish God's kingdom in hearts and minds of individuals called into community with one another. With that perspective, we may justly applaud the end of Christendom in the sense that it was never God's intention to begin with. Further we may recognize that the fight to preserve it has in many senses distracted Christians from the task originally given—making

35. Ibid.,14.

disciples—and not preserving the vestiges of a "Christian era" now past. As Murray observes, "The end of Christendom means, in the long run, *imposing Christianity does not work*; only if we celebrate this and move beyond dismissing Christendom to a more repentant response will we be truly free to develop a different strategy."[36]

2. Recognize the Size of the Challenge Ahead

Once the church—Pentecostal and otherwise—is able to embrace the demise of the Christendom narrative and structure, sober thought will be required to discern how the church might shift its view of mission when the assumed foundational structure of Christendom is no longer present. Further, the Church must recognize the change in cultural milieu occurring as the demise of Christendom corresponds to the same in Modernity. As we've noted, a post-Christendom Canadian culture also exhibits signs of postmodern thinking. Shane Simms, writing about the significance of this change in thinking via his doctoral thesis on the Missional church in Newfoundland, notes:

> Penetrating a pagan or saturated culture that thinks in terms of post-modernity is one of the biggest challenges the church has ever faced in its history. Even though the postmodern milieu is potentially open to the narrative of God's Kingdom, it does not largely accept the role of the church in that narrative. The church needs to discover ways to be about the work of the Kingdom of God, not to proclaim itself as superintending the work of the Kingdom of God. *This change in ecclesiastical mindset may post a more significant challenge than actually reaching a postmodern generation with the message of Christ.*[37]

Newbigin argues that a Christian response to secularism must involve more than simply affirming the way of salvation for the individual. Rather, the central call and life of the Church must be to call men and women into discipleship. Acknowledging Christ's sovereignty over the personal and domestic issues of life, and the life of the Church, also implies acknowledging the Lordship of Christ over the public life of society. Believers cannot simply seek to follow Christ in their personal lives without also challenging the assumptions that govern the worlds of economics, politics, education, government, and culture. He observes:

---

36. Murray, *Post-Christendom*, 208.
37. Shane A. Simms, "Moving Forward in Mission," 54–55. Italics mine.

The Church can never settle down to being a voluntary society concerned merely with private and domestic affairs. It is bound to challenge in the name of the one Lord all the powers, ideologies, myths, assumptions, and worldviews which do not acknowledge him as Lord. If that involves conflict, trouble, and rejection, then we have the example of Jesus before us and his reminder that a servant is not greater than his master.[38]

3. Remain Orthodox: Resist Assimilation and Isolationism

We observe that neither the conservative nor the liberal responses to the Enlightenment throughout the nineteenth century helped the cause of Christianity. "Conservatives, rejecting scientific explanations, and trying to maintain a stranglehold on debate, weakened its appeal by associating Christianity with obscurantism and blinkered traditionalism. Liberals, attempting to reconfigure Christianity to fit comfortably into the culture of scientific rationalism, produced an anaemic religion that attracted little commitment and decreasing numbers."[39] Some groups in the 20th century sought to fortify their position in Christendom by withdrawing into the church walls, avoiding contact with "evil culture." In a culture that has moved beyond bounded set thinking, and desires to *belong* before it will *believe*, this approach simply will not work.

Other Christian groups sought to navigate the changes in culture by seeking to eradicate any position or doctrine offensive to a secularist demographic. Belief in the Scriptures as authoritative, the divinity of Christ, and any talk of Christ's atoning blood shed for "sinners" were among the first casualties. While these attempts to placate the supposed demands of a secular culture and bridge the gap between the message of Christ and the notions acceptable to the modern, educated person, would seem wise, in reality the strategy has the opposite effect.

The correct approach seems to be in the middle of these two extremes: neither *Christ Against Culture* nor *Christ of Culture* approaches will serve the church well in a post-Christendom society. Rather, church groups would do well to hold strongly to conservative theology that demands something of the individual, while still striving to engage culture. We must recognize that Christ followers will need to work as harmoniously with culture as possible, even as they seek to embody and promote the truth of Christ. Finke and Stark note, "People tend to value religion according to how much it costs

---

38. Newbigin, *The Gospel in a Pluralist Society*, 220–21.
39. Murray, *Post-Christendom*, 181.

... because 'reasonable' and 'sociable' religion costs little, it is not valued greatly."[40] Bibby agrees, stating "In short, the more mainline a denomination becomes, the lower the value of belonging to it, resulting eventually in widespread defection."[41] Commenting on the failure of the secularization theory, Leslie Newbigin observes,

> The facts are well known. The strongly conservative and evangelical elements in the Protestant church have undergone a remarkable renaissance, while the churches which have tried to adjust their beliefs and practices to the temper of modernity are in decline . . . It would seem to be proved beyond doubt that human beings cannot live in the rarefied atmosphere of pure rationality as the post-Enlightenment world has understood rationality. There are needs of the human spirit which simply must be met. It seems that those religious bodies which have tried to accommodate as much as possible of the rationalism of the Enlightenment are those which are in decline, and that those which have maintained a strong emphasis on the supernatural dimensions of religions have flourished.[42]

In their work *Acts of Faith: Explaining the Human Side of Religion*, sociologists Rodney Stark and Roger Finke argue that a key component of any resurgence of the Christian faith is new, highly committed clergy. These new clergy in turn call their congregations to high levels of commitment while emphasizing traditional religious content.[43] I agree; the challenge however is achieving the proper balance. For example, it is now popular to speak of "belonging before believing." Many churches have discovered that, whatever theology seeking individuals may hold, their need to belong must be met before they are ready to adjust beliefs. But it will not serve us well, however, to forget the whole purpose behind belonging or believing. Post-Christendom churches must spend more time nurturing their core values and community life than defining and patrolling their boundaries. They must be welcoming places where those exploring faith options and searching for authentic relationships feel comfortable; communities of faith that refrain from quick judgment, and where all manner of doubts, questions, criticism, and fears are embraced. "They will also need to embody core values that

---

40. Stark and Finke, *Acts of Faith*, 238–50.

41. Bibby, *Beyond the Gods & Back*, 39.

42. Newbigin, *The Gospel in a Pluralist Society*, 212–13. This is the key point of Reeves, *The Empty Church*.

43. Stark and Finke, *Acts of Faith*, 259–74. I must confess, as the Director of a program that trains young men and women for Pentecostal ministry, I believe (and hope) this is correct!

are attractive, clear, demanding, and deeply owned. The term 'centred set' (rather than 'bounded set') is now popular to describe communities that welcome people to 'belong before they believe' but it is not always clear that the 'centred set' has a centre!"[44] We can hold strong to Christ as the centre while still ensuring that the margins are flexible and open.

Stuart Murray makes the excellent point that it is the surviving interest in the person of Jesus, exhibited in contemporary culture by individuals who have long given up on the church—and even on the Jesus portrayed by Christendom—that offers the greatest asset to the post-Christendom church. "In a society that is heartily and understandably sick of institutional Christianity, Jesus still commands interest and respect. However garbled his teaching may have become, and however little his story is known, many people suspect Jesus is good news, despite the shortcomings they see in our churches and the distaste for which they regard our evangelistic activities."[45] We must rediscover how to tell the story of Jesus without compromise, while recognizing that many previous attempts have fallen short and portrayed him in the vein acceptable to the institutional church. We cannot reduce Jesus to simple statements of dogmatism, a feel-good message to assuage guilt so few even feel anymore, or a safe "establishment Jesus" who came to make believers feel comfortable and secure. Rather, "we must present Jesus as (among much else) friend of sinners, good news to the poor, defender of the powerless, reconciler of communities, pioneer of a new age, freedom fighter, breaker of chains, liberator, and peacemaker, the one who unmasks systems of oppression, identifies with the vulnerable, and brings hope."[46]

4. *Rejoice! Post Christendom Need Not Mean Post Christian*

Some may fear that celebrating or even accepting the demise of Christendom automatically entails a tacit acknowledgment that we must de facto enter a post-Christian era also. In fact, the opposite may well be the case. The end of Christendom may in reality place the church in a context where the gospel as Christ intended—without the trappings of official Christianity—may once again be clearly heard. John Webster Grant, in *The Church in Canada, 1867–1967*, writes, "The end of Christendom does not imply the end of Christianity or necessarily even any diminution of the influence

---

44. Murray, *Post-Christendom*, 310. Sociologist Paul Hiebert first used these terms in Hiebert, "Conversion, Culture and Cognitive Categories." Also see Hiebert, "Sets and Structure," in Hasselgrace, *New Horizons in World Missions*.

45. Murray, *Post-Christendom*, 316.

46. Ibid., 316–17.

of the church on its members or on society . . . A period of exile to the periphery of power might well release Christian energies that have been smothered for centuries."[47]

We might argue that while the Church relied on the position and influence afforded by the overarching narrative of Christendom she was less creative than might otherwise have been the case. Why seek earnestly for the creative empowerment of the Holy Spirit to engage culture, when one could count on Parliament to enact the laws needed to preserve the semblance of a Christian nation? With the structure of Christendom collapsing, the Church will be forced to once again rely upon the Spirit's guidance and power.

Stuart Murray declares:

> But post-Christendom need not mean post-Christian. The near future will be difficult for Christians in a society that has rejected institutional Christianity and is familiar enough with the Christian story not to want to hear it again. Inherited assumptions and Christendom models will not help us respond creatively to the challenges ahead. But perhaps—if we have the courage to face into this future rather than hankering after a fading past, if we resist short-term strategies and pre-packaged answers, if we learn to be cross-cultural missionaries in our own society, and if we can negotiate the next forty years—whatever culture emerges from the ruins of Christendom might offer tremendous opportunities for telling and living out the Christian story in a society where this is largely unknown. Whether post-Christendom is post-Christian will depend on whether we can re-imagine Christianity in a world we no longer control. Christendom is dying, but a new and dynamic Christianity could rise from its ashes.[48]

Niebuhr and Pentecostalism: Conclusion

It should be apparent that neither antagonism towards culture, nor the confusion of Christ's message with cultural norms, will be effective in a post-Christendom context. Surely the transformation of culture is a laudable goal, but from my perspective only if culture is first defined as the "whole world" that God so loved—individuals primarily and not institutions. Transformed individuals will in ways small and large transform the culture around them,

---

47. Grant, *The Church in the Canadian Era*, 216–17.
48. Murray, *Post-Christendom*, 8.

but more in the sense of the human networks they are associated with than in terms of institutions, media, or government. While the transformation of culture in the larger sense may be a commendable goal, and some may insist that restricting God's mission solely to saving souls is far too narrow, the top-down approach of Christendom was not the correct approach. "It was compromised by confusing between the institutional church and God's kingdom, coercive methods, a moralising tone, unrealistic expectations of what was achievable in the present age and inability to distinguish Christendom ideology from the original Christian story."[49]

The road forward, in my estimation, is best navigated through a combination of the *Christ Above Culture*, and *Christ and Culture in Paradox* approaches described above, if by culture we mean the institutions and structures that govern our society. The *Christ Above Culture* position has the benefit of recognizing that Christ is within culture (via the incarnation) even while remaining outside (as God who sustains culture.) The extremes of pitting Christ against culture, or having Christ disappear within culture are avoided. We might also desire to embrace the wisdom in the *Christ and Culture in Paradox* option. This view desires the ideals of the *Christ Above Culture* approach, but wishes to acknowledge that the road ahead will not be smooth, but full of paradox where a conflict arises between Christ and culture, as the culture is sinful. In Christ's dealings with culture, we see both sin and grace, and therein, the paradox. This view rightly observes the tension inherent in the biblical description of Christians living *in* the world—a world they are not to be *of*. Christian engagement with the world will in fact be a "dynamic process, not a static rejection or acceptance of culture of the previous 'models' but rather we sense, almost from experience, that our dealing with culture is fraught with pain and peace."[50]

Conclusion

In this chapter we have explored themes five (reclaiming the supernatural) and six (embracing post-Christendom). We have done so via our discussion on the appropriate Pentecostal response to what as been described as the "double whammy" of postmodernism and post-Christendom.[51] We observed that though the postmodern rejection of the concept of absolute truth is indeed troublesome, the openness to an epistemology that is not bound to rationalism brings tremendous opportunities for Pentecostalism. For the

49. Ibid., 132.
50. "'Christ and Culture' by Richard Niebuhr: Book Summary."
51. Murray, *Post-Christendom*, 254.

first time in several centuries, culture has shifted away from Enlightenment rationalism in terms of faith experiences, towards openness to experiencing the miraculous. As was shown, this generation of spiritual seekers may be leaving the practice of institutional religion in large number, but they are still interested in spirituality that connects them with the supernatural. Pentecostals dare not miss this important opportunity to be unashamedly and boldly Pentecostal. As we will discuss in chapter 9, Pentecostalism must return to a focus of a rich life in the Spirit, complete with the full range of spiritual gifts, without employing the reductionism that occurs when our message and raison d'etre are reduced to tongues-speech.

This chapter has also suggested a Pentecostal response to the secularism already observed in Europe, Great Britain, Canada, (and increasingly in the United States). The era of Christendom has passed, and tremendous new opportunities come in its wake. Recognizing the paradox inherent in our attempts to engage culture, we may nonetheless understand Christ to be above culture, even while we seek to engage culture via a relationship with our neighbours and communities. With a full understanding of the complexities of the road ahead, and a dedication to remain fully orthodox in our doctrine and practice, we may face the future with the confidence that the gospel of Christ may actually fare better in a postmodern, post-Christendom world than it ever could under the Modernist influence within Christendom. We close this section with a prescient thought from Stuart Murray:

> Christianity is remarkably adaptable, having been translated into numerous cultures and eras. Postmodernism offers both challenges and opportunities. Christians will dissent from some aspects of postmodernism; others we will affirm—including its critique of the pretensions of modernism—as offering fresh possibilities for telling the Christian story. But Christendom is inflexible; its values, structures and models are even less appropriate in postmodernity than in modernity. Postmodernism sounds its death-knell. For Christianity to thrive in postmodernity, Christendom assumptions and attitudes must go....Post-Christendom is our future.[52]

We have explored the types of external issues that Pentecostalism must seriously address and immediately if it desires to remain a relevant voice in an increasingly secular culture. Both postmodern thought and the demise of Christendom represent the new everyday realities in our societal context. We cannot afford to remain silent or fail to think critically on these

---

52. Ibid., 183, 216.

important matters. We must be willing to reclaim our heritage of experiencing the supernatural if we wish to engage postmoderns in their areas of greatest need. Further, we must cease our tendency to mourn the loss of the Christendom structure that was never God's intention, and refocus our energies from fighting for the survival of Christendom to creatively engaging a culture that though rife with secularism, still exhibits signs of spiritual hunger. With wisdom and discernment, Pentecostals can indeed engage culture on the significant issues of our day, and do so in a God-honouring fashion.

I have intentionally saved for last what are perhaps the most difficult conversations for Pentecostals. It is now time to truly look inward at who we are. Without considerable self-evaluation relative to our final themes—*beliefs vs. values*, and *essence not distinctives*—our efforts to be creative, missional, and engaging will be seriously hampered.

— 9 —

Themes 7 & 8: Essence over Distinctives / Beliefs VS. Values

Differentiating Beliefs vs. Values and the "Distinctives" of Pentecostalism

SECTION THREE HAS EXPLORED practical models for Pentecostals to ponder as they move forward into the next century. Our focus in this final chapter will consider issues inside the movement—internal issues that nevertheless profoundly influence Pentecostalism's ability to speak to the world around them. We will begin with a discussion on the most sacred of Pentecostal doctrines—Spirit baptism (including initial evidence and subsequence)—as an example of internal conversations that must occur within Pentecostalism. We will explore how a new understanding of this cherished experience must unfold on a going-forward basis. This will address our seventh theme—*Essence over Distinctives*. Second, and flowing out of our discussion on Pentecostal distinctives, this chapter will highlight the importance of differentiating *Beliefs* from *Values*—our final theme. Although not complicated or particularly profound, I am persuaded that a failure to distinguish between what one believes, and what one values, has in recent years negatively impacted Pentecostal piety and praxis at unprecedented levels. The goal here is to provide a sample of the types of issues that, regardless of particular sensitivities, or long-established refusals to engage these matters, must be openly discussed and lacunas addressed should Pentecostalism desire to reverse declining fortunes in the decades to come.

A. Re-Thinking Pentecostal Distinctives

As has been demonstrated, classical Pentecostalism in popular understanding has become virtually indistinguishable from its deeply held theology of

Baptism in the Holy Spirit. In the Pentecostal interpretation, this experience is logically, if not chronologically, distinct from the salvation event, and is evidenced primarily and physically by glossolalia. Despite enduring continued opposition from some quarters[1], Pentecostals generally continue to place strong emphasis on their "distinctives" *even if this now comes more in the form of beliefs than values*—a point we will take up in the latter part of this chapter. Macchia suggests, "I believe that the enduring significance of Spirit baptism for Pentecostals is due to a complexity of reasons, one of which is that it provides them with a way of levelling a critique toward the church of what they perceive as a lack of charismatic awareness, and conscious participation in the diverse and vibrant witness of the Spirit."[2] Unfortunately, however, while Pentecostals may continue to believe in this sacred doctrine of Pentecostalism, it would seem it is no longer valued, as numbers of those professing Spirit baptism are very low for an experience many would consider the "distinctive" of the movement. For example, the PAONL in 2012 recorded just 79 Spirit baptisms in 108 assemblies reporting, for a ratio of 0.73 Spirit baptisms per church.[3]

Simon Chan notes,

> It is one thing to show that there was some historical evidence of occurrences of prophetic gifts including tongues, but quite another to show from history that it had the same significance that modern Pentecostals have given to it. No wonder theologically it is becoming something of an embarrassment, even while classical Pentecostals continue to maintain its special place of importance. Increasingly, even ordinary lay people are questioning if it is really that important. When there is no strong theological underpinning for a practice it will eventually fall into disuse. As

---

1. One need only consider John MacArthur's conference entitled "Strange Fire," held October 2013, and the considerable discussion surrounding his continued support of Cessationism.

2. Macchia, *Baptized in the Spirit*, 22. To my mind, this is an excellent point, and one I will address in the coming discussion. The Pentecostal desire to challenge the church in terms of its lack of charismatic practice is a worthwhile goal, though better accomplished through a renewed focus on *life in the Spirit*, rather than the specific doctrines of subsequence and initial evidence.

3. *Report of the Discipleship Commission* (Pentecostal Assemblies of Newfoundland and Labrador, 2012). The number of salvations was only marginally higher, at 404, or 3.74 per assembly. Although the numbers are not available, it would be interesting in light of 404 conversions to note how many funerals were conducted in the same period. A former student of mine now pastoring a rural PAONL assembly, reports that in a congregation of less than 200, they are conducting their 3rd funeral in four weeks, 16 in total since beginning their pastorate 14 months ago.

we have already noted, signs of its practical abandonment are already apparent in Pentecostal churches.[4]

Further, scholarly attention to the doctrines of subsequence and initial evidence has been diminishing in recent years. ". . . [T]he doctrine of Spirit baptism is waning in significance among the most prolific among Pentecostal theologians. Spirit baptism is no longer regarded as the most distinctive Pentecostal doctrine or as having central significance to Pentecostal theology without qualification or even rejection among leading Pentecostal theologians and historians today."[5]

Frank Macchia[6], in his excellent *Baptized in the Spirit: A Global Pentecostal Theology*, believes that scholars have ceased giving priority to that which has traditionally been distinctively Pentecostal, for fear that it would mitigate against current efforts to engage a more ecumenical vision of theological reflection. He cautions, however, that abandoning our distinctives may leave us with little to offer the ecumenical conversation.[7] Rather, Pentecostals should once again embrace Spirit baptism, but recognize that, "Pentecostalism has been blessed and gifted by God with certain theological and spiritual accents. We do other Christian families a disservice if we do not preserve and cherish these, and seek to bless others with them. Thus, ideal would be a reworking of our distinctives in a way that cherishes our unique accents but expands them in response to the broader contours of the biblical witness and the diversity of voices at the ecumenical table."[8]

Further, I would add, Pentecostals must reconsider their distinctives in such a way that better connects with the younger generations, fully engaged as they are with postmodern thought. Using Macchia's work as a guide, this section will seek to assist Pentecostals with a re-framing of their distinctives doctrines. This effort should serve to help Pentecostals connect with believers of other persuasions and also connect the best of Pentecostal Spirit baptism theology with younger generations for whom the traditional language of Subsequence and Initial Evidence no longer makes sense.

---

4. Chan, *Pentecostal Theology and the Christian Spiritual Tradition*, 40.

5. Macchia, *Baptized in the Spirit*, 23. By way of example, of the 43 volumes released in the *Journal of Pentecostal Theology Supplementary Series* since its inception in 1993, only two have focused specifically on Spirit baptism. See Menzies, *Empowered for Witness*; Stronstad, *The Prophethood of All Believers*. Healing, Pneumatology, Ecclesiology, Eschatology, Ecology, Exorcism, and Hermeneutics have been popular topics of late.

6. Adding applause from afar, Anthony Thiselton describes Macchia as "one of the most forward-looking, open, and ecumenically concerned Pentecostal leaders . . ." Thiselton, *The Holy Spirit*, 456.

7. Macchia references Terry Cross' excellent article, "The Rich Feast of Theology."

8. Macchia, *Baptized in the Spirit*, 25.

With Macchia, I wish to clearly state:

> *There can be no doubt that Spirit baptism will need to be defined more broadly than it has among most classical Pentecostals if it is to continue to function as central to Pentecostal theology.*[9]

The Displacement of Spirit Baptism in the Academy: Four Reasons

Before moving to prognosis, it will serve us well to first properly diagnose the issue. Macchia gives four reasons in particular for the displacement of Spirit baptism as the "chief theological distinctive" among Pentecostal theologians. As his observations serve our own goals for reframing the discussion on Pentecostal distinctives, we will explore these in detail, and provide corresponding observations from our present perspective.

A. Fragmentation

Ever since Wesley's followers advocated a "second blessing" for sanctification, or Finney championed Spirit baptism as a second blessing for empowerment, there have been issues with the separation of the conversion-initiation event from the later sanctification or charismatic empowering. As noted in chapter 2, Pentecostals embraced the second blessing understanding of the holiness folk, but adapted the purpose from sanctification to empowerment; many Pentecostals today struggle with integrating this charismatic empowering with sanctification.[10] As Macchia notes, "A fragmented twofold or threefold initiation into the life of the Spirit is difficult to justify in Scripture . . . Exegetically, Pentecostals faced the difficulty of advocating two or three separate receptions of the Spirit in one's entry into life of the Spirit."[11] In recent years, Pentecostal scholars have sought to mitigate against this difficulty by observing a charismatic intention in the pneumatology of Luke, without disregarding the obviously soteriological pneumatology of Paul. In essence, we may know that Luke intends to teach a second blessing for

---

9. Ibid., 26. Italics mine.

10. There remains latent within Pentecostalism a mixture of the two theologies. While none doubt that Spirit baptism is for empowering, one will often hear in the narratives the understanding that Spirit baptism will assist with the believer's holiness. Simon Chan concurs; we will explore this in greater detail below.

11. Macchia, *Baptized in the Spirit*, 26, 28.

empowerment, because his whole theology is charismatic in focus; he is not attempting to replicate Paul's good work on the Spirit's salvific role.[12]

Macchia argues that Dunn's focus on the, "basic continuity of emphasis throughout the New Testament on the Spirit as the hallmark of Christian identity . . . seems compelling and potentially relevant to the task of granting Spirit baptism a major place in Christian theology."[13] He views the compartmentalizing of the work of the Spirit into regeneration (Paul) and charismatic empowering (Luke) as far less compelling.[14] This separation is in part a response to Gordon Fee's insistence on authorial intent when establishing normative theology from narratives.[15] As I demonstrated in an earlier work, Fee's detractors essentially conceded the point when they sought to demonstrate that it was chiefly Luke's *intent* to teach Spirit baptism as a subsequent experience, evidenced by glossolalia.[16] Only in this way could they ensure that the Pentecostal reading of Acts did not conflict with the more unified approach preferred by Dunn.[17]

---

12. Menzies, *Empowered for Witness*; Stronstad, *Charismatic Theology of St. Luke*; Menzies, "Luke and the Spirit."

13. See Dunn, *Baptism in the Holy Spirit*. With Dunn on this is Pentecostal scholar Gordon Fee: "Ask any number of people today from all sectors of Christendom to define or describe Christian conversion or Christian life, and the most noticeable feature of that definition would be its general lack of emphasis on the active, dynamic role of the Spirit. It is precisely the opposite in the New Testament. The Spirit is no mere addendum. Indeed, he is the *sine qua non*, the essential ingredient, of Christian life." Fee, *Gospel and Spirit*, 111.

14. Macchia, *Baptized in the Spirit*, 29.

15. Fee's three principles for determining what is normative from narratives are: 1) Authorial intent is the chief factor in determining normative values from narratives. 2) That which is incidental to the primary intent of a narrative cannot have the same didactic value as the intended teaching, though it may provide insight into the author's theology. 3) For historical precedent to have normative value, it must be demonstrated that such was the specific intent of the author. If the author intended to establish precedent, then such should be regarded as normative. Fee, *Gospel and Spirit*, 92.

16. Noel, "Gordon Fee and the Challenge to Pentecostal Hermeneutics."

17. The approach taken by Fee on this point is worth noting. "That this experience was for them usually a separate experience in the Holy Spirit and subsequent to their conversion is in itself probably irrelevant. Given their place in the history of the church, how else might it have happened? Thus the Pentecostal should probably not make a virtue out of necessity." Fee, *Gospel and Spirit*, 119. In personal conversation, he offered the following: "I do not throw out initial evidence, I throw out the language, because it is not biblical, and therefore irrelevant. From a reading of Luke and Paul, I would expect people to speak in tongues when they are empowered by the Spirit. The reception of the Spirit is most commonly evidenced by speaking in tongues. It is very normal. I expect people to be empowered by the Spirit for witness. For most people this will be a subsequent experience, because they will have become Christians without realizing that this is for them." Gordon Fee, interview with author, December 5, 1997.

Further, as Macchia observes, in the Pentecostal understanding inherited from Pietism, revivalism becomes the model for the spiritual life. As we observed in chapter 2, revivalistic influence on the Holiness movement transformed Wesley's more process-oriented understanding into a powerful crisis experience. In my experience, the following describes perfectly the spirituality resident within the PAONL[18] subculture:

> The entire Christian life [tends] to be viewed as a series of crisis moments of renewal in which the born-again experience can be recaptured and affirmed . . . Believers can end up living between moments of renewal in fear, not knowing the precise nature of their status in between the altar experiences by which they make things right once more with God.[19]

As noted above (and will be discussed further in our next section), one of the key challenges in promoting biblical growth and discipleship within classical Pentecostalism is the high value placed upon the ecstatic experience at the altar. The idea that growth comes slowly, through faithfulness, and the spiritual disciplines, measured via the Fruit of the Spirit in the believer's life, seems passé and even spiritually dry, compared to God's "quick fixes" through the work of the Spirit around Pentecostal altars. A quick survey of the media and publications of the charismatic world in particular will demonstrate the Pentecostal preference for the Gifts of the Spirit over the Fruit.

Further, the combination of sanctification and Spirit baptism as an ecstatic experience, coupled with the ability to speak in tongues, can lead the recipients to quickly believe they occupy an elevated position in the Body of Christ. It easily appears elitist, both to those who have enjoyed the experience, and perhaps particularly to those who have not.[20] With an eye towards the youngest generation[21] of Pentecostals, I would have to concur. Millennials are not wont to parse the theological distinctions that avoid the appearances of first and second-class Christians inherent in Pentecostal Spirit baptism theology. Further, many young students of Pentecostal theology

---

18. This would be particularly true of the older generations, and less so for GenX and the Millennials. My conversations with fellow Pentecostals from other Pentecostal denominations in North America suggest that this is a common theme.

19. Macchia, *Baptized in the Spirit*, 29.

20. Ibid., 32.

21. In teaching Pneumatology and/or Pentecostal Distinctives now for more than a decade at the Bible College level, I am aware that every year, significant numbers of Pentecostal students confess their struggle with the doctrines of subsequence and initial evidence.

confess their struggle with seeing Spirit baptism as a normative experience based on three, maybe four, maybe five narratives in Acts.[22]

Having taught courses in Pentecostal Distinctives and Pneumatology at a Pentecostal denominational Bible College for many years, Peter Neumann sought to quantify the attitudes of students in training for Pentecostal ministry relative to these doctrines.[23] Of the 162 students who voluntarily completed the survey, a full 32 percent strongly disagreed/disagreed that glossolalia is the Initial Evidence of Spirit-baptism, while 38 percent agreed/strongly agreed; the group was almost split on the issue. Subsequence faired much better: just 5 percent strongly disagreed/disagreed with 78 percent reporting they agreed/strongly agreed. When asked if Spirit baptism was important for Christian leaders in carrying out their ministry, 23 percent strongly disagreed/disagreed while 52 percent agreed/strongly agreed. The most challenging find for Classical Pentecostal denominations, however, came when students were asked if they agreed with the policy that Spirit-baptism (including glossolalia as evidence) was required for credentials with the denomination. A full 60 percent strongly disagreed/disagreed, with just 24 percent indicating they agreed/strongly agreed. Millennials are given to a strong sense of justice[24] and profess an abhorrence of elitism. The idea that the gift of Spirit baptism is given to some but not others, is a difficult pill to swallow. If Spirit baptism is to retain its central role in Pentecostal theology and pastors in the coming decades, a significant re-visioning will be required.

B. The Challenge of Global Diversity

Second, Pentecostals have discovered within their ranks an amazing diversity of theological viewpoints,[25] variants that were not apparent until the full

22. We have in view here Acts 2:1–4 (Pentecost); 8:1–25 (Samaritans); 9:1–19 (Saul's Conversion); 10 (Cornelius and the Gentiles); and 19:1–6 (Ephesian disciples).

23. Neumann, "Spirit Baptism in Communal Perspective."

24. The PAONL, Pentecostal Assemblies of Canada, and Assemblies of God (USA) all require applicants for credentials to confirm Spirit baptism by acknowledging their personal experience of glossolalia. Nothing seems to grate the sensibilities of Millennials more than to know that despite clear evidence of a calling into ministry, and having completed the required years of ministry training (often with tens of thousands of debt incurred!), their friend (or themselves) will be denied credentials because they have not spoken in tongues - a situation which they in and of themselves are powerless to remedy!

25. Indeed, the theme of the 2012 annual meeting of the Society for Pentecostal Studies was "Pentecostalisms, Peacemaking, and Social Justice/Righteousness." The concept that there are, in reality, a multiplicity of Pentecostalism(s) was present

global span of the movement was appreciated. Macchia reports that Walter Hollenweger's classic, *The Pentecostals*,[26] "fell like a bombshell" on Pentecostal groups who were surprised by the global diversity of Pentecostalism. Hollenweger observed:

> There is . . . a broad spectrum of opinion [on] . . . the definition of baptism in the Spirit, social and individual ethics, the question of biblical hermeneutics, the doctrine of the Trinity and Christology. Therefore, talk of "the doctrine" of the Pentecostal churches is highly problematic. What unites the Pentecostal churches is not a doctrine but a religious experience, and this can be interpreted and substantiated in many different ways.[27]

The significant work by Harvey Cox on Pentecostalism, appropriately entitled *Fire From Heaven*,[28] focused heavily on Pentecostalism's ability to adapt creatively to a variety of cultural settings across the globe due to its emphasis on a very "primal" religious experience. "A discussion of the Pentecostal belief in Spirit baptism as 'subsequent' to regeneration was not given the time of day in Cox's extremely insightful book."[29] Though there is no universal agreement on the doctrines of Subsequence and Initial Evidence, a case may be made that the understanding of Spirit baptism as distinct from the conversion experience has been accepted by a sufficient number of Pentecostal groups worldwide that it may be regarded as a Pentecostal distinctive. Most believe this experience provides greater power for witness and a more intense awareness of God's presence. While a majority of Pentecostals in North America, at least, view speaking in tongues as the indisputable evidence that Spirit baptism has occurred, this belief is far from consistent throughout Pentecostalism, even while the *experience* of glossolalia is widely enjoyed.[30] The tremendous diversity in the Pentecostal

---

throughout.

26. Hollenweger, *The Pentecostals*. Hollenweger's 1966 doctoral thesis, *Handbuch der Pfingstbewegung* (Handbook on Pentecostals) totaled ten volumes, and is considered the standard work on Pentecostalism. It, along with numerous publications in the decades since, established him as one of the preeminent interpreters of the Pentecostal movement.

27. Hollenwager, "From Azusa Street to the Toronto Phenomena," in *Pentecostal Movements*.

28. Cox, *Fire from Heaven*.

29. Macchia, *Baptized in the Spirit*, 33.

30. Macchia observes, "Actually, initial evidence tends to be most rigidly adhered to among white Pentecostal denominations in the United States. Outside of these boundaries, attitudes towards it vary." I would note that white Pentecostal denominations in Canada are generally indistinguishable from their American counterparts on

movement worldwide has caused some Pentecostals to consider the importance of a "distinctive" doctrine, if unanimity does not exist on the doctrines supposedly at the heart of Pentecostalism.

C. Theological Method

Macchia notes that Hollenweger has argued throughout his many works on Pentecostalism that the most distinctive aspect of Pentecostalism is its conceptualization of the theological task as largely oral, narrative, and dramatic.[31] What is distinctive theologically about Pentecostalism therefore, is secondary to how Pentecostal theology is actually conceived in the first place. This focus, by such an influential scholar of Pentecostalism, helped move Pentecostalism from a narrow and ecumenically irrelevant focus on tongues-speech, to the forefront of theological initiative unburdened by the chains of post-Enlightenment standards of rationalism. In a theological world navigating the waters of postmodern thought, Pentecostalism was able to move from the periphery to the main stage of ecumenical discourse. Because of Hollenweger's work, Macchia argues, it became very difficult to publish a work that concentrated specifically on Spirit baptism as subsequent to conversion, evidenced by glossolalia, without appearing " . . . provincial in one's theology and completely off the mark in terms of what is really ecumenically significant about global Pentecostalism."[32] Macchia writes,

> That which is really distinctive or most significant about Pentecostal theology for Hollenweger consists of forms of expression that lie close to the heartthrob of human experience of the divine . . . From this kind of concern, Hollenweger almost single-handedly shifted the direction of thinking about Pentecostal distinctives . . . to what seemed for many to be the more ecumenically relevant orality of liturgy, narrativity of theology and witness, maximum participation in reflection, prayer and decision-making within reconciling communities, inclusion of dreams and visions into personal and public forms of worship,

---

this issue. Ibid., 37. Canadian Pentecostal scholar Andrew Gabriel, in reviewing Macchia's book, notes, " . . . that which has traditionally been understood within North America as *the* classical Pentecostal doctrine of Spirit Baptism is really only *the North American* classical Pentecostal doctrine of Spirit Baptism (or perhaps even only one of a few North American Pentecostal views). Gabriel, "Review of Frank Macchia," 121.

31. See Hollenweger, *The Pentecostals*; idem, *Pentecostalism*; idem, "The Black Roots of Pentecostalism"; idem, "Theology of the New World." Noted in Macchia, *Baptized in the Spirit*, 27–28.

32. Macchia, *Baptized in the Spirit*, 50.

and a correspondence of mind and body through healing and the dance.[33]

By way of personal example, I direct a program that trains students for Pentecostal ministry in Newfoundland and Labrador. I do so at Tyndale University College and Seminary, which boasts more than 50 different denominations on its campus. As the Pentecostal students begin to mix with the students from a myriad of other denominations, there are the usual stories about differing views on eschatology, predestination, and, always on, Spirit baptism. The most significant difference observed by students, however, is in praxis: other students sometimes seem to lack the expectancy of an encounter with God that Pentecostals bring into worship. That God can, and often will be encountered both in worship, and at unexpected times during the day, has permeated the worldview of these Pentecostal students; they recognize its absence when it is missing.[34]

D. A Movement Toward Eschatology

Finally, as the variety of Pentecostal Spirit baptism theologies became apparent, a number of scholars shifted their focus to eschatology as that which most clearly defined the whole of Pentecostalism. The fourth reason for the neglect of Spirit baptism is therefore its movement into a secondary role for defining Pentecostalism, subservient to eschatology. Key scholars of Pentecostalism such as Donald Dayton, in *The Theological Roots of Pentecostalism*,[35] and Bill Faupel in *The Everlasting Gospel*,[36] argued that the Pentecostal "distinctive" was much larger than subsequence and initial evidence, even if those were the doctrines that later defined the movement. Both observed that Pentecostalism was notably defined by its devotion to

---

33. Ibid., 51. See. Hollenweger, "Priorities in Pentecostal Research", in *Experiences of the Spirit*, 9–10.

34. I was not at Tyndale very long when, despite the many chapel services held each week for the student body, Newfoundland students began asking for their own chapel in which they could worship freely, as Pentecostals. As we experimented with format, it quickly became clear that their worship songs would be the same as those loved by all Millennials, regardless of denomination. The difference sought was not therefore in the songs, or the sermons. It was in the expectancy; the format adjusted so that time was never a factor in the seeking of God's presence. Students longed to worship for one, two, or three hours as they felt led. When God began to move in their midst, as they expected, it was imperative that this take priority above all other plans or schedules.

35. Dayton, *The Theological Roots of Pentecostalism*.
36. Faupel, *The Everlasting Gospel*.

the "four-fold" gospel of Jesus as Saviour, Healer, Baptizer, and Coming King, though it was the fourth element that provided early Pentecostals with the impetus to share the good news of the other three.[37] As noted earlier, early Pentecostals clearly viewed themselves as experiencing the Latter Rain outpouring of the Holy Spirit; their worldview was thoroughly shaped by this understanding. Faupel quotes an early Pentecostal source as stating, "Salvation, the Baptism in the Holy Spirit, Divine Healing, the ministrations of the Holy Spirit among us are features of a program . . . The Second Coming of the Lord Jesus Christ is not a feature of the program . . . it is THE program. The . . . others . . . are features of this program leading up to the grand and glorious fulfillment."[38]

Macchia writes,

> . . . I find Faupel's reference to an eschatological narrative of the outpouring of the Spirit at the heart of Pentecostal distinctives rather compelling as a historical thesis. But Spirit baptism for Pentecostals is the experience that brings to realization personally what the eschatological latter rain of the Spirit brings corporately to an era of time . . . In other words, the latter rain of the Spirit assures that Spirit baptism is not just an individual experience but has implications for how we view the entire church and its mission in the world . . . Rather than subordinate Spirit baptism to the latter rain, it would seem truer to Pentecostal theology to view the latter rain of the Spirit as the setting against which the broader implications of Spirit baptism should be understood and even developed theologically . . . Spirit baptism should be expanded and reinvigorated by the eschatological nature of the Pentecostal vision of the latter rain rather than subordinated to it.[39]

The Displacement of Spirit Baptism in the Pew

We have explored four significant reasons for the relegation of Spirit baptism theology to the back of the theological burner, at least as pertains to scholars of Pentecostalism. But a key question remains: why then have we observed the increasing decline of actual Spirit-baptisms in the Pentecostal

---

37. The PAONL was no different in this regard. See Newman, "The Eschatology of Newfoundland and Labrador Early Pentecostals."

38. Mcdowell, "The Purpose for the Second Coming of the Lord" Cited in Faupel, *The Everlasting Gospel*, 43. Cf. Macchia, *Baptized in the Spirit*, 39.

39. Macchia, *Baptized in the Spirit*, 40.

pew? On some levels, certainly, we may conclude that as goes the academy, so goes the church. When a shift has occurred in theological circles, and students in training for Pentecostal ministry observe this change in focus, it naturally transfers to the congregations of these new Pentecostal ministers. To be fair, however, while there may be elements of all four reasons cited above present in the weakening of this experience in our congregations, I am convinced that it is the lack of eschatological focus in particular that is impacting the pew.

Early Pentecostals believed they were experiencing the Latter Rain outpouring of the Holy Spirit. Why? To prepare God's people to spread the Gospel and reach lost souls before Jesus' soon return. Why was this important? Early Pentecostal writings and sermons are replete with references to both Heaven and Hell. These pioneers firmly believed what they sang: "This world is not my home . . . I'm just passing through." Souls who were not "right with the Lord" could expect to spend an eternity in Hell, separated forever from the love of God. Therefore, to empower believers to gather the harvest of souls in the last days, God baptized them with the Holy Spirit. The outward sign that this had occurred was tongues-speech. But we may note that in many respects, neither Spirit baptism nor tongues was the focus; it was the soon return of Christ. We may illustrate it as follows:

1. Jesus' return is imminent, therefore:

2. Those who do not know him are bound for Hell. Therefore:

3. To gather in as many as possible, God baptizes believers with the Holy Spirit to empower them for witness. Therefore:

4. We speak in tongues as a sign this has occurred.

We will immediately observe that glossolalia was actually three steps removed from the key point—the soon return of Christ for his bride. As noted in chapter 2, however, in the decades following Azusa, partly in response to those who challenged Pentecostals on the doctrines of subsequence and initial evidence as found in points 3 and 4 above, Pentecostalism undertook a defense of its cherished experience of Spirit baptism to the extent that the Pentecostal "distinctive" shifted from an eschatological to an experiential focus. Other authors see this shift as occurring in part due to the waning among Pentecostals of the expectation of the immediacy of Christ's return. Writing as an outsider, and largely critical of the movement, Robert Anderson noted,

> Once the belief in a Second Coming ceased to be an immediate individual expectation, it could no longer hold the central

place in Pentecostal thought. Thus, speaking in tongues, which retained its immediacy, moved to the center of Pentecostal ideology . . . Speaking in tongues then ceased to be primarily an eschatological sign and a means for hastening the Second Coming . . . Rather, speaking in tongues became an end in itself, and the central teaching of the Pentecostal movement.[40]

Indeed, by the time I was attending a Pentecostal youth group and youth camps in the 1980s, Spirit baptism was more likely to be presented as:

1. You should get your Spirit baptism[41] because,
2. You are Pentecostal.
3. And, by the way, it gives us great power for witness.

Although perhaps a touch jaded, this nonetheless represents the reality for several generations of younger Pentecostals in Newfoundland and Labrador, and I suspect, throughout Canada and the United States. As we have seen, GenX and Millennials are far less denominationally focused than their forebears, and generally less loyal to "brands" than preceding generations. The idea that one should seek Spirit baptism simply to identify with being "Pentecostal" is one that might have worked 50 years ago, but certainly will not work with any effectiveness today. Younger generations will require something beyond denominational identification to justify their belief in, and pursuit of, gifts such as Spirit baptism. I believe, however, that it so happens that the original Pentecostal understanding of this gift—as eschatologically focused—will serve us very well in the 21st century.

The Way Forward: Five Suggestions

I would suggest five courses of action for Pentecostalism should it wish to reinvigorate the important doctrine (and experience) of Spirit baptism among its people in the coming decades. Naturally, this list does not pretend to be exhaustive, or even conclusive. But it does represent significant steps Pentecostals can take to help connect one of their most important doctrines with a post-Christendom and secular culture.

---

40. Anderson, *Vision of the Disinherited*, 96. While I disagree with much of the tenor of Anderson's work, I believe he has accurately represented this point.
41. Or worse, "You should get your tongues."

1. Re-Connect Spirit Baptism to Eschatology

First, as described above, we must once again become a people consumed with the eschatological reality of Christ's soon return, and the resultant implications for those unreached with the Gospel. Anecdotal evidence abounds of the lack of emphasis on eschatology in Pentecostal churches.[42] With tongues viewed simply as evidence of Spirit baptism, and Spirit baptism thought to be little more than identification with a Pentecostal denomination, younger generations have not, nor will ever view Spirit baptism properly or with the importance it deserves. Pentecostals must again recognize the essential role of eschatological expectation in the gift of Spirit baptism.[43] While youth today are less loyal to brands than ever, they are also strongly motivated to effect change in their communities, and indeed, in the world. Presenting the historically Pentecostal (and I would add, biblical) understanding of Spirit baptism to youth and young adults will help reverse the decline Pentecostal denominations have witnessed in this important gift.[44]

Norris and Inglehart argue that religion will thrive where the society is less secure, and decline where security is abundant.[45] Clearly, the personal and financial security of a Canadian society that has known fifty consecutive years of peacetime has not contributed to the need of individuals to look

---

42. In teaching Eschatology for many years at the undergraduate level, I've often had students complete an assignment whereby they were to interview a number of PAONL Pastors with more than 25 years in the ministry, and a number of parishioners who have attended PAONL churches for more than 25 years. Parishioners were asked whether they heard as many sermons on eschatology in recent times as they did decades ago. To a person, the answer was "no." Pastors were asked if they preached or taught on the end times as often as they did in their early ministry. Again to a person, the answer was "no." When asked why this was so, the most common answer was that there were too many other pressing concerns of contemporary import, such as marriage, sexuality, or family concerns.

43. In so doing, we may have to revisit the dogmatism with which we've held to the Dispensational model of the end times. See for example, Sheppard, "Pentecostals and the Hermeneutics of Dispensationalism." Two new works in the Journal of Pentecostal Theology Supplementary Series seek to assist with this endeavor. Thompson, *Kingdom Come*; McQueen, *Toward a Pentecostal Eschatology*.

44. For 15 years now I have been the morning theology teacher at the two PAONL youth camps. Each year, I cycle through a variety of doctrinal issues with Junior and Senior Highs, including Spirit baptism. We have observed that when Spirit baptism is properly linked to its eschatological *raison d'être*, youth are easily and quickly baptized in the Spirit. We have witnessed dozens of teenagers Spirit baptized in just one evening. I believe the key is their understanding of this gift as connected to Jesus' soon return and the missional purpose of the Church to spread the Kingdom of God.

45. Norris and Inglehart, *Sacred and Secular*, 12–14.

outside of themselves for assistance and reassurance. Early Pentecostals were able to proclaim the promise of an eschatological system that understood the days were dark and difficult, but consoled believers with the conviction that God was in full control of human history, and would soon convincingly break in upon world affairs in dramatic fashion. Those days may soon be upon us again, and Pentecostalism must be ready with an appropriate biblical message.[46]

Finally, as Macchia observes, re-uniting Spirit baptism theology with eschatology can help us mend the current fracture in Pentecostal theology between the "soteriological" emphasis of Paul, and the "charismatic" emphasis of Luke. Though we may conclude that there are a variety of emphases in Scripture upon the outcomes of Spirit baptism, they may be united under the umbrella of God's eschatological purposes in inaugurating his kingdom. "As a pneumatological concept, the kingdom is inaugurated and fulfilled as Spirit-baptism . . . the highest description possible of the substance of Spirit-baptism as an eschatological gift is that it functions as an outpouring of divine love. This is the final integration of the soteriological and charismatic."[47]

2. Replace "Evidence" with "Sign"

Second, we must recapture the language of "sign" instead of "evidence" for glossolalia. Younger generations in particular, affected as they are by postmodern thought, will not connect with language that refers to evidence, and is presented as rational proof. Understanding a "sign" as something that directs us to a greater reality, but is not in itself that reality, will prove tremendously useful as a theological assist for younger Pentecostals who seek a proper understanding of the traditional Pentecostal distinctive. Glossolalia may, therefore, be understood not as the goal in and of itself, but as the sign pointing towards the reality of Christ's imminent return and the mandate of all believers to represent the Kingdom of God to a world in spiritual darkness.[48] Macchia proposes, ". . . shifting to the language of 'sign' (rather than

---

46. In an article that is both interesting and provocative, Robert Kaplan asserts that just as Late Antiquity was not able to recognize the epochal shifts in world affairs that came as a result of the collapse of the Roman Empire, so too we are not able to properly discern the incredible changes in the geo-political world we are currently witnessing. He further argues that now as then, religion will play an incredibly important role in world stability as it is able to take the place of known authority structures that give way, at times to tribalism and even chaos. Kaplan, "Rome's Fall and Late Antiquity."

47. Macchia, *Baptized in the Spirit*, 17.

48. Useful here is Macchia, "Sighs Too Deep for Words."; idem, "Tongues as a

'evidence,' which is not a biblical term) concerning tongues and focusing on the theological rather than a legalistic connection between them."[49]

3. Increase Focus on the Reality to Which the Sign Points

Simon Chan, in *Pentecostal Theology and the Christian Spiritual Tradition*, suggests that the way glossolalia is experienced "cries out" for a better explanation than the one typically given by Pentecostals and charismatics. With Macchia, Chan believes that the Pentecostal understanding of Spirit-baptism must be broadened to incorporate both the soteriological and charismatic dimensions. Once integrated properly, he suggests that Spirit baptism is "better understood primarily in terms of revelation and personal intimacy, and only derivatively, as empowerment for mission."[50] Although I am not fully persuaded by Chan's position, I believe he has captured something that was native to classical Pentecostal spirituality in its earliest days. Chan observes,

> Pentecostals seek to capture a unique reality with a unique sign: they see glossolalia as an appropriate symbol of this spiritual reality. Thus, within the Pentecostal community at least, glossolalia as initial evidence makes good sense. It makes even better sense when evidential tongues are interpreted within the broader context of the Christian mystical tradition where silence signals a certain level of intimacy with God. Silence and tongues have the same logical function within the respective communities. At this level it becomes apparent that glossolalia, like silence, bears a much stronger relationship to Spirit-baptism than just being an appropriate symbol. The relationship is of such a kind that one is quite justified to call it 'the initial evidence.' But ultimately, glossolalia makes the best sense when it is understood as signifying a reality which configures gracious and powerful affections in a distinctively Pentecostal way. Its truth must finally be seen in terms of transformed persons and communities.[51]

I believe this to be a point worthy of further reflection. As we have noted, a significant shift occurred in the focus on Spirit baptism from the time of Wesley to that of the Azusa revival. Perhaps, in adjusting the focus from holiness to power, a proper balance was lost. My early memories of

---

Sign."
49. Macchia, *Baptized in the Spirit*, 36.
50. Chan, *Pentecostal Theology and the Christian Spiritual Tradition*, 41.
51. Ibid.

personal testimonies while growing up in Pentecostalism convince me that these Pentecostal pioneers understood Spirit baptism very clearly as providing both a richer spiritual experience and empowerment for mission. Spirit baptism was variously described as an entrance into a deeper experience of God's love, an increased thirst for holiness, prayer, and reading of the Scriptures, and the birthing of a powerful passion for reaching the lost with the Gospel of Christ. With the rise of denominationalism within Pentecostalism in the mid 20th century, the raison d'etre shifted from this very subjective and emotive expression, to one simply based on power for service. In this move, something important was lost.

4. Open and Forthright Discussion

Fourth, we must be willing to have open and transparent theological discussions about this "white elephant" of classical Pentecostalism. Cecil Robeck has demonstrated that even though considerable diversity existed in early North American Pentecostalism on the doctrines of Subsequence and Initial Evidence, successive generations of denominational leadership have essentially quashed any open discussion on these matters.[52] In my opinion, one of the foremost reasons for the decline of this doctrine (and experience) in North American Pentecostalism is the reticence on the part of leadership to have the open and honest conversations required for increasingly educated young Pentecostals to move forward with a level of theological confidence and intellectual integrity.[53] As we do so, I suggest we will find that

---

52. Robeck, "An Emerging Magisterium." My own experience in the PAONL has mirrored Robeck's claims. A number of years ago I submitted an article to the PAONL for publication in *Good Tidings*. The article sought to clarify current understandings of Spirit baptism. It was declined, not because my assertions were incorrect, but rather because it was deemed we were not ready for that discussion via that medium.

53. By way of anecdotal evidence, during the course of this writing a former student contacted me about his application for Ordination with the PAONL. On the application relative to his understanding of Initial Evidence, he wished in part to write, "In terms of accurately conveying the heart of Pentecostalism, using the term 'evidence' emphasizes tongues over the importance of Spirit Baptism for the empowerment of the believer. Spirit Baptism is for the empowerment of the believer to witness Jesus to the lost, not to receive tongues. If I say something is 'evidence', this puts an over-importance on that something. If I say something is a 'sign', it makes an individual ask the question, 'a sign to what?' More importantly, tongues as a sign reflects the historical Pentecostal notion that no language would be a barrier to witness, it was a sign to a greater Spirit-fueled global awakening. I guess the question is, do I seek evidence for my Spirit Baptism, or do I seek empowerment for witness?" My opinion was sought in the context of wondering whether or not this would disqualify him for Ordination. Despite my assurances that it would not, he remained unconvinced.

recent expressions of Subsequence and Initial Evidence have been overly dogmatic, and unnecessarily difficult for younger generations to embrace. I concur wholeheartedly with Fee:

> ... I am convinced that the dynamic, empowering dimension of life in the Spirit was the "norm" in the early church, and that they simply would not have understood the less-than-dynamic quality of life in the Spirit (without the Spirit?) that has been the "norm" of so much of the later church ... Precisely because I understand this dimension of life in the Spirit to be the New Testament norm, I think it is repeatable, and should be so, as the norm of the later church. Where I would tend to disagree with my tradition in the articulation of this norm is when they use language that seems more obligatory to me than I find in the New Testament documents themselves.[54]

Pentecostal leadership must recognize that an openness to comprehensive discussions on the validity of the Spirit baptism doctrine, and a willingness to step back from some of the theological dogmatism surrounding Subsequence and Initial Evidence, will not in the long run cause the demise of this doctrine, *but may in fact preserve it.* Younger, more educated generations will simply not be willing to "tow the line" on doctrinal positions without a more thorough examination and discussion. The days of honest, but uneducated, Pentecostal believers exclaiming, "The Bible says it, and that settles it" have passed. I believe that the Pentecostal experience of Spirit baptism will not only survive into the future, but thrive—IF we are willing to take a fresh look at our expressions of this biblical gift.

5. Emphasize the Essence more than the Distinctives

For too long, classical Pentecostalism in North America has been largely defined theologically by the twin doctrines of Subsequence and Initial Evidence. Important as these doctrines and resultant experience have been for Pentecostal growth, such significant focus on Spirit-baptism has left Pentecostalism with a truncated and reductionist pneumatology. To be sure, Pentecostals do believe in the full expression of the Spirit's manifestations and leading in the life of the church. Unfortunately, however, our ability to express our belief in the comprehensive role of the Holy Spirit in both the church and the world has been unnecessarily hampered. It is my belief

---

54. Fee, *Gospel and Spirit*, 102–3. For further discussion, see Noel, "Gordon Fee's Contribution to Contemporary Pentecostalism's Theology of Baptism in the Holy Spirit."

that Pentecostalism would be well served to refocus our pneumatological efforts to express more broadly the *essence* of Pentecostalism instead of just its *distinctives*. While the distinctives are undoubtedly an important part of the whole, they are just that—one component of the whole picture.

The essence of Pentecostalism, as I understand it, may be described as the invitation to participate in a full orbed *life in the Spirit*. Pentecostals believe the Holy Spirit was given to the Church for far more than tongues-speech. It is time we truly begin to understand ourselves, and express to a searching culture, the essence of the movement. To provide but a brief list, we must once again focus on the roles of the Holy Spirit as taught in the biblical account. Among other things, the Spirit:

a) *Is our teacher.* Jesus promised that the Holy Spirit would teach believers what was necessary to know and understand: "All this I have spoken while still with you. But the Counselor, the Holy Spirit, whom the Father will send in my name, will teach you all things and will remind you of everything I have said to you."[55]

b) *Helps us live by grace.* During the decades when Pentecostalism was highly "legalistic" as described above, believers knew what was expected of them; practices deemed sinful were regularly highlighted during the weekly sermons. When the Pentecostal congregation began to move away from their understanding of holiness as tied to clothing choices and abstinence from "worldly" activities, however, a correct understanding of biblical holiness did not always arise in its place. Older congregants will complain that Pentecostalism moved from prohibiting its members to cook their meals on Sunday, to having younger members skip church to attend the movie theatre—all within a generation. Missing often from the discussion is the role of the Holy Spirit in leading believers into God-honoring holiness. Ezekiel looked ahead to this when he prophesied God declaring, "I will give you a new heart and put a new spirit in you; I will remove from you your heart of stone and give you a heart of flesh. And I will put my Spirit in you and move you to follow my decrees and be careful to keep my laws."[56]

c) *Helps us put to death the sinful nature.* "Therefore, brothers, we have an obligation—but it is not to the sinful nature, to live according to it. For if you live according to the sinful nature, you will die; but if by the Spirit you put to death the misdeeds of the body, you will live . . ."[57]

55. John 14:25–26
56. Ezek 36:26–28
57. Rom 8:12–14

Pentecostals today, particularly in the younger generations, may be less familiar with the older language of "flesh" and "spirit" and the description of the ongoing battle between them, a narrative so common in the testimonies and witness of more senior Pentecostals. A key aspect of right living and practice is the recognition that temptations of the flesh cannot be conquered by willpower alone; the Holy Spirit provides the strength necessary for wise choices.

d) *Helps us to pray.* Every believer has had the experience of desiring to pray, but being unsure of how or what to pray. Paul wrote, "In the same way, the Spirit helps us in our weakness. We do not know what we ought to pray for, but the Spirit himself intercedes for us with groans that words cannot express. And he who searches our hearts knows the mind of the Spirit, because the Spirit intercedes for the saints in accordance with God's will."[58]

e) *Gives spiritual gifts to the church.* "Now to each one the manifestation of the Spirit is given for the common good. To one there is given through the Spirit the message of wisdom, to another the message of knowledge by means of the same Spirit, to another faith by the same Spirit, to another gifts of healing by that one Spirit, to another miraculous powers, to another prophecy, to another distinguishing between spirits, to another speaking in different kinds of tongues, and to still another the interpretation of tongues. All these are the work of one and the same Spirit, and he gives them to each one, just as he determines."[59] The decline of the manifestation of the Gifts of the Spirit in Pentecostal churches should provoke serious concern. That this is occurring simultaneously with the greatest cultural openness to spirituality and the supernatural is supremely unfortunate. Those seeking a faith experience or religious involvement that provides an authentic experience of the divine, should need look no farther than Pentecostalism. In many Pentecostal contexts, tongues and interpretation alone survive with relative frequency in Sunday services.

Pentecostals should once again "seek earnestly" these Gifts for two important reasons. First, as was mentioned, those seeking a faith journey or religious experience in the postmodern or post-Christendom culture will likely seek one that allows them to experience God directly. While this is the goal in all areas of the Christian life, the free flow of these spiritual Gifts within the Body are an important outward testimony to the world of God's presence experienced in the Church.

58. Rom 8:26–27
59. 1 Cor 12:7–11

Second, Paul teaches that these Gifts are meant to edify the Body. Surely a case can be made that Pentecostalism throughout the Western world is weaker than could be. God's pattern for edification must once again be embraced by Pentecostals seeking maturity and growth in their congregations.

f) *Grows His Fruit in believers.* Finally, Pentecostals seeking to engage culture in a post-Christendom era would do well to give this point significant attention. I am convinced that for all of the attention given the Gifts including tongues, healing, and prophecy, in the contemporary Pentecostal and Charismatic world, and as appealing as these may be to a postmodern mindset, our greatest tool for witness comes from a transformed character. In a post-Christendom world that is rocked with financial insecurity, war, health challenges, and threat of terrorism, observing the Body of Christ powerfully exhibiting such uncommon traits as love, peace, joy, patience, and self-control, may lead to a variety of opportunities for authentic relationship and eventual witness to the gospel.

Summary

Throughout this section we have observed both the reasons for the decline in practice of the doctrines of Subsequence and Initial Evidence, and a variety of steps that Pentecostals can take to address this weakness. For all of the challenges presented, and solutions prescribed, however, little will matter if Pentecostalism does not arrest the trend to celebrate *belief* in the areas described above, with little evidence that these foundational doctrines and practices of Pentecostalism are *valued*. To the difference in *beliefs* and *values* and the implications present in our failure to move from the former to the latter, we now turn.

B. Beliefs vs. Values

Pentecostals in North America have been privy to discussion from their leadership concerning the various challenges we face, including the fact that overall, the Pentecostal movement in North America is not growing anywhere near the pace of other continents, and is in decline in some areas. For a revival movement based on the empowering of the Holy Spirit for witness, this information cannot be met with passive acceptance. In addition, and crucial to the subject of this work, there is evidence that the encroachment of secularism is occurring not just in the world, but also in the church itself. Norris and Inglehart, in *Sacred and Secular,* observe that "The most persuasive evidence about secularism in rich nations concerns values and behavior: the critical test is what people say is important to their lives and what they actually *do*."[60] They further define secularism as "a systematic erosion of religious practices, values and beliefs..."[61]

The Difference Between Beliefs and Values

Pentecostal leadership have initiated a variety of responses to this challenge, including once again focusing the attention of membership on our Core Values—those deeply held convictions that should guide us as an organization, but only after they have directed us as individual believers. In the PAONL for example, as noted earlier, the following five core values have been established:

> We value God: His Word, His Creation, His redemptive purposes in His son, his presence through the Holy Spirit and the imminent return of Christ.
>
> We value "the lost" to whom we owe the compassion of Christ, an opportunity to receive the gospel, and entrance into Christian fellowship.
>
> We value believers, their commitment to personal discipleship, their baptism in the Holy Spirit, their Christian family life, and their Christ-like example and witness.
>
> We value the local assembly marked by sound doctrine, anointed proclamation, fervent prayer, divine healing, Spirit-led worship, authentic relationships, every-member ministry, Holy Spirit-empowered evangelism and practical expression of Christian faith in the world.
>
> We value a cooperative fellowship that enhances the church's ability to fulfill its missional mandate, through servant leadership, a shared vision, positive communication, relevant ministry and strategic mobilization of its resources.[62]

Why such a refocus on values that have long been held? First, to remind congregants that beliefs and values are simply not the same thing. Beliefs are basically assumptions that we make about God, the Bible, and the world; these grow from what we see, hear, experience, read and think

---

60. Norris and Inglehart, *Sacred and Secular*, 2.
61. Ibid.
62. "Pentecostal Assemblies of Newfoundland and Labrador: We Believe..."

about. From our beliefs we derive our values. Our values are things that we deem important and can include ideas such as equality, honesty, education, a Spirit-filled life, perseverance, loyalty, faithfulness, Scripture, the Church, and youth.

Second, leadership has refocused upon these values because it is our values that shape our actions. Far too often, our actions do not equal our beliefs, solely because our beliefs have not translated into values. J. Barton Cunningham notes,

> Every human action illustrates the influence of a person's values and beliefs. Beliefs and values are both assumptions that describe what people hold to be true. A value is an assumption of what ought to be, while a belief is an assumption of what is or will result. While a person may value participating in a cause to change the world, he or she may not believe that participation will actually improve the environment.[63]

Put another way, "A *belief* is an internal feeling that something is true, even though that belief may be unproven or irrational . . . A *value* is a measure of the worth or importance a person attaches to something; our values are often reflected in the way we live our lives. An *attitude* is the way a person expresses or applies their beliefs and values, and is expressed through words and behaviour."[64]

The relationship between beliefs, values, and our actions, might be displayed thusly: our values are based on our beliefs, and our actions are based on our values.

---

63. Cunningham, *Researching Organizational Values and Beliefs*, 4.
64. Anderson and De Silva, *Beliefs, Values and Attitudes*, 1.

```
Beliefs
  ↓
Values
  ↓
Action
```

If we do not translate our beliefs into values, we will not act properly, or we will not act at all, as we see in the following:

```
Beliefs
  ↓
Absence of Values
  ↓
Action
Not Equal to Beliefs
```

I believe this failure to translate beliefs into values is more prevalent in Pentecostalism than has been heretofore recognized. For example, I may visit a local Pentecostal assembly and ask for a show of hands as to how many present believe that the Bible is God's Word, and is therefore authoritative and exceptionally important for guiding our lives. I'm certain almost every hand would be raised. Now, were I to continue by asking for a show of hands as to how many present not just read, but studied their Bibles on a daily basis, there is evidence that the number would be much lower.[65] Why? While we *believe* that God's Word is important, this has not always translated into a *value*, and therefore, not into proper *action*.

Similarly, most Pentecostals would agree that children's and youth ministry is the key to the Church's future. If I were then able to determine how many made special effort to attend whatever "youth emphasis services" on Sunday they possibly could, to support these youth which they believe are so significant, the numbers may be much lower. Why? Because belief not translated into value does not produce proper action. While we believe youth are important, what we sometimes value are Sunday services that appeal to our own styles of worship and music—and not the "noise" that youth services are known for!

Bring Transformation

Beliefs alone may bring behaviour modification, but not character transformation. Because of the holiness background of much of Pentecostalism, behaviour modification was often acceptable—individuals gave up alcohol and tobacco, dancing, and made other lifestyle and clothing changes. If we wish to see Pentecostalism moving forward, we need to move from beliefs to values because only values bring character transformation. People with modified behaviours will appear to be Christians, but not always act like it, thus often hindering the growth of the local church. People with transformed characters, who exhibit the Fruit of the Spirit in their lives, are far more likely to advance the Kingdom of God.[66]

For example, our youth are taught a belief system, but it sometimes doesn't translate into values, and therefore not into transformation. This is why young men can be on our youth leadership teams, leave home to attend university, and promptly engage in activities contrary to the teaching they have received. They may have *believed* these things to be wrong, but never translated their beliefs into the *values* and resultant positive actions.

65. "Bible Engagement in Churchgoers' Hearts."
66. See, for example, Willard and Simpson, *Revolution of Character*.

The Bible prophesies that a time would arise when people would hold *beliefs* but these would not translate into *values*.

> But mark this: There will be terrible times in the last days. People will be lovers of themselves, lovers of money, boastful, proud, abusive, disobedient to their parents, ungrateful, unholy, without love, unforgiving, slanderous, without self-control, brutal, not lovers of the good, treacherous, rash, conceited, lovers of pleasure rather than lovers of God—having a form of godliness but denying its power. Have nothing to do with them.[67]

Having a form of godliness but denying its power may well be understood as beliefs without value.

The Pentecostal Challenge

As noted above, a key aspect of Pentecostal spirituality is emphasis on the supernatural, particularly as manifested during worship times. Daniel Albrecht notes, "Experiencing God is the fundamental goal of the Pentecostal service. This experiencing or encountering God is often symbolized as a felt presence of the divine. The sense of the divine presence is a primary component of, an aim, of Pent/Char spirituality."[68] Pentecostals therefore have another, perhaps unique, struggle in determining beliefs and values. Consider this saying, which has been fairly common in Pentecostal circles in Newfoundland and Labrador: *"We had such an awesome service! The altar service was so powerful that we didn't have any preaching!"*

For many older Pentecostals, this was the metric used to evaluate everything from the "success" of Sunday services, to the effectiveness of the pastor. When juxtaposed against the value we assign to the preaching of the Scriptures, for example, this common expression explains much. We may say that we value the Word, but all too often we simply believe that the Word is important, authoritative, or inspired.

What we actually value, and therefore act upon, is the moving of the Holy Spirit in our lives and around our altars. The metric by which we often measure Pastoral success, therefore, is not making disciples, teaching sound doctrine, or preaching expository sermons. The yardstick is whether the altar service goes "over the top;" whether we "feel" the presence of God.

Every Pentecostal church is pastored by someone who is very much human and in need of encouragement from those to whom they are called

---

67. 2 Tim 3:1–5
68. Albrecht, *Rites in the Spirit*, 149.

to shepherd. Pastors may find themselves under tremendous pressure to have services in which the altar call is suitably powerful, and sadly, not always under much pressure to ensure that their people are fed a solid diet of the Word of God, complete with regular expository preaching.[69] In too many cases, Pastors have concluded that they will not be criticized for weak sermons, as long as the service is sufficiently emotional and concludes with a "powerful" time around the altar.

As Pentecostals endeavour to engage a culture that exhibits increasing signs of secularism, we must guard against two extremes. On one side, when we have mere *belief* in the Word but *value* spiritual manifestations, we may be left with an emotional Christianity, subject to trendiness with a lack of doctrinal maturity. On the other, when we place *value* in the Word but merely *believe* in spiritual manifestations we may unwillingly espouse a rational Christianity, full of doctrinal head knowledge, but which lacks openness to God's Spirit. We find balance when we value God's Word and value the moving of the Holy Spirit. Then we will produce Pentecostal believers who are well grounded in Scripture and doctrine, are mature, not subject to whims and trends, and are fully open to God's Spirit via all manifestations and direction. These are the type of Christians who will bring Christ with them into the world, and change their context for God's Kingdom.

How might Pentecostals create this kind of disciple? How might we bring our people to a place where they are willing to employ creative methods fraught with risk, in the vein of Sister Aimee? How will we inspire our people to move from an attractional model of church, to one that sees all of life as mission and engages the community on its own ground? How will we appropriate the lessons learned from the Emergent church, while embracing the shift to the post-Christendom context? Where will we find the courage to focus once again on the essence of Pentecostalism, boldly pursuing a life in the Spirit in the midst of a postmodern context longing for authentic spirituality?

Ephesians 4: Pastors as Equippers

While there is no simple or pat answer that will suit every congregation and context, I believe much can be mined from Paul's teaching in Ephesians 4:11–16 on Christ's gifts to the Church. Though perhaps only one piece of the equation, the outcomes Paul suggests in this passage mirror closely the desired goals of Pentecostalism to help its people grow in spiritual and

---

69. See, for example, Magruder, "Why Pentecostals Don't Preach Expository Sermons."

theological maturity. Speaking of the Pentecostal tendency to separate "spiritual experiences" from structured learning, Adam White suggests, "We can see then an educational ideal in Paul, and indeed, the whole NT. The means to counter heresy, the method of producing maturity, the process by which we attain the fullness of God is all found in 'Christian paideia.' Moreover, in Ephesians 4.11–14, we see this constellation of terms come together in a beautiful picture of what Paul (and indeed Christ) desires for the church."[70] Paul wrote:

> So Christ himself gave the apostles, the prophets, the evangelists, the pastors and teachers, to equip his people for works of service, so that the body of Christ may be built up until we all reach unity in the faith and in the knowledge of the Son of God and become mature, attaining to the whole measure of the fullness of Christ. Then we will no longer be infants, tossed back and forth by the waves, and blown here and there by every wind of teaching and by the cunning and craftiness of people in their deceitful scheming. Instead, speaking the truth in love, we will grow to become in every respect the mature body of him who is the head, that is, Christ. From him the whole body, joined and held together by every supporting ligament, grows and builds itself up in love, as each part does its work.[71]

Ephesians chapters 1–3 contain Paul's description of the Christian calling; in 4:1–6 he transitions to practical instructions on how the Christian life should be lived. Next, Paul discusses the need for "each one" in the Body to work to attain the particular unity that is already generally present in the sense that the Body is God's creation. The power to achieve this goal comes not from the believers, but from the victorious Christ. The first section of this paragraph focuses on the Christ who has defeated the powers of evil, and includes the much-debated description of Christ who "descended" into the lower regions of the earth. Our passage continues this theme with a description of the gifts given by the victorious Christ to his Body, that it might be built up in the faith, and properly equipped for ministry.[72]

A full discussion on the five (or four)[73] fold ministry is beyond the scope of this study; we will focus specifically on the role of the Pastor.[74] It is

---

70. White, "Knowledge and Transformation."

71. Ephesians 4.11–14.

72. Thielman, *Ephesians*, 262–63.

73. Some scholars see only four groups due to the Greek syntax involved. See Combs, "The Biblical Role of the Evangelist," fn 29.

74. Much has been written of late on the five-fold ministry, and the desire to restore

my experience that in many cases, Pastors have assumed the responsibilities outlined by Paul as belonging to the Body. Due in part to consumerist attitudes first made commonplace by Baby Boomers, I believe Pastors are often viewed simply as "paid staff" whose job it is to meet the needs of both the congregation and the community.[75] When additional areas of ministry are needed and it is determined that the Pastor cannot be expected to assume the added duties, the automatic response (if finances deem possible) is to hire another staff member to care for the perceived needs, in areas such as Worship, Children's ministry, or Visitation. In essence, congregations with a consumerist mentality view the Church as something that should meet their needs. As tasks and needs arise, congregations will pay individuals to complete the work, resulting in a view of Pastors as little more than paid "employees."[76]

As we may quickly observe, this approach does not resonate with Paul's teaching given above. Pastors are "gifts" to the Church, and their key role is to "equip the people for works of service."[77] Once the congregation and Pastor fall into the trap of the Pastor doing all the works of service, however, with the congregants as little more than spectators or consumers, a vicious cycle begins. Pastors are therefore no longer able to properly equip the saints as they are too busy doing the work of the ministry.[78] The people are poorly equipped therefore, and combined with their natural tendency to view the staff as those paid to run the ministries of the Church, congregants further shrink from their biblical duties. With few enabled or willing to embrace the ministerial call that is the privilege of every believer, the works of service fall once again to the pastoral staff—and the cycle continues.

Apostles and Prophecy specifically to the Church. See for example, Cartledge, *The Apostolic Revolution*; Wagner, *Apostles and Prophets*.

75. See for example Piper, *Brothers, We Are Not Professionals*.

76. I addressed this issue recently in our denominational publication. Noel, "What Is a Pastor?."

77. There is some discussion in the literature on whether Paul is listing three purposes for which Christ gave these five gifts—the equipping of the saints, the work of the ministry, and the edification of the body—or whether we are to understand their role as equipping the saints for the work of the ministry, which edifies the body. I stand with commentators who hold to the latter interpretation. Cf. Thielman, *Ephesians*, 277–80. Contra Lincoln, *Ephesians*, 253.

78. This is particularly true for congregations where the Sunday preaching time is still viewed as the key source of discipleship. 62 of the 75 respondents in the 2009 survey on discipleship I completed among PAONL pastors indicated that the Sunday service and mid-week Bible Study meeting were the chief drivers of discipleship in their assemblies.

In sum, when the pattern Paul suggests is reversed, Pastors are not properly equipping the people, but are instead very often finding themselves exhausted caring for the works of service themselves.[79] Quite striking about the reversal of the pattern Paul has taught are the outcomes that we may anticipate. Taking Paul's outcomes listed above and viewing them in the reverse, we see that without people properly equipped and doing the work of the ministry, we may expect:

- A lack of unity in the faith and in the knowledge of Christ.
- Failure to attain maturity and the whole measure of Christ's fullness.
- Congregants who act like infants, blown to and fro by every new trend.
- We will fail to speak the truth in love.
- We will fail to grow into the mature body of Christ, the head of the Church.

Of course, when the pattern is reversed and Pastors once again become equippers, we may hope to observe increased maturity, unity, and stability in our people, as the Body grows together in Christ and fulfills its biblical mandate. Pastors tired from dealing with petty issues and "putting out fires" in their congregations, Pastors discouraged because handling so many situations with kid gloves leaves little time to discuss vision and ministry dreams, will enjoy new maturity and unity in their people. To be sure, rewiring the expectations of congregations who have long viewed the Pastor as an employee may be neither simple nor pleasant. Pastors may be viewed as seeking to shirk from their duties, or worse, as lazy. There is little doubt in my mind, however, that this is a task worth engaging, for passive, consumerist congregations will never fulfill the call of God to advance his Kingdom, and further, they will often destroy their "gift"—the Pastor—in the process.

As we consider the differences in beliefs and values, and seek to grow congregations that are fully involved in ministerial service, we may reflect upon a largely unnoticed verse in Philemon 1:6:

> "I pray that you may be active in sharing your faith, so that you will have a full understanding of every good thing we have in Christ."

---

79. By way of personal anecdote, I taught on this passage with our pastors at a recent PAONL conference. When I listed the consequences of failing to follow God's pattern in this regard, some Pastors sat with tears running down their faces as we described the outcomes of childishness and immaturity that pervade congregations who treat their Pastors as employees and themselves as spectators.

While many wait for this full understanding before engaging acts of service, we observe Paul once again teaches the opposite approach: begin doing the works of service, and we will observe ourselves growing in the faith, and understanding of Christ. With this understanding, our people will move from a faith that is largely based in belief, to one that is valued and compels them into mission.

Conclusion

This chapter has explored our two final themes—*essence* over *distinctives* and *beliefs vs. values*. We have observed the need for Pentecostals to shift their pneumatological focus from the more narrow aspects of Spirit baptism to a wider message of life in the Spirit. We can accomplish this without in any way diminishing the proper place of Spirit baptism (including glossolalia) in our midst. In so doing, we will serve both our constituency well, in terms of discipling properly the church, and also the many seekers looking for spiritual reality. In the second half, we explored the differences in beliefs and values, and observed the challenges with Christians who have not allowed beliefs important to the faith to translate into values—which then influence action. Though the movement from beliefs to values and corresponding right action does not come easily, I believe that the active participation of Christ's followers in the mission of the Church mitigates significantly the tendency for the faith to reside solely in the arena of belief.

— 10 —

Conclusion, Summary and Limitations

THIS WORK HOPES TO be a primer for Pentecostal pastors and leaders who like the men of Issachar[1] seek to understand their times and adjust ministry approaches and methods accordingly. I have sought to help define and explain cultural trends including the proliferation of secularism, and the turn to a post-Christendom era in the West. The goal of this study was to explore the significant changes that have occurred in Western (particularly Canadian) culture, predominantly in the area of attitudes towards and the practice of Christianity. We sought to gauge the changes in terms of the move to a post-Christendom era, and explored the rise of secularism and postmodern thought within the Canadian context. It is my contention that attitudes towards religion and faith have shifted so considerably in the West in the last 50 years, that anything less than a thorough rethinking of church life and ministry will not serve us well as we seek the continued growth of God's kingdom. Our purpose therefore was to provide a primer for Pentecostal pastors and leaders who are seeking to understand the times and culture in which they live and minister.

Summary

To accomplish this task, we provided the background necessary for the discussion. Our first undertaking was to supply a foundational understanding of Pentecostalism in the West. Beginning with the theology of John Wesley, we traced the development of "second work" theology through the Holiness movement, into the thought of Finney, and Torrey, concluding with the shift in emphasis from holiness to power that characterized the early Pentecostal movement. We explored the Azusa Street revival and observed the spread of Pentecostalism throughout the globe. Characteristics of early

1. 1 Chr 12:32

Pentecostalism were noted, including its identification with the *Latter Rain* outpouring of the Holy Spirit, and we described the shift in Pentecostal self-understanding from an eschatological to pneumatological focus. The Charismatic movement was highlighted, and we discussed its influence upon Pentecostal identity today.

Chapter 3 sought to complete our background information by exploring recent changes in Western culture, focusing in particular upon Canada as a middle ground in the march towards post-Christendom. Finding itself several decades earlier than the experience of the United Kingdom, but several decades later in the process than the United States, Canada is in an excellent place to learn from the example of the U.K. while able to speak into the fears of Pentecostals in the U.S. We introduced the concept of post-Christendom, and observed both statistical and anecdotal evidence of the rise of secularism within the Canadian context, even while disputing the "secularism thesis." To complete our survey of significant societal change, we explored some basic tenets of postmodern thought, including anti-foundationalism, deconstructionism, the preference for relativism over absolutes, and the rise of community over individuality. We critiqued postmodern thought from an evangelical perspective, but also observed areas of beneficial interaction.

Having provided sufficient background for our discussion we then sought to ensure the conversation remained more concrete than theoretical by examining the struggles of one small classical Pentecostal denomination as it seeks to navigate the cultural shifts described in chapters 2 and 3. Chapter 4 told the story of the Pentecostal Assemblies of Newfoundland and Labrador, and its efforts to stem the tide of declining numbers, while ensuring vibrant and effective ministry to future generations.

Chapter 5 began a series of five chapters that examine eight different themes I propose Pentecostals must consider and engage as they aspire to contextual relevancy. Theme one investigated the six generations that currently worship together in our churches, and noted the varying ways each is affected by cultural changes, and what each generation may in fact learn from the others. While I believe that generation-specific ministry has its place within Pentecostal churches, young and old must be willing to learn from each other if we are to successfully traverse the challenges ahead. Chapter 6 introduced theme two, describing the life and ministry of Aimee Semple McPherson as a Pentecostal who engaged culture on all levels, and was willing to use whatever creative methods she could find or create to spread the Gospel, even at considerable risk to herself and her ministry.

Our third theme focused on the need for Pentecostal churches to continue the move from an attractional to missional model of church life and mission. We described the major concepts of the missional conversation, and noted natural points of convergence between the areas of missional focus and those that Pentecostalism ought to embrace in the future. Though Pentecostal churches are moving in a missional direction, much remains to be done as patterns of attractional thinking run deep and are pervasive. We then sought to explore the Emergent church as an example of those who seek to engage culture on all fronts, and by so doing brought focus to our fourth theme of influencing culture. Chapter 7 concluded with areas where Pentecostalism would do well to learn from its Emergent brothers and sisters, and other areas where we have cause for concern.

Chapter 8 brought our next two themes (reclaiming our supernatural heritage) and (embracing post-Christendom) to the fore. We accomplished this via another look at two topics introduced earlier—postmodernism and post-Christendom. Having introduced these shifts in culture, we now desired to explore how Pentecostals could embrace what is best about these trends away from Modernity and Christendom, recognizing what is beneficial from these important realignments in societal beliefs and attitudes. Pentecostalism may yet thrive in an era unbound by the shackles inherent within Modernity and Christendom in a manner unequalled since its history. It is my contention that though not without challenges, the postmodern and post-Christendom mindset will prove a tremendous advantage to churches and denominations willing to understand the times and adjust their approach accordingly.

Our final chapter explored our two remaining themes, areas of discussion that are perhaps the closest to the Pentecostal heart. Pentecostalism has become known for its focus on Spirit-baptism as much as anything else, and while important, I believe the recent trends towards declining numbers of Pentecostals experiencing this gift is testimony to the need to reconfigure our methodology. I suggested five paths forward that I believe will help Pentecostalism recapture the vibrancy of this precious gift, while simultaneously realigning the message of Pentecostalism from that of a narrow focus on Spirit-baptism to the wider experience of life in the Spirit. To accomplish this, Pentecostal leadership will have to take seriously the challenges of discipleship, and focus on the maturity of Pentecostal people to the effect that simple intellectual beliefs are transformed into values, and therefore, actions. Though the process of discipleship is not complicated, neither is it easy in a Pentecostal sub-culture accustomed to quick "spiritual" fixes that has increasingly moved to a view of pastors as employees. Restoring a biblical recognition of pastors and church leaders as gifts to the Body of Christ, and re-establishing pastors as the "equippers of the Saints," are two important steps to ensure the proper discipling of God's people, bringing the promised maturity, unity, and growth in obedience to Christ.

For Further Study

As with any study of this nature, there are a number of limitations herein, some as deficits that others may wish to address in future endeavours, and some which have been sufficiently covered elsewhere. First, due to the scope of this project, there are areas of significance that did not receive the attention they would otherwise be due. As noted in chapter 1, as others have made excellent cases for a biblical rationale for cultural engagement, I sought simply to show that from the creation mandate in Genesis 1, through to the teachings of Jesus about being "salt and light," to the confession of Paul that "to the Jew I became as a Jew," there is ample biblical support in the wider picture of biblical theology. Second, our study focuses in particular upon the Canadian context, with passing references to the situation in Western Europe, Great Britain or the United States. Though it is beyond the scope of this work to engage each of these locales, it is my hope that this study is able to speak to Pentecostals seeking to navigate changing cultural norms wherever they may be found. More study can be done on the rise of post-Christendom in the United States, even though I believe my suggestions herein will serve American Pentecostals well. Finally, my attempts to traverse a wide range of topics and concerns in the latter chapters necessitated a lighter touch on some substantial theological issues than I would have preferred. Each of the theological topics discussed in the section on the Emergent church, for example, could warrant a chapter of its own; space in this study permitted only a cursory examination sufficient to interact briefly with Pentecostalism.

Conclusion

To the Pentecostals, who wish to take up the challenge of cultural engagement via missional ministry, who will embrace the challenges of secularism and welcome the post-Christendom mindset: God's instructions to the Israelites who found themselves in a foreign land are instructive. Going back to a passage we highlighted in chapter 1, we read of God's directions to those in Babylonian captivity:

> This is what the Lord Almighty, the God of Israel, says to all those I carried into exile from Jerusalem to Babylon: "Build

houses and settle down; plant gardens and eat what they produce. Marry and have sons and daughters; find wives for your sons and give your daughters in marriage, so that they too may have sons and daughters. Increase in number there; do not decrease. Also, seek the peace and prosperity of the city to which I have carried you into exile. Pray to the Lord for it, because if it prospers, you too will prosper." Yes, this is what the Lord Almighty, the God of Israel, says: "Do not let the prophets and diviners among you deceive you. Do not listen to the dreams you encourage them to have. They are prophesying lies to you in my name. I have not sent them," declares the Lord.

This is what the Lord says: "When seventy years are completed for Babylon, I will come to you and fulfill my good promise to bring you back to this place. For I know the plans I have for you," declares the Lord, "plans to prosper you and not to harm you, plans to give you hope and a future."[2]

Pentecostals (and other believers) love to quote verse 11; God's promise of good plans, prosperity, hope and a great future seem to ring true with our own fond hopes for our lives. While we may debate whether a promise of God to his people in Babylonian exile may be claimed with integrity by North American Pentecostals in the twenty-first century, the context of the promise in verse 11 is terribly instructive. We observe that God's people found themselves in a strange land, a culture where their faith system was not adhered to or even acknowledged in the public sphere. Other gods had full reign in Babylon. In that sense, the shift from living in Israel to the Babylonian empire might be compared to that of moving from Christendom to post-Christendom. That which was comforting and familiar about the Jewish faith was also present in the wider Israelite culture; in Babylon little was familiar or comforting. While Canada in the 1950s might have been a very safe place for Pentecostal believers to practice their faith while Christendom was at its height, the same surely cannot be said for the current era. In this sense, many Pentecostals may feel as if they are themselves, exiled to Babylon. We can hear the cry today that was recorded from the lips of God's people millennia ago: "How can we sing the song of the Lord in a strange land?"[3]

We observe, then, God's command to the Israelites while in this strange land: "Build houses and settle down; plant gardens and eat what they produce. Marry and have sons and daughters; find wives for your sons and give your daughters in marriage, so that they too may have sons and daughters.

2. Jeremiah 29:4
3. Ps 137:4

Increase in number there; do not decrease. Also, *seek the peace and prosperity of the city to which I have carried you into exile. Pray to the Lord for it, because if it prospers, you too will prosper."* The Israelites were to fully engage in the normal routines of life while in exile. Further, they were to pray that the culture around them would thrive; they were not to withdraw, adopt isolationist tendencies, or retreat from city life. This is the context out of which God's promise of verse 11 can be found: full engagement with the foreign culture, praying for its prosperity, even while living out the faith in the normalcy of life. I believe that followers of Christ who engage this world, with its secularism and increasingly post-Christendom attitudes and ways, may expect to receive the same promises of hope and a prosperous future.

Appendix 1

First PAONL Survey 2007

Tabulation Discipleship Questionnaire – 120 total

1. From the list below, please indicate how often you've taught on the following in your pastoral ministry (include Sunday services and others such as Prayer Meetings):

	Every Quarter	*Every Year*	*In the Past Five Years*	*Rarely / Never*
The Doctrine of Christ: Fully God and Fully Man	31	61	19	8
The Authority of Scripture	33	64	20	3
Salvation: Is Jesus the Only Way to God?	92	30	1	0
Understanding Scripture: How to Interpret the Bible	10	54	38	15
Worship	61	53	4	2
Healing	46	46	7	7
Evangelism	81	36	3	1
Prayer	81	37	3	0
Giving/Stewardship	27	68	15	6

APPENDIX 1

	Every Quarter	Every Year	In the Past Five Years	Rarely / Never
The Baptism of the Holy Spirit	47	64	9	1
The Fruit of the Spirit	27	72	21	4
The Gifts of the Spirit	19	69	23	5
Holiness: Inward vs. Outward	53	60	6	1
The Church	48	56	13	5
Water Baptism/ The Lord's Supper	39	67	13	4
End Time Theology	34	58	18	7
Creation	6	42	44	31

2. For those topics in which you've checked "in the last 5 years" or "rarely/never," why do you believe this to be the case? (Check 2 or less)

Too many other "hot issues" needing attention (relationships, homosexuality, etc.)	I don't have time to adequately prepare for these topics.	I feel unprepared to deal with these topics; I'm not sure how to approach the topic.	My congregation is uninterested in such "theological" topics.	I am not convinced that these topics are of substantial importance
38	30	21	12	4

3. From your interaction with the congregation you're currently pastoring, do you generally feel they have been well-taught on the above topics in the last 20-30 years? (Check one)

Very Well (Most in my congregation could defend/share their beliefs in all of the above)	Adequately (Most in my congregation could defend/share their beliefs some of the above)	Poorly (Some in my congregation could defend/share their beliefs in some of the above)	Very Poorly (Few in my congregation could defend/share their beliefs in some of the above)
7	61	42	7

4. Have you recognized a need in your own ministry to increase the teaching of our essential doctrines and made plans to do the same?

Yes I have	I hadn't thought of it before now	No, I feel I am on track with the teaching I'm currently doing
88	11	17

APPENDIX 2

Second PAONL SURVEY 2009

Discipleship Questionnaire
Pentecostal Assemblies of Newfoundland and Labrador
May 2009

1. How satisfied are you with the level of discipleship occurring in your local assembly? (circle one)

   1. Very Dissatisfied — 1
   2. Dissatisfied — 15
   3. Mixed Feelings — 40
   4. Satisfied — 19
   5. Very Satisfied — 0

2. How do you measure your effectiveness at making disciples?

   - Attendance: growth = discipleship — 5
   - I preach and let the Holy Spirit take care of the rest — 4
   - By the testimonies I hear — 5
   - I look for increased growth of the Fruit of the Spirit — 42
   - Demand for discipleship classes (Alpha, Bible Studies) — 7
   - To be honest, I'm not sure how to measure it! — 12
   - Other:
     - Christlikeness.
     - If believers come to be discipled and if they are being and making disciples.
     - As it becomes worked out in their commitment.

- I measure it by believers becoming soul winners and resembling Jesus in their character.
- Disciples making disciples.
- An increase of spiritual maturity.

3. What is the primary source of discipleship in your local assembly?

- Pulpit preaching during Sunday services — 38
- Sunday school — 6
- Small Groups during the week — 8
- Departmental Ministries (youth, children's, Women's etc.) — 16
- One-on-one discipleship — 9
- Outside the local assembly (TV, other programs, etc.) — 0
- Mid-week Prayer and Bible Study — 24

4. Does your assembly have an intentional ministry for discipling new believers? (Check one)

- Yes (if Yes, please describe)
    - Sunday School
    - New believers Bible Study Course
    - Project Esther — good for all new believers regardless of age and gender.
    - New convert class
    - Foundations for Christian Living
    - Members are encouraged to foster these individuals and follow up ministry
    - One-on-one discipleship
    - We stay close to new believers and spend a lot of time ministering to them one on one
    - New believers class — Foundations for Faith.
- Yes — 6
    - A 9 week Discipleship Program
    - Christian Growth Class — Tuesdays as well as Mid-Week Bible Study

- One on one in our home
- Just started a Christian Growth Class — both new converts and "old saints" attend
- Small groups (spin off from Alpha model)
- Pastor does discipleship course with all new converts, great motivation
- Besides small group, a personal course one on one is suggested as well

- No — 41
- Yes, but it needs improvement — 9
- No, but we are in the process of starting one — 5

5. What does your assembly offer (or has recently offered)?

- Small groups — 18
- Prayer Meeting (with Bible Study) — 66
- A separate Bible Study night — 16
- Mini courses in doctrine or theology — 16
- Sunday School — 35
- Departmental programs (i.e., Men's Ministry, children's, youth) — 53

6. Does your assembly offer an "Introduction to Membership" course?

- Yes — 11
- No — 60 (We don't have anyone with a Doctorite Degree)?
- No, but we plan to begin one soon — 1

7. Which of these discipleship methods do you feel is most effective?

- Preaching —11
- Teaching — 38
- Small Groups — 21
- A program such as *Alpha* — 1
- Mid-week Bible Study and Prayer — 13
- The individual's personal devotions — 3
- Sunday School — 2

8. What do you consider to be the main challenge in moving our assemblies forward in discipleship?

- Lack of relationships — 10
- Lack of biblical knowledge — 8
- Lack of application of preaching — 5
- Lack of commitment — 35
- Lack of intentionality — 12
- Lack of Pentecostal focus and power — 5
- Lack of resources — 4
- Lack of personal devotional time — 9

9. What area of discipleship do you feel needs to be more clearly addressed?

- Vision casting — 7
- Relevant resources —
- Daily spiritual resources — 3
- Spiritual applications — 5
- More intentional teaching of doctrine — 7
- Opportunity for discussion and deeper questions — 8
- Re-thinking how we do discipleship altogether — 5
- All of the above — 19
- Other:

10. Additional comments you may wish to add:

- As important as Discipleship is, it seems we know it but fail to implement it. Fear, time, unsure, etc. are many factors.
- The biggest challenge I face on discipleship at my church is trying to take an approach that's applicable across generational gaps.
- We need to be on the same page in Doctrine, Administration Policies and Procedures.
- One on one is so time consuming but so transforming
- In our situation we have such a mixture of people at different levels it is hard to devote to one level.

- There should be a measuring tool to see where each assembly is in their Discipleship. Also, some assemblies and pastors need help starting.
- For retention - Discipleship is a must.

This information is based on 75 questionnaires received.
Some had multiple answers checked.

APPENDIX 3

Third PAONL Survey 2011

Discipleship Questionnaire
Pentecostal Assemblies of Newfoundland and Labrador
June 2011

Thank-you for participating!

The goal of this survey is to determine trends and practices within the PAONL regarding young adults in our assemblies. *We will define a young adult/young family as an individual or couple between the ages of 19 and 39 years old.* When answering the questions, keep in mind that we are collecting information for the purpose of better helping the Pastors and other leaders of our assemblies fulfill God's call to make disciples. The survey is anonymous and we appreciate your honest answers!

176 surveys were completed

Question 1
How satisfied are you with the number of young adults (age 19-39) in your local assembly?

- 35% (62) reported to be very dissatisfied with the number of young adults in their local assembly
- 36% (63) reported to be dissatisfied
- 16% had mixed feelings
- 10% were satisfied
- 2% were very satisfied
- 1% did not answer this question

Question 2
Please state the percentage of your congregation you believe to fit that profile.

- 3.5% are 0–12 years of age
- 10% are 13–18 years of age
- 5% are 18–27 years of age
- 20% are 27–45 years of age
- 30% are 46–65 years of age
- 32% are 65 and older

Question 3
How do you integrate young adults and young families into your assembly?

- 61% have young adults lead worship in their churches
- 37% have changed the start times and style of their services
- 25% have a young adult group
- 21% have a small group study for young adults
- 2% chose other
- 24% did not answer this question
- Others include:
    - Strong emphasis on involvement in various ministries
    - We get together from time to time
    - Social events
    - Children's emphasis
    - Activities such as bowling etc.
    - They minister in backup singing and sound
    - Ball hockey, and a program for moms with small children
    - Monthly services with children involved
    - Young couples bi-weekly social group
- Comments:
    - "We have no youth."
    - "Programs are conducted with them in mind."

- "We are a family church. All ages attend all events."
- "Those who attend are involved in all aspects of ministry."
- "Doing work in this area."
- "Not age specific because we are a small church but using multimedia power point etc. in a teaching mode on a Sunday morning."
- "Just hired a Family Ministries Pastor."
- "Other Church involvement. Currently discussing this need on a leadership level."

Question 4
We have one or more individuals of this age on our church board.

- 23% said yes
- 24% said yes and would like more
- 33% said no
- 12% said they cannot get anyone that age to let their stand
- 2% said no, despite their willingness, no one that age receives enough votes
- 6% did not answer this question

Question 5
What ministries to young families do you offer?

- 22% offer a small group for young families
- 64% offer nursery facilities
- 10% offer a parenting course
- 15% offer a marriage enrichment course
- 24% do not offer any of the above

Question 6
When I consider the changes in society in the last 40 years, I feel:

- 34% said they had a decent handle on what's happening and how to minister in this context
- 8% said that NL culture is changing too fast for them to keep up with: they're unsure how to proceed

- 51% said that they would like to better understand how to interact with our changing culture
- 2% said that there's too much talk of change; people are basically the same today as they were 40 years ago
- 5% did not answer this question

Question 7
Why do you think young families sometimes avoid church?

- 11% thought one of the reasons was due to boring preaching
- 42% thought one of the reasons was lack of personal maturity and commitment
- 27% thought one of the reasons was because of small children = inconvenience
- 65% thought one of the reasons was because they prefer leisure activities to church
- 30% thought one of the reasons was because the service is too traditional; worship is irrelevant
- 47% though one of the reasons was that they are too busy
- 31% thought one of the reasons was because they think they can be "spiritual" without attending church regularly
- 14% thought one of the reasons was because church is too formal and stuffy
- Comments:
  - "I would also say — their views of Spirituality have shifted from 'formal' church connections to 'relational' connections and friendships. The Church has not done well to shift in that area."
  - "They all say they are the 'only one their age' instead of setting an example they'd rather follow."
  - "They have no interest what so ever!"
  - "Church is not part of their tradition. Non-Pentecostal, past hurts, not on radar"
  - "Many have not yet had a real experience with Christ – They have a dozen other 'gods'"
  - "Many have been offended and hurt in the past."

- "They don't see the need/relevancy."
- "Question people 'Christians' sitting in pew feel they are just as good."
- "The vast majority of the out port churches are older (traditionally). Rapid change is having a tendency to leave older saints behind (resulting in inner conflict)."
- "We have to adopt and change with our time – Please help us do so!"
- Other reasons include; past hurts, backslidden, and church is lacking in priorities.
- "Legalism from by gone years."
- "The loss of testimony. The church has gotten in the way of Christ."
- "This age group has been hurt/offended across the board"
- "I wonder if our leadership is committed and these young people use them as role models."
- "Are we really relevant in worship? Testimonies? Preaching? I don't think so."
- "Not accepted within church context."

Question 8
How do you think young families would answer question 7?

- 13% chose that young families would say they avoid church because of boring preaching
- 13% chose that young families would say they avoid church because of lack of maturity and commitment
- 40% chose that young families would say they avoid church because of small children/inconvenience
- 49% chose that young families would say they avoid church because they prefer leisure activities to church
- 34% chose that young families would say they avoid church because the service is too traditional; worship is irrelevant
- 54% chose that young families would say they avoid church because they are too busy
- 44% chose that young families would say they avoid church because they can be spiritual without attending church regularly

- 22% chose that young families would say they avoid church because it is too formal and stuffy
- Comments:
  - "Let's connect and be open and be available to change."
  - "They want to attend church at their own convenience."
  - "You can believe what you want and I'll believe what I want."
  - "They don't see the need/relevancy."
  - "Been offended/hurt in the past."
  - "They're totally unaware of what we offer."
  - "No interest."
  - "The usual statement on attending Sunday p.m. is young children and work the next day."

Question 9
What are your greatest frustrations with this age group?

- 79% say they are frustrated with this age group because they are not committed
- 29% say they are frustrated with this age group because they do not give their time or money
- 44% say they are frustrated with this age group because they do not take their faith seriously
- 31% say they are frustrated with this age group because of their declining levels of holiness
- 17% say they are frustrated with this age group because of their lack of appreciation for their heritage and traditions
- 35% say they are frustrated with this age group because of their weak understanding of what it means to be a Pentecostal
- 5% are either not frustrated with this age group, or just did not answer this question
- Comments:
  - "It is unclear if they are really strongly loyal to the church or the Lord."
  - "They have no concept of Salvation. They don't need what we are selling."

- "This age group is declining in rural areas and is very small in our community."
- "Not so much frustrated with this age group as with the older age group who are making it difficult for them."
- "I could check more than three. They all apply."
- "I don't think any of these apply to our local church. They are a very strong group in our church."
- "Not frustrated! This age group is very connected in church."
- "Younger pastors do not have the same commitment which filters through to the younger families."
- "They don't help us reach the lost."
- "Their focus is spiritual not necessarily on traditional faith."
- "They are hard to reach with the gospel."
- "They want their children to be saved, but have no interest in salvation."
- "Rurally speaking, many Pentecostal young people leave the communities. We grow them and pass them on — how I wish they could stay and be a part of church life after high school."
- "Busy lives."

Question 10
What do you think young adults would list as their #1 frustration with the church?

- 27% said hypocrisy of members
- 31% said church services are irrelevant to their lives and where they are
- 1% said the preaching is for seniors; they cannot get into the style or content
- 10% said all the church worries about is what happens within its four walls
- 14% said it is far too judgemental
- 6% said the church does not care about the important social issues such as poverty, AIDS, injustice towards homosexuals and others
- 11% did not answer this question

- Comments:
  - "Making faith relevant in the context of the post-Modern may be lacking in our preaching/teaching."
  - "A feeling of hypocrisy not just of today but a learning and understanding of how the church has been in hundreds of years prior."
  - "Just isn't important."
  - "Rather it seems young adults struggle here — they too seem very 'self centered' in action but 'social in speech only.'"

Question 11
Do you or your assembly intentionally follow up on teens when they leave home for University or work?

- 57% said yes
- 28% said no
- 15% did not answer this question

Question 12
How old are you?

- 13% were between the ages of 20–30
- 15% were between the ages of 30–40
- 26% were between the ages of 40–50
- 26% were between the ages of 50–60
- 17% were 60 and over
- 3% did not answer this question

Additional Comments

- "Within our church, two things come into play: 1) This age group feels unaccepted and judged and 2) an importance is on kids receiving spirituality NOT the parents."
- "These young adults have huge potential. I think that if we do not bridge the gap, our church will suffer the loss of a whole generation. We need to take the focus off of how we like church and change to how church should be."

- "I think this survey is an amazing tool and needs to be done. Our age group (30–40) is absent from far too much."
- "We have started a coffee house to help get to know the young people. We haven't had any young person leave since we came."
- "This is an un-established church with a community background that the community church 'non-Pentecostal' dominates the community."
- "Our assembly is vibrant with young families; I'm sure we are not 'average' in this area."
- "Thank you! Looking forward to the results. We are moving in this direction."
- "Thank you for this survey!"
- "We have a positive percentage of this age group, but they are not interested for the most part in Church life. They need to be motivated to grow in Jesus."
- "I believe that this needs to be a focus of the church, trying to reach this age bracket."
- "It is frustrating trying to minister to young adults but I have learned that when you get to know them and their hearts, they are hungry for more of God. Great survey Brad!"
- "I commend the effort to investigate and further understand this age group. My frustration is with the fact that having pastored two large churches in the last 15 years that I/we have tried 'almost everything' but with little success. It leaves me feeling that I'm 'chasing the mouse around the room'! But I have every intention to catch the mouse! Amen!"
- "We are just not seeing the group connect with church. Kids are struggling to connect with church most of the way through. When youth ministry age is done they drop out it seems."
- "Part of the reason that the 19–39 age group is not well represented in our church is that this is the age that they move out for education or work, which means St. John's or Alberta. They do not return until they are ready to retire."
- "To be honest the young adults in my church are very reliable. A lot of them are in leadership positions and we are very much involved. They may lack in areas of holiness, but overall they are good Christians."

- "I feel we have a healthy young adult ministry; however, service aspect on a bi-weekly basis is not well attended. They are too busy with family and life to attend regularly."
- "This age group has been neglected too long."
- "Please help us step in the right direction!"
- "We are looking at starting Alpha as a means for young adults to ask the hard questions and get some real answers."
- "We are trying some activities to reach out to young couples such as: sweetheart banquets, bowling nights, etc."
- "Many young adults are moving away. Still those that stay need to be a part of the church."
- "There are a lot of changes taking place in our society and the church seems to be trying to keep up with these changes and in doing so 'I believe' the church has lost its way in the world. Therefore, it (the church) is making very little impact on society."
- "I am living in a community of mostly retirees but there are a number of new families moving into the community. Praying for direction and have made contact with several of them."
- "I think our church is trying to be pro-active with this age group because the Y/A say they want things for them and for something to be practical and relevant. However, they are so hard to make happy because at the end of the day they will always have a better reason not to attend the functions you put off to cater to them, very non-committed!"
- "Making the church relevant to their community has always been a challenge in every generation. Folk have to understand that when we talk about the church, one has to realize they speak of ourselves. People are the church — not a structure."

APPENDIX 4

Provincial Survey of PAONL Membership 2012

PAONL Discipleship Survey

Thank you for participating in this anonymous survey on discipleship for the PAONL. Please note we are seeking your opinion only; there are no right or wrong answers. Definitions for certain terms are provided for your reference in answering the questions. For each of the questions below, please circle only one answer which represents the opinion which most closely represents your own. If the question is not relevant to you, please circle "N/A" as your response.

Vision
A clear vision reflects what the congregation believes, provides a direction, and charts a way to get there. Vision requires a strong sense of identity.

On a scale from 1 to 5, where 1 is "Strongly Disagree" and 5 is "Strongly Agree", please indicate how strongly you agree or disagree with each of the statements.	Strongly Disagree				Strongly Agree	
1. As Pentecostals, we know who we are.	1	2	3	4	5	N/A
2. Within our church, we have a strong sense of identity.	1	2	3	4	5	N/A
3. Our church has a clear idea of our direction for the future.	1	2	3	4	5	N/A

On a scale from 1 to 5, where 1 is "Strongly Disagree" and 5 is "Strongly Agree", please indicate how strongly you agree or disagree with each of the statements.	Strongly Disagree				Strongly Agree	
4. Our church is aware of the key elements of our beliefs which must remain constant as we move into the future.	1	2	3	4	5	N/A
5. I am able to tell someone what the vision of our church is.	1	2	3	4	5	N/A
6. I am confident in the leadership provided by our church.	1	2	3	4	5	N/A
7. I believe the mission of our church is clear.	1	2	3	4	5	N/A
8. The core values of our church are the same today as they were in the past.	1	2	3	4	5	N/A

Relationships

Through relationships the church attracts people to Christ and connects them to each other and to God. Through relationships people begin their journey in faith and deepen spiritually. Through relationships people are encouraged to engage in their area of ministry.

On a scale from 1 to 5, where 1 is "Strongly Disagree" and 5 is "Strongly Agree", please indicate how strongly you agree or disagree with each of the statements.	Strongly Disagree				Strongly Agree	
9. Our church is as concerned with reaching out to the community as it is with what's going on within its four walls.	1	2	3	4	5	N/A
10. Our church has a clear strategy for reaching out to the people of our community.	1	2	3	4	5	N/A
11. When a new person comes to our church they receive a warm welcome.	1	2	3	4	5	N/A

On a scale from 1 to 5, where 1 is "Strongly Disagree" and 5 is "Strongly Agree", please indicate how strongly you agree or disagree with each of the statements.	Strongly Disagree				Strongly Agree	
12. Our church has an effective program for following up with a newcomer.	1	2	3	4	5	N/A
13. I have as many strong relationships with people outside the church as I do with people inside our church.	1	2	3	4	5	N/A
14. Our congregation has opportunities to share with one another what God is doing in our lives.	1	2	3	4	5	N/A
15. I would describe our church as a warm and caring place.	1	2	3	4	5	N/A
16. I would be comfortable approaching a member of the pastoral staff with a concern or issue.	1	2	3	4	5	N/A
17. Our church leadership has a burden for the lost.	1	2	3	4	5	N/A
18. I feel comfortable inviting someone from my relationships outside church to come to church with me.	1	2	3	4	5	N/A
19. In our church, individual and/or group conflicts are resolved in a Christ-like way.	1	2	3	4	5	N/A
20. Within our church mature Christians mentor new believers into following and growing in Christ.	1	2	3	4	5	N/A
21. Our church leadership encourages practices that unify the church.	1	2	3	4	5	N/A
22. Our church leadership reflects character traits that engender trust in our people.	1	2	3	4	5	N/A
23. A healthy relationship exists in our church between the pastoral staff and the congregation.	1	2	3	4	5	N/A

On a scale from 1 to 5, where 1 is "Strongly Disagree" and 5 is "Strongly Agree", please indicate how strongly you agree or disagree with each of the statements.	Strongly Disagree				Strongly Agree	
24. Our church provides an opportunity for people to engage in a discipleship program.	1	2	3	4	5	N/A
25. Our congregational leaders reflect servanthood, morality and respect for all persons.	1	2	3	4	5	N/A
26. Our church leaders provide a process for people to shape a vision for the church.	1	2	3	4	5	N/A
27. Our leaders share information and authority needed to empower others to engage in ministry.	1	2	3	4	5	N/A
28. Our leaders help the church to celebrate God's blessing on the ministry of the church.	1	2	3	4	5	N/A
29. People are encouraged to develop devotional time and a vibrant prayer life.	1	2	3	4	5	N/A

Programs

The programs of the church reflect its identity and vision for ministry. Programs depend upon the involvement of both the leadership and lay members of the church, and must meet the real social, emotional and spiritual needs of the people.

On a scale from 1 to 5, where 1 is "Strongly Disagree" and 5 is "Strongly Agree", please indicate how strongly you agree or disagree with each of the statements.	Strongly Disagree				Strongly Agree	
30. Our church has a vibrant and effective youth ministry.	1	2	3	4	5	N/A
31. Our church has a vibrant and effective children's ministry.	1	2	3	4	5	N/A

On a scale from 1 to 5, where 1 is "Strongly Disagree" and 5 is "Strongly Agree", please indicate how strongly you agree or disagree with each of the statements.

	Strongly Disagree				Strongly Agree	
32. There are Christian education opportunities for all ages in our church.	1	2	3	4	5	N/A
33. During our worship services an unchurched individual would likely sense the presence of the Holy Spirit.	1	2	3	4	5	N/A
34. New members to our church receive basic training on the fundamentals of Pentecostal doctrine.	1	2	3	4	5	N/A
35. Prayer is a regular part of our worship services.	1	2	3	4	5	N/A
36. Our church places a strong emphasis on the power and importance of prayer.	1	2	3	4	5	N/A
37. Regular Bible study is featured in our ministry programs.	1	2	3	4	5	N/A
38. In our church we encourage the sick to be anointed and prayed for.	1	2	3	4	5	N/A
39. The gifts of the Holy Spirit are regularly manifested in our services.	1	2	3	4	5	N/A
40. Believers are encouraged to be baptized in water.	1	2	3	4	5	N/A
41. The Baptism in the Holy Spirit is emphasized in our church.	1	2	3	4	5	N/A
42. Our church uses programs that are creative and invigorating.	1	2	3	4	5	N/A
43. Our church provides relevant programs for all ages.	1	2	3	4	5	N/A
44. Our church's music ministry effectively leads us into worship.	1	2	3	4	5	N/A
45. People in our church are encouraged to engage in intercessory prayer ministry.	1	2	3	4	5	N/A

On a scale from 1 to 5, where 1 is "Strongly Disagree" and 5 is "Strongly Agree", please indicate how strongly you agree or disagree with each of the statements.

	Strongly Disagree				Strongly Agree	
46. Sermons are devoted to the work of the Holy Spirit in our lives.	1	2	3	4	5	N/A
47. Believers are given an understanding of end times events.	1	2	3	4	5	N/A
48. Our people have a strong set of principles based on Scripture.	1	2	3	4	5	N/A

Management

Management is concerned with how decisions are made in administering the resources of the church.

On a scale from 1 to 5, where 1 is "Strongly Disagree" and 5 is "Strongly Agree", please indicate how strongly you agree or disagree with each of the statements.

	Strongly Disagree				Strongly Agree	
49. Our church ministries reflect successful planning and organization.	1	2	3	4	5	N/A
50. Most of the decisions in our church are made by the pastoral staff and church board.	1	2	3	4	5	N/A
51. Congregational members are given opportunity to influence how church ministries are developed and carried out.	1	2	3	4	5	N/A
52. Our pastors seek the help of others to provide support in ministry areas where they are not gifted.	1	2	3	4	5	N/A
53. Our congregation is fully informed of the goals that will shape our future ministries.	1	2	3	4	5	N/A

On a scale from 1 to 5, where 1 is "Strongly Disagree" and 5 is "Strongly Agree", please indicate how strongly you agree or disagree with each of the statements.

	Strongly Disagree				Strongly Agree	
54. The Annual General Meeting provides the main opportunity for the review of church ministries.	1	2	3	4	5	N/A
55. Our leadership encourages lay members to develop and use their knowledge and skills in running church ministries.	1	2	3	4	5	N/A

56. Of the four major elements, *Vision, Relationships, Programs,* and *Management,* which *one* element would you consider to be the strongest component of your local assembly? *(Circle only one answer)*

   1. Vision
   2. Relationships
   3. Programs
   4. Management

Based on the definitions provided above, on a scale from 1 to 5, where 1 is "very weak", and 5 is "very strong", please indicate how strong or weak you believe each of these elements are for your local assembly.

	Very Weak				Very Strong	
57. Vision	1	2	3	4	5	N/A
58. Relationships	1	2	3	4	5	N/A
59. Programs	1	2	3	4	5	N/A
60. Management	1	2	3	4	5	N/A

This final section collects broad demographic information and will be used to categorize responses.

61. Do you hold membership with this local assembly?

    1. Yes
    2. No
    3. Unsure
    4. Our church does not have membership

62. Which of the following best describes your attendance at this local assembly?

    1. Regularly Attend (one per week)
    2. Periodically Attend (once per month)
    3. Rarely Attend (several times per year)
    4. Visitor

63. Are you a member of a Small Group / Bible Study within this local assembly?

    1. Regularly Attend (most meetings)
    2. Periodically Attend
    3. Do Not Attend

64. Do you have children currently attending this local assembly?

    1. Yes
    2. No
    3. I do not have children

65. Into which of the following general ranges does your age fall?

   1. Less than 14
   2. 14 – 24
   3. 25 – 44
   4. 45 – 64
   5. 65 and over

66. Which of the following best describes your current marital status?

   1. Single
   2. Married
   3. Divorced
   4. Widowed
   5. Other

67. Are you:

   1. Male
   2. Female

Works Cited

"2011 National Household Survey: Data Tables" http://www12.statcan.gc.ca/nhs-enm/2011/dp-pd/dt-td/Rp-eng.cfm?LANG=E&APATH=3&DETAIL=0&DIM=0&FL=A&FREE=0&GC=0&GID=0&GK=0&GRP=0&PID=105399&PRID=0&PTYPE=105277&S=0&SHOWALL=0&SUB=0&Temporal=2013&THEME=95&VID=0&VNAMEE=&VNAMEF=.

"Benedict XVI Signals Support for Ecclesial Movements." http://www.zenit.org/en/articles/benedict-xvi-signals-support-for-ecclesial-movements.

"Bible Engagement in Churchgoers' Hearts, Not Always Practiced." *Lifeway Research* (2013). http://www.lifewayresearch.com/2013/11/15/bible-engagement-in-churchgoers-hearts-not-always-practiced-2/.

"The Charismatic Movement and Orthodoxy." http://orthodoxinfo.com/inquirers/charmov.aspx.

"Charter Affirming the Values of State Secularism and Religious Neutrality and of Equality between Women and Men, and Providing a Framework for Accommodation Requests." http://www.nosvaleurs.gouv.qc.ca/medias/pdf/Charter.pdf.

"'Christ and Culture' by Richard Niebuhr: Book Summary." In *Regeneration: A Tryst with (Indian) Theology*, 2014.

"Christianity Reborn." http://www.economist.com/node/8401206.

"Community Covenant Agreement: Our Pledge to One Another." http://twu.ca/studenthandbook/twu-community-covenant-agreement.pdf .

"Discipleship: Helping Jesus' Followers Become His Closest Friends." http://ag.org/discipleship_downloads/what_is_discipleship.pdf.

"Generational Comparisons." http://www.bellarmine.edu/documents/Generational Comparisons.pdf.

"History of Catholic Charismatic Renewal." http://www.diolaf.org/index.cfm?load=page&page=734 .

"Leadership in the Life Cycle" http://www.docstoc.com/docs/54004759/Leadership-in-the-Life-Cycle.

"No Gay-Free Law School Should Stand in Canada." http://www.theglobeandmail.com/globe-debate/editorials/no-gay-free-law-school-should-stand-in-canada/article8356107/.

"'Nones' on the Rise." http://www.pewforum.org/2012/10/09/nones-on-the-rise/-.UHSMWEgSEQ4.facebook.

"O Come All Ye Faithful." http://www.economist.com/node/10015239/print.

"Pentecostal Assemblies of Newfoundland and Labrador: We Believe…" http://www.paonl.ca/content/beliefs.

"Post Christian Society: What Is Meant by the Term "Post-Christian?" http://www.spiritrenewalministries.com/Post Christian.html.

"Quebec Religious Symbols Ban Proposal Roundly Condemned." http://news.ca.msn.com/top-stories/quebec-religious-symbols-ban-proposal-roundly-condemned.

"School Cross to Be Removed after Parent Complaint." http://www.cbc.ca/news/canada/newfoundland-labrador/school-cross-to-be-removed-after-parent-complaint-1.1321152.

"Town of Hampstead Won't Apply 'Racist' Quebec Charter." http://www.cbc.ca/news/canada/montreal/town-of-hampstead-won-t-apply-racist-quebec-charter-1.2448915.

"Weird Babble of Tongues on Azusa Street." *Los Angeles Times*, April 18 1906.

"What Is the Likely Future of Generation AO in 2020?" *Imagining the Internet: A History and Forecast*. http://www.elon.edu/docs/e-web/predictions/expertsurveys/2012survey/PIP_Future_of_Internet_2012_Gen_Always_ON.pdf.

Adams, Michael. *Stayin' Alive: How Canadian Baby Boomers Will Work, Play, and Find Meaning in the Second Half of Their Adult Lives.* Toronto: Viking Canada, 2010.

Albrecht, D.E. *Rites in the Spirit: A Ritual Approach to Pentecostal/Charismatic Spirituality.* Journal of Pentecostal Theology Supplementary Series 17, edited by John Christopher Thomas, Rickie D. Moore and Steven J. Land. Sheffield, UK: Sheffield Academic, 1999.

Alexander, Estrelda. *Limited Liberty: The Legacy of Four Pentecostal Women Pioneers.* Cleveland, TN: Pilgrim, 2008.

Anderson, Allan. "The Origins of Pentecostalism and Its Global Spread in the Early Twentieth Century." http://www.ocms.ac.uk/docs/Allan Anderson lecture20041005.pdf.

Anderson, Allan. *An Introduction to Pentecostalism*. Cambridge: Cambridge University, 2004.

Anderson, Allan. "To All Points of the Compass: The Azusa Street Revival and Global Pentecostalism." *Enrichment*, (2013).

Anderson, Allan. "Transformation of World Christianity: Challenges and Opportunities for Pentecostalism." Lecture, Annual Meeting of the Society for Pentecostal Studies, Lakeland, FL, 12–14 March, 2015.

Anderson, Myra and Stephen De Silva. *Beliefs, Values and Attitudes.* PSHE Strategies and Skills, Edited by Hilary Dixon. Sedbergh, Cumbria, UK: Me-and-Us, 2009.

Anderson, Robert Mapes. *Vision of the Disinherited: The Making of American Pentecostalism*. Peabody: Hendrickson, 1979.

Archer, Kenneth J. "Pentecostal Story: The Hermeneutical Filter for the Making of Meaning." *Pneuma* 26, no. 1 (2004): 36–59.

Baklinski, Thaddeus. "Ontario Tribunal Bans Bible Distribution Unless School Board Also Gives out Atheist Texts" http://www.lifesitenews.com/news/ontario-tribunal-bans-bible-distribution-unless-school-board-also-gives-out.

Barfoot, Chas H. *Aimee Semple McPherson and the Making of Modern Pentecostalism, 1890-1926.* London: Equinox, 2011.

Barna, George. *The Barna Report: What Americans Believe - an Annual Survey of Values and Religious Views in the United States.* Ventura, CA: Regal Books, 1991.

Barrett, D.B. and T.M. Johnston. "Global Statistics." In *The New International Dictionary of Pentecostal and Charismatic Movements*, edited by S.M. Burgess and E.M. Van der Mass. Grand Rapids: Zondervan, 2002.
Barth, Karl. *God in Action: Theological Addresses*. Translated by E.G. Homrighausen and K.J. Ernst. New York: Round Table, 1936.
Bartleman, Frank. *Azusa Street*. S. Plainfield, NJ: Bridge Publishing, 1980.
Bartleman, Frank. *Another Wave of Revival*. Revised ed. Springdale, PA: Whitaker House, 1982.
Baucham Jr., Voddie. *The Ever-Loving Truth: Can Faith Thrive in a Post-Christian Culture?* Nashville, TN: Broadman & Holman, 2004.
Bauerlein, Mark. *The Dumbest Generation: How the Digital Age Stupefies Young Americans and Jeopardizes Our Future*. New York: Penguin, 2009.
Beaman, Lori G. *Religion and Canadian Society: Traditions, Transitions, and Innovations*. Toronto: CSP, 2006.
Beaman, Lori Gail and Peter Beyer. *Religion and Diversity in Canada*. Vol. 16. Boston: Brill, 2008.
Beaudoin, Tom. *Virtual Faith: The Irreverent Spiritual Quest of Generation X*. San Francisco: Jossey-Bass, 1998.
Bell, Rob. *Love Wins: A Book About Heaven, Hell, and the Fate of Every Person Who Ever Lived*. New York: Harper Collins, 2011.
Bennet, Dennis. *Nine O'clock in the Morning*. Plainfield, NJ: Bridge Publishing, 1970.
Berends, Kurt O. *A Divided Harvest: Alice Belle Garrigus, Joel Adams Wright, and Early New England Pentecostalism*. Department of Bible and Theology, Wheaton College Graduate School, 1993.
Berends, Kurt O. "Cultivating for a Harvest: The Early Life of Alice Belle Garrigus." *Pneuma* 17, no. 1 (1995): 37–49.
Berger, Peter L. *The Noise of Solemn Assemblies*. Garden City, NY: Doubleday, 1961.
Berger, Peter L. *The Sacred Canopy: Elements of a Sociological Theory of Religion*. Garden City, NY: Anchor Doubleday, 1967.
Berger, Peter L. *The Desecularization of the World: Resurgent Religion and World Politics*. Grand Rapids: Eerdmans, 1999.
Beverley, James A. *Holy Laughter and the Toronto Blessing: An Investigative Report*. Grand Rapids: Zondervan, 1995.
Bibby, Reginald W. *Restless Gods: The Renaissance of Religion in Canada*. Toronto: Novalis Publishing, 2004.
Bibby, Reginald W. *The Boomer Factor: What Canada's Most Famous Generation Is Leaving Behind*. Toronto: Bastion Books, 2006.
Bibby, Reginald W. *The Emerging Millennials: How Canada's Newest Generation Is Responding to Change and Choice*. Lethbridge, AB: Project Canada Books, 2009.
Bibby, Reginald W. *The Resilience & Restructuring of Religion in Canada*. Lethbridge, AB: Project Canada Books, 2012.
Bibby, Reginald W. "Continuing the Conversation on Canada: Changing Patterns of Religious Service Attendance." *JSSR Journal for the Scientific Study of Religion* 50, no. 4 (2011): 831–837.
Bibby, Reginald W. *Fragmented Gods: The Poverty and Potential of Religion in Canada*. Toronto: Irwin Publishing, 1987.
Bibby, Reginald W. *Beyond the Gods & Back: Religion's Demise and Rise and Why It Matters*. Lethbridge, AB: Project Canada Books 2011.

Bibby, Reginald W. and Donald C. Posterski. *Teen Trends: A Nation in Motion*. Toronto: Stoddart 1992.

Bliese, Richard. "The Mission Matrix: Mapping out the Complexities of a Missional Ecclesiology." *Word and World* 26, no. 3 (2006): 237–248.

Blumhofer, Edith. *Aimee Semple McPherson: Everybody's Sister*. Grand Rapids: Eerdmans, 1993.

Blumhofer, Edith. "Reflections on the Source of Aimee Semple McPherson's Voice." *Pneuma* 17, no. 1 (1995): 21–24.

Blumhofer, Edith. "Sister." *Christian History* 58, (1998). https://www.christian historyinstitute.org/uploaded/50cf83d3192469.20505915.pdf.

Borlase, Craig. *William Seymour: A Biography*. Lake Mary, FL: Charisma House, 2006.

Bosch, David J. *Transforming Mission: Paradigm Shifts in Theology of Mission*. Maryknoll, NY: Orbis Books, 1991.

Bowen, Kurt Derek. *Christians in a Secular World: The Canadian Experience*. McGill-Queen's Studies in the History of Religion, Edited by Donald Harman Akenson. Montreal: McGill-Queen's University, 2004.

Boyd, Gregory. *Oneness Pentecostals and the Trinity*. Grand Rapids: Baker, 1992.

Brown, Derek. "Is Cultural Engagement Biblical?" In *Rediscovering the Kingdom of God*, 2011.

Brown, Peter. *The Rise of Western Christendom: Triumph and Diversity, AD 200-1000*. Vol. 1. Toronto: John Wiley & Sons, 2012.

Bruce, Steve, ed. *Religion and Modernization: Sociologists and Historians Debate the Secularization Thesis*. Oxford: Oxford University, 1992.

Brueggemann, Walter. *The Word That Redescribes the World: The Bible and Discipleship*. Minneapolis: Fortress, 2006.

Brumback, Carl. *What Meaneth This?: A Pentecostal Answer to a Pentecostal Question*. Springfield, MO: Gospel Publishing House, 1947.

Bryum, Russell. *Holy Spirit Baptism and the 2nd Cleansing*. Anderson, IN: Gospel Trumpet, 1923. Reprint, Guthrie, OK: Faith Publishing House, n.d.

Bullard, George. "The Life Cycle and Stages of Congregational Development." http://www.kingdomworksonline.org/uploads/stages_of_church_life_bullard_1_.pdf.

Cannon, William R. *The Theology of John Wesley*. New York: University of America, n.d.

Carlson, Elwood. "20th Century U.S. Generations." *Population Reference Bureau* (March 2009). http://www.prb.org/Publications/Reports/2009/20thcenturyusgen erations.aspx.

Carlson, Jason, "Emerging Vs. Emergent Churches: Clearing up the Confusion" http://www.worldviewweekend.com/worldview-times/article.php?articleid=1645-sthash.JHebzlYf.dpuf.

Carson, D. A. *Becoming Conversant with the Emerging Church: Understanding a Movement and Its Implications*. Grand Rapids: Zondervan, 2005.

Carson, D. A. *Christ and Culture Revisited*. Grand Rapids: Eerdmans, 2008

Carter, Craig A. *Rethinking Christ and Culture: A Post-Christendom Perspective*. Grand Rapids: Brazos, 2007.

Cartledge, David. *The Apostolic Revolution: The Restoration of Apostles and Prophets in the Assemblies of God in Australia*. Chester Hill, Australia: Paraclete Institute, 2000.

Chalke, Steve and Alan Mann. *The Lost Message of Jesus*. Grand Rapids: Zondervan, 2003.

Chan, Simon. *Pentecostal Theology and the Christian Spiritual Tradition*. Journal of Pentecostal Theology Supplementary, Edited by John Christopher Thomas, Rickie D. Moore and Steven J. Land. Sheffield, UK: Sheffield Academic, 2000.

Chan, Simon. *Pentecostal Ecclesiology: An Essay on the Development of Doctrine*. Journal of Pentecostal Theology Supplementary, Edited by Rickie D. Moore, John Christopher Thomas, Steven J. Land. Blandford Forum, UK: DEO Publishing, 2011.

The Charismatic Movement and Lutheran Theology. A Report of the Commission on Theology and Church Relations of the Lutheran Church - Missouri Synod, 1972.

Christenson, Larry. "The Charismatic Movement: An Historical and Theological Perspective." http://www.lutheranrenewal.org/The_Charismatic_Movement2.pdf.

Christie, Nancy and Michael Gauvreau. *Christian Churches and Their Peoples, 1840-1965: A Social History of Religion in Canada*. Toronto: University of Toronto, 2010.

Cimino, Richard and Christopher Smith. "The New Atheism and the Formation of the Imagined Secularist Community." *Journal of Media and Religion* 10, no. 1 (2011): 24–38.

Cohen, Michael Lee. *The Twenty-Something American Dream: A Cross-Country Quest for a Generation*. New York: Dutton, 1993.

Combs, William W. "The Biblical Role of the Evangelist." *Detroit Baptist Seminary Journal* 7, (2002): 23–48.

Cox, Harvey Gallagher. *Fire from Heaven: The Rise of Pentecostal Spirituality and the Reshaping of Religion in the Twenty-First Century*. Reading, MA: Addison-Wesley Pub, 1995.

Craven, Michael. "The Church in Post-Christendom." *The Christian Post* (2008). http://www.christianpost.com/news/the-church-in-post-christendom-31585/.

Cravit, David. *The New Old: How the Boomers Are Changing Everything... Again*. Toronto: ECW, 2008.

Cross, Terry. "The Rich Feast of Theology: Can Pentecostals Bring the Main Course or Only the Relish?" *Journal of Pentecostal Theology* 8, no. 16 (2000): 27-47.

Crysdale, Stewart and Les Wheatcroft, eds. *Religion in Canadian Society*. Toronto: MacLean Hunter, 1976.

Cunningham, J. Barton. *Researching Organizational Values and Beliefs: The Echo Approach*. Westport, CT: Greenwood Publishing Group, 2001.

Davidson, Janet, "Are We Living in Post-Religious Times?" http://www.cbc.ca/news/canada/are-we-living-in-post-religious-times-1.1362828.

Davis, Richard B. "Can There Be an "Orthodox" Postmodern Theology?" *Journal of the Evangelical Theological Society* 45, no. 1 (2002): 111–124.

Dawe, R.H. "Denominational Education in Newfoundland and Labrador: An Analysis of the Effects of Sociopychological Factors on Attitudes toward Church Involvement in Education and Educational Change." Memorial University of Newfoundland, 1995.

Dawkins, Richard. *The God Delusion*. Boston: Houghton Mifflin Co., 2006.

Dayton, Donald W. *The Theological Roots of Pentecostalism*. Peabody: Hendrickson, 1987.

Dayton, Donald W. "The Limits of Evangelicalism: The Pentecostal Tradition." In *The Varieties of American Evangelicalism*, edited by Donald W. Dayton and Robert K. Johnston. Downers Grove: IVP, 1991.

Del Colle, Ralph. "Postmodernism and the Pentecostal-Charismatic Experience." *Journal of Pentecostal Theology* 8, no. 17 (2000): 97–116.

Dempster, Murray W., et al. *The Globalization of Pentecostalism: A Religion Made to Travel*. Irvine, CA: Regnum Books International, 1999.

Dempster, Murray W., Byron D. Klaus and Douglas Petersen, eds. *Called and Empowered: Global Mission in Pentecostal Perspective*. Grand Rapids: Baker Books, 1991.

DePaul, Michael R. *Resurrecting Old-Fashioned Foundationalism*. Lanham, MD: Rowman & Littlefield, 2000.

Derrida, Jacques. *Of Grammatology*. Translated by Gayatri Chakravorty Spivak. Baltimore: Johns Hopkins University, 1976.

Derrida, Jacques. *Margins of Philosophy*. Translated by Alan Bass. Chicago: University of Chicago, 1982.

Derrida, Jacques. "Force of Law: The Mystical Foundations of Authority." In *Deconstruction and the Possibility of Justice*, edited by Drucilla Cornell, Michel Rosenfield and David Gray Carlson. New York: Routledge, 1992.

DeYoung, Kevin and Ted Kluck. *Why We're Not Emergent: By Two Guys Who Should Be*. Chicago: Moody Publishers, 2008.

Di Giacomo, Michael. "Aimee Semple McPherson: 'Shot in the Arm' for French-Canadian Protestantism." In *Winds from the North: Canadian Contributions to the Pentecostal Movement*, edited by Peter Althouse and Michael Wilkinson. Boston: Brill, 2010.

Dieter, Melvin E., et al. *Five Views of Sanctification*. Grand Rapids: Zondervan, 1987.

Douglas, James Dixon and Robert G. Clouse. *New 20th Century Encyclopedia of Religious Knowledge*. 2nd ed. Grand Rapids: Baker Publishing Group, 1991.

Duncan, Kent. "Emerging Engagement: The Growing Social Conscience of Pentecostalism." *Enrichment Journal*. http://enrichmentjournal.ag.org/201201/201201_EJO_Emerg_Engag.cfm.

Dunn, James D. G. *Baptism in the Holy Spirit: A Re-Examination of the New Testament Teaching on the Gift of the Spirit in Relation to Pentecostalism Today*. Philadelphia: Westminster, 1970.

Dunn, James D.G. "Spirit-Baptism and Pentecostalism." *Scottish Journal of Theology* 23, (1970): 397-399.

Dyck, Drew. "The Leavers: More Than in Previous Generations, 20-and 30-Somethings Are Abandoning the Faith. Why?" *Christianity Today*, November 2010, 40.

Dyck, Drew. *Generation Ex-Christian: Why Young Adults Are Leaving the Faith...And How to Bring Them Back*. Chicago: Moody, 2010.

Eco, Umberto. *Postscript to the Name of the Rose*. Translated by William Weaver. New York: Harcourt Brace Jovanovich, 1989.

Egerton, George. "Trudeau, God, and the Canadian Constution: Religion, Human Rights, and Government Authority in the Making of the 1982 Constitution." In *Rethinking Church, State, and Modernity: Canada between Europe and America*, edited by David Lyon and Marguerite Van Die. Toronto: University of Toronto, 2000.

Ellyson, E.P. *Doctrinal Studies*. Kansas City: Nazarene Publishing House, 1936.

Epstein, Daniel Mark. *Sister Aimee: The Life of Aimee Semple McPherson*. San Diego: Harcourt Brace & Co., 1993.

Erickson, Millard J. *Truth or Consequences: The Promise & Perils of Postmodernism.* Downers Grove: InterVarsity, 2001.

Erickson, Millard J. *The Postmodern World: Discerning the Spirit of Our Age.* Wheaton: Crossway, 2002.

Faupel, D. William. *The Everlasting Gospel: The Significance of Eschatology in the Development of Pentecostal Thought.* Journal of Pentecostal Theology Supplementary Series 10. Edited by John Christopher Thomas, Rickie D. Moore and Steven J. Land. Sheffield, UK: Sheffield Academic, 1996.

Fee, Gordon D. *Gospel and Spirit: Issues in New Testament Hermeneutics.* Grand Rapids: Baker 1991.

Ferrin, Scott Ellis, et al. "From Sectarian to Secular Control of Education: The Case of Newfoundland." *Journal of Research on Christian Education* 10, (2001): 411–430.

Finger, Thomas. "Modernity, Postmodernity-What in the World Are They?" *Transformation: An International Journal of Holistic Mission Studies* 10, no. 4 (1993): 20–26.

Finney, Charles G. *Memoirs.* New York: A.S. Barnes & Co., 1876.

Finney, Charles Grandison. *Lectures on Revivals of Religion.* NewYork: Leavitt, Lord & Company, 1835.

Flew, Robert Newton. *The Idea of Perfection in Christian Theology.* London: Oxford University, 1934.

Flower, J. Roswell. "Pentecostal Commission." *Pentecostal Evangel,* June 12, 1920.

Foucault, Michael. *The Archeology of Knowledge and Language.* Translated by A.M. Sheridan Smith. London: Tavistock, 1969.

Foucault, Michael. *Power/Knowledge: Selected Interviews and Other Writings.* Translated by Colin Gordon et al. New York: Pantheon Books, 1980.

Gabriel, Andrew. "Review of Frank Macchia, 2006. Baptized in the Spirit: A Global Pentecostal Theology. Grand Rapids: Zondervan." *Canadian Journal of Pentecostal-Charismatic Christianity* 1, no. 1 (2010): 116–130.

Galli, Mark. "Rob Bell's Bridge Too Far." *Christianity Today* 55, no. 4 (2011). http://www.christianitytoday.com/ct/2011/april/lovewins.html.

Garrigus, Alice Belle. *Walking in the King's Highway.* http://www.mun.ca/rels/pent/texts/king.html.

Gee, Donald. *Pentecost.* Springfield, MO: Gospel Publishing House, 1932.

Gerson, Jen, "'This Isn't Supposed to Be a Christian Country': Atheist to Get Human Rights Hearing against Politician's Dinner Blessing" http://life.nationalpost.com/2013/02/20/human-rights-commission-to-look-at-complaint-by-atheist-offended-by-saskatoon-councillors-dinner-blessing/.

Gibbs, Eddie. *The Rebirth of the Church: Applying Paul's Vision for Ministry in Our Post-Christian World.* Grand Rapids: Baker Academic, 2013.

Gibbs, Eddie and Ryan K. Bolger. *Emerging Churches: Creating Christian Community in Postmodern Cultures.* Grand Rapids: Baker Academic, 2005.

Gidney, R.D. and W.P.J. Millar. "The Christian Recessional in Ontario's Public Schools." In *Religion and Public Life in Canada: Historical and Comparative Perspectives,* edited by Marguerite Van Die. Toronto: University of Toronto, 2001.

Gitlin, Todd. "The Postmodern Predicament." *The Wilson Quarterly (1976-)* 13, no. 3 (1989): 67–76.

Goff, James R. *Fields White Unto Harvest: Charles F. Parham and the Missionary Origins of Pentecostalism.* Fayetteville; AK: University of Arkansas, 1988.

Goff, James R. "Parham, Charles Fox." In *The New International Dictionary of Pentecostal and Charismatic Movements*, edited by S.M. Burgess and E.M. Van der Mass. Grand Rapids: Zondervan, 2002.

Grant, John Webster. *The Church in the Canadian Era*. Revised and Expanded ed. Vancouver: Regent College Publishing, 1998.

Grenz, Stanley J. *A Primer on Postmodernism*. Grand Rapids: Eerdmans, 1996.

Gresham, John L. *Charles G. Finney's Doctrine of Baptism in the Holy Spirit*. Peabody: Hendrickson, 1994.

Grigg, Viv. "The Spirit of Church and the Postmodern City." University of Auckland, 2005.

Guder, Darrell L., ed. *Missional Church: A Vision for the Sending of the Church in the Twenty-First Century*. Grand Rapids: Eerdmans, 1998.

Hagner, Donald A. *Matthew 1-13*. Word Biblical Commentary. Edited by Bruce M. Metzger. Nashville: Thomas Nelson, 1993.

Hammond, J.W. *The Joyful Sound: A History of the Pentecostal Assemblies of Newfoundland and Labrador*. J.W. Hammond, 1982.

Hare, Douglas R. A. *Matthew*. Interpretation. Edited by James Luther Mays. Louisville: Westminster John Knox, 2009.

Harvey, David. *The Condition of Postmodernity*. Vol. 14. Cambridge, MA: Blackwell Oxford, 1989.

Hattie-Longmire, B. "Sit Down, Brother! Alice B. Garrigus and the Pentecostal Assemblies of Newfoundland." Mount Saint Vincent University, 2001.

Henry, Carl F.H. "Postmodernism: The New Spectre?" In *The Challenge of Postmodernism*, edited by David S. Dockery. Grand Rapids: Baker, 2001.

Herrin, Judith. *The Formation of Christendom*. Princeton: Princeton University, 1989.

Hiebert, Paul. "Conversion, Culture and Cognitive Categories." *Gospel in Context* 1, no. 4: 24-29.

Hiebert, Paul. "Sets and Structures: A Study in Church Patterns." In *New Horizons in World Missions: Evangelicals and the Christian Mission in the 1980s*, edited by David Hasselgrace. Grand Rapids: Baker, 1979.

Hirsch, Alan. *The Forgotten Ways: Reactivating the Missional Church*. Grand Rapids: Brazos, 2006.

Hitchens, Christopher. *God Is Not Great: How Religion Poisons Everything*. New York: Twelve Hachette Book Group, 2009.

Hocken, Peter D. "Charismatic Movement." In *The New International Dictionary of Pentecostal and Charismatic Movements*, edited by S. M. Burgess and E.M. Van der Mass. Grand Rapids: Zondervan, 2002.

Hollenwager, Walter J. "From Azusa Street to the Toronto Phenomena: Historical Roots of the Pentecostal Movement." In *Pentecostal Movements as an Ecumenical Challenge*, edited by Jurgen Moltman and Karl-Josef Kuschel. London: SCM, 1996.

Hollenweger, Walter J. "Theology of the New World." *The Expository Times* 87, no. 8 (1976): 228–232.

Hollenweger, Walter J. "Priorities in Pentecostal Research: Historiography, Missiology, Hermeneutics and Pneumatology." In *Experiences of the Spirit*, edited by J.A.B Jongeneel. Bern: Peter Lang, 1989.

Hollenweger, Walter J. *Pentecostalism: Origins and Development Worldwide*. Peabody: Hendrickson, 1997.

Hollenweger, Walter J. "The Black Roots of Pentecostalism." In *Pentecostals after a Century: Global Perspectives on a Movement in Transition*, edited by Allan Anderson and Walter J. Hollenweger. Sheffield, UK: Sheffield Academic, 1999.

Hollenweger, Walter J. *The Pentecostals*. Grand Rapids: Zondervan, 1973.

Hollenweger, Walter J. *Pentecostalism*. Peabody: Hendrickson, 1988.

Howe, Neil and William Strauss. *13th Gen: Abort, Retry, Ignore, Fail?* New York: Vintage Books, 1993.

Hudson, Neil. "British Pentecostal's Past Development and Future Challenges." http://salfordelimchurch.org/heritage.php

Hunter, Harold D. and Cecil M. Robeck. *The Azusa Street Revival and Its Legacy*. Cleveland, TN: Pathway, 2006.

Hurst, John Fletcher. *The History of Methodism*. Vol. III. New York: Eaton & Mains, 1902.

Hyatt, Eddie, ed. *Fire on the Earth: Eyewitness Reports from the Azusa Street Revival*. Lake Mary, FL: Creation House, 2006.

Jacobson, Douglas. *Thinking in the Spirit: Theologies of the Early Pentecostal Movement*. Bloomington, IN: Indiana University, 2003.

Jaichandran, Rebecca and B.C. Madhav. "Pentecostal Spirituality in a Postmodern World." *Asian Journal of Pentecostal Studies* 6, no. 1 (2003): 39.

Janes, Burton K. *The Lady Who Came: The Biography of Alice Belle Garrigus, Newfoundland's First Pentecostal Pioneer*. St. John's, NL: Good Tidings, 1982.

Janes, Burton K. *The Lady Who Stayed: The Biography of Alice Belle Garrigus, Newfoundland's First Pentecostal Pioneer*. St. John's, NL: Good Tidings, 1983.

Janes, Burton K. *From Hinder's Hall to Emmanuel*. St. John's, NL: Robinson-Blackmore Print. & Pub., 1996.

Janes, Burton K. *History of the Pentecostal Assemblies of Newfoundland*. St. John's, NL: Good Tidings, 1996.

Janes, Burton K. *Reflections from Ship Cove Pond to the Harbour Hills: The History of the Pentecostal Tabernacle, Port De Grave, Newfoundland*. St. John's, NL: Good Tidings, 2000.

Janes, Burton K. *The Ancient Landmarks of Happy Cove and the Faithful Seven: The History of Beacon Tabernacle, Birchy Bay, Newfoundland*. St. John's, NL: Robinson-Blackmore Printing and Pub., 2001.

Janes, Burton K. *The Jug in the Window: The History of the Pentecostal Church, Springdale, Newfoundland and Labrador*. St. John's, NL: Print Atlantic, 2003.

Johns, Jackie David. "Pentecostalism and the Postmodern Worldview." *Journal of Pentecostal Theology* 7, (1995): 73.

Johns, Jackie David. "Yielding to the Spirit: The Dynamics of a Pentecostal Model of Praxis." In *The Globalization of Pentecostalism: A Religion Made to Travel*, edited by Murray W. Dempster, Byron D. Klaus and Douglas Peterson. Irvine, CA: Regnum Books International, 1999.

Johnson, Megan and Larry Johnson. *Generations, Inc. From Boomers to Linksters - Managing the Friction between Generations at Work*. New York: AMACOM, 2010.

Jones, Andrew. "11 Common Characteristics of the Church Emerging." http://tallskinnykiwi.typepad.com/tallskinnykiwi/2006/04/the_dewaaypagit.html.

Jones, Tony. *Postmodern Youth Ministry: Exploring Cultural Shift, Creating Holistic Connections, Cultivating Authentic Community*. Grand Rapids: Youth Specialties, 2001.

Jones, Tony. *The New Christians: Dispatches from the Emergent Frontier.* San Francisco: Jossey-Bass, 2008.

Jones, Tony. "Society for Pentecostal Studies Paper: What Pentecostals Have to Learn from Emergents." (2010). http://www.patheos.com/blogs/tonyjones/2010/03/09/society-for-pentecostal-studies-paper-what-pentecostals-have-to-learn-from-emergents/.

Kaplan, Robert D., "Rome's Fall and Late Antiquity: A Specter for America?" http://www.startribune.com/opinion/commentaries/235805621.html.

Kean, Gary, "Religious School Assembly Concerns Parent." http://www.thewesternstar.com/News/Local/2013-04-05/article-3214082/Religious-school-assembly-concerns-parent/1.

Kilbourn, William. *Religion in Canada; the Spiritual Development of a Nation.* Toronto: McClelland and Stewart, 1968.

Kimball, Dan, "Origin of the Terms 'Emerging' and 'Emergent' Church - Part 1" http://dankimball.typepad.com/vintage_faith/2006/04/origin_of_the_t.html.

Kimball, Dan. *The Emerging Church: Vintage Christianity for New Generations.* Grand Rapids: Zondervan, 2003.

Knight, Henry H. "From Aldersgate to Azusa: Wesley and the Renewal of Pentecostal Spirituality." *Journal of Pentecostal Theology* 4, no. 8 (1996): 82–98.

Kurtzhan, Stephen F. C. "Exegesis of Matthew 28:18-20." http://www.wlsessays.net/files/KurtzahnMatthew.pdf.

Kydd, Ronald A.N. "The Impact of the Charismatic Renewal on Classical Pentecostalism in Canada." *Pneuma* 18, no. 1 (1996): 55–67.

Land, Steven Jack. *Pentecostal Spirituality: A Passion for the Kingdom. Journal of Pentecostal Theology Supplementary Series 1.* Edited by John Christopher Thomas, Rickie D. Moore, and Steven J. Land. Sheffield: Sheffield Academic, 1993.

Letson, Harry. "Pentecostalism as a Paradigm Shift." *The Journal of the European Pentecostal Theological Association* XXVII, (2007): 104–117.

Lewis, Paul W. "Towards a Pentecostal Epistemology: The Role of Experience in Pentecostal Hermeneutics." *Spirit and Power* 2, no. 1 (2000): 95125.

Lincoln, Andrew T. *Ephesians.* Word Biblical Commentary. Edited by David A. Hubbard and Glenn W. Barker. Dallas: Word Books, 1990.

Lindstrom, Harald. *Wesley and Sanctification.* Grand Rapids: Francis Asbury Publishing, 1980.

Lyons, Gabe. *The Next Christians: The Good News About the End of Christian America.* New York: Doubleday Religion, 2010.

Lyotard, Jean-Francois. *The Postmodern Condition: A Report on Knowledge.* Translated by Geoff Bennington and Brian Massumi. Vol. 10 Theory and History of Literature. Minneapolis: University of Minnesota, 1984.

Macchia, Frank D. "Sighs Too Deep for Words: Toward a Theology of Glossolalia." *Journal of Pentecostal Theology* 1, no. 1 (1992): 47–73.

Macchia, Frank D. "Tongues as a Sign: Towards a Sacramental Understanding of Pentecostal Experience." *Pneuma* 15, no. 1-2 (1993): 1–2.

Macchia, Frank D. "God Present in a Confused Situation: The Mixed Influence of the Charismatic Movement on Classical Pentecostalism in the United States." *Pneuma* 18, no. 1 (1996): 33–54.

Macchia, Frank D. *Baptized in the Spirit: A Global Pentecostal Theology.* Grand Rapids: Zondervan, 2006.

MacIlvaine III, W. Rodman. "What Is the Missional Church Movement?" *Bibliotheca Sacra* 167, (2010): 89.

Mackay, Hugh. "One for All and All for One: It's a Tribal Thing." *Sydney Morning Herald*, July 13, 2002.

Magruder, Jeff C., "Why Pentecostals Don't Preach Expository Sermons." http://www.preaching.com/resources/articles/11547311/.

McClung, Grant. "Explosion, Motivation, and Consolidation: The Historical Anatomy of the Pentecostal Missionary Movement." *Missiology: An International Review* 14, no. 2 (1986): 159–172.

McDowell, D.H. "The Purpose for the Second Coming of the Lord." *Pentecostal Evangel*, (May 2, 1925).

McGee, Gary B. "Assemblies of God Mission Theology: A Historical Perspective." *International Bulletin of Missionary Research* 10, no. 4 (1986): 166.

McGill, Jena, et al, "Counterpoint: Why Trinity Western University Should Not Have a Law School." http://fullcomment.nationalpost.com/2013/01/24/counterpoint-why-trinity-western-university-should-not-have-a-law-school/.

McIntosh, Gary L. *One Church, Four Generations: Understanding and Reaching All Ages in Your Church.* Grand Rapids: Baker, 2002.

McKim, Donald K., ed. *Westminster Dictionary of Theological Terms.* Louisville: Westminster John Knox, 1996.

McKnight, Scot. "Five Streams of the Emerging Church." *Christianity Today* 51, no. 2 (2007). http://www.christianitytoday.com/ct/2007/february/11.35.html.

McLaren, Brian D. *A Generous Orthodoxy.* Grand Rapids: Zondervan, 2004.

McLaren, Brian D. *A New Kind of Christianity: Ten Questions That Are Transforming the Faith.* New York: HarperOne, 2010.

McLaren, Brian D. and Tony Campolo. *Adventures in Missing the Point.* Grand Rapids: Zondervan, 2006.

McPherson, Aimee Semple. *This Is That: Personal Experiences, Sermons, and Writings.* Los Angeles: Bridal Call Publishing House, 1919.

McPherson, Aimee Semple. *In the Service of the King: The Story of My Life.* New York: Boni and Liveright, 1927.

McPherson, Aimee Semple. *The Story of My Life.* Waco, TX: Word Publications, 1973.

McPherson, Joseph D. "John Wesley's Views of Spirit Baptism Accurately Reflect New Testament Teaching." *The Arminian Magazine,* 2010.

McQueen, Larry. *Toward a Pentecostal Eschatology: Discerning the Way Forward.* Journal of Pentecostal Theology Supplement Series 39. Edited by John Christopher Thomas, Rickie D. Moore and Steven J. Land. Blandford Forum, UK: Deo Publishing, 2012.

McQuilkin, Robertson and Bradford Mullen. "The Impact of Postmodern Thinking on Evangelical Hermeneutics." *Journal of the Evangelical Theological Society* 40, no. 1 (1997): 69–82.

Menzies, Robert P. *Empowered for Witness: The Spirit in Luke-Acts.* Journal of Pentecostal Theology Supplementary Series 6. Edited by John Christopher Thomas, Rickie D. Moore and Steven J. Land. Sheffield, UK: Sheffield Academic, 1994.

Menzies, Robert P. "Luke and the Spirit: A Reply to James Dunn." *Journal of Pentecostal Theology* 2, no. 4 (1994): 115–138.

Menzies, William W. "The Methodology of Pentecostal Theology: An Essay on Hermeneutics." In *Essays on Apostolic Themes*, edited by Paul Elbert. Peabody: Hendrickson, 1985.

Menzies, William W. and Robert P. Menzies. *Spirit and Power: Foundations of Pentecostal Experience*. Grand Rapids: Zondervan, 2000.

Michel, David. "Aimee Semple McPherson and the Reconfiguration of Methodism in America, 1916-1922." In *Winds from the North: Canadian Contributions to the Pentecostal Movement*, edited by Peter Althouse and Michael Wilkinson. Boston: Brill, 2010.

Miller, Donald E. and Tetsunao Yamamori. *Global Pentecostalism: The New Face of Christian Social Engagement*. Los Angeles: University of California, 2007.

Miller, John D. *Active, Balanced, and Happy: These Young Americans Are Not Bowling Alone*. The Longitudinal Study of American Youth. University of Michigan, 2011.

Miller, Thomas William. *Canadian Pentecostals: A History of the Pentecostal Assemblies of Canada*. Mississauga, ON: Full Gospel Publishing House, 1994.

Milley, David B. *A Study of the Pentecostal Assemblies of Newfoundland's Message of Separation*. Providence Theological Seminary, 1999.

Mohler Jr., R. Albert. "What Should We Think of the Emerging Church? Part One." *Christian Post* (2005). http://www.christianpost.com/news/what-should-we-think-of-the-emerging-church-part-one-6355/ .

Moody, Dwight L. *Secret Power*. New York: Fleming H. Revell, 1881. Reprint, Ventura, CA: Regal Books, 1987.

Murray, Stuart. *Post-Christendom: Church and Mission in a Strange New World*. Milton Keyes, UK: Paternoster, 2004.

Myers, Ken. *All God's Children and Blue Suede Shoes: Christians & Popular Culture*. Westchester, IL: Crossway Books, 1989.

Myland, David Wesley. *The Latter Rain Covenant with Pentecostal Power and Testimonies of Healings and Baptism*. Chicago: Evangel Publishing House, 1910.

Nelson, P.C. *Bible Doctrines*. Springfield, MO: Gospel Publishing House, 1948.

Newbigin, Lesslie. *The Other Side of 1984: Questions for the Churches*. Geneva: World Council of Churches, 1983.

Newbigin, Lesslie. *The Gospel in a Pluralist Society*. Grand Rapids: Eerdmans, 1989.

Newman, David Lorne. "The Eschatology of Newfoundland and Labrador Early Pentecostals: 'Jesus Is Coming Soon,' 1910–1949." Memorial University of Newfoundland, 2012.

Niebuhr, H. Richard. *Christ and Culture*. New York: Harper, 1951.

Noel, Bradley Truman. "What Is a Pastor?" *Good Tidings*, September-October 2012, 5-6.

Noel, Bradley Truman. "The Historical Roots of the Second Work Doctrine." In *Full of the Holy Spirit and Faith: Essays Presented in Honour of Dr. Allison A. Trites, Pastor, Teacher, Scholar*, edited by Scott A Dunham. Gaspereau, NS: Gaspereau, 1997.

Noel, Bradley Truman. "Gordon Fee's Contribution to Contemporary Pentecostalism's Theology of Baptism in the Holy Spirit." Acadia University, 1998.

Noel, Bradley Truman. "Gordon Fee and the Challenge to Pentecostal Hermeneutics: Thirty Years Later." *Pneuma* 26, no. 1 (2004): 60–80.

Noel, Bradley Truman. *Pentecostal and Postmodern Hermeneutics: Comparison and Contemporary Impact*. Eugene, OR: Wipf and Stock, 2010.

Noll, Mark A. *A History of Christianity in the United States and Canada.* Grand Rapids: Eerdmans, 1992.

Noll, Mark A. *What Happened to Christian Canada?* Vancouver, BC: Regent College Publishing, 2007.

Norris, P. and R. Inglehart. *Sacred and Secular: Religion and Politics Worldwide.* Cambridge, UK: Cambridge University, 2004.

Nuttall, Geoffery F. *The Holy Spirit in Puritan Faith and Experience.* Chicago: University of Chicago, 1992.

O'Connor, Edward D. *The Pentecostal Movement in the Catholic Church.* Notre Dame, IN: Ave Maria, 1971.

O'Toole, Roger. "Religion in Canada: Its Development and Contemporary Situation." *Social Compass* 43, no. 1 (1996): 119–134.

Oden, Thomas C. *After Modernity—What? An Agenda for Theology.* Grand Rapids: Zondervan, 1992.

Oden, Thomas C. *Two Worlds: Notes on the Death of Modernity in America & Russia.* Downers Grove: InterVarsity, 1992.

Owens, Robert R. *The Azusa Street Revival: Its Roots and Its Message.* Longwood, FL: Xulon, 2005.

Pagitt, Doug. "The Emerging Church and Embodied Theology." In *Listening to the Beliefs of Emerging Churches: Five Perspectives*, edited by Robert Webber. Grand Rapids: Zondervan, 2007.

Pagitt, Doug and Tony Jones. *An Emergent Manifesto of Hope.* Grand Rapids: Baker, 2007.

Palmer, Phoebe. *The Promise of the Father.* Boston: H.V. Degen, 1859.

Palmer, Phoebe. *Pioneer Experiences.* New York: W.C. Palmer Jr., 1868.

Parham, Charles Fox. *Kol Kare Bomidbar: A Voice Crying in the Wilderness.* n.p.: n.p., 1902. Reprint, Baxter Springs, KS: Robert L. Parham, 1944.

Parham, Charles Fox. *The Everlasting Gospel.* Baxter Springs, KS: Apostolic Faith Bible College, n.d. [1911].

Pearson, Birger A. "The Gospel According to the Jesus Seminar." Claremont Graduate School, 1996.

Percesepe, Gary John. "The Unbearable Lightness of Being Postmodern." *Christian Scholar's Review* 20, (1990): 118–35.

Perrin, Norman. *The Kingdom of God in the Teaching of Jesus.* Philadelphia: Westminster, 1963.

Perrin, Norman. *Rediscovering the Teaching of Jesus.* London: SCM, 1967.

Perrin, Norman. *The Promise of Bultmann.* Philadelphia: Lippincott, 1969.

Piper, John. *Brothers, We Are Not Professionals: A Plea to Pastors for Radical Ministry.* Nashville, TN: Broadman & Holman, 2002.

Piper, John. "What Is the Emerging Church?" (2008). http://www.desiringgod.org/resource-library/ask-pastor-john/what-is-the-emerging-church.

Poloma, Margaret M. "The Spirit Bade Me Go: Pentecostalism and Global Religion." In *Association for the Sociology of Religion.* Washington, D.C., 2000.

Putnam, Robert D. *Bowling Alone: The Collapse and Revival of American Community.* New York: Simon and Schuster, 2000.

Quebedeaux, Richard. *The New Charismatics: The Origins, Development, and Significance of Neo-Pentecostalism.* Garden City, NY: Doubleday, 1976.

Rainer, Thom S. and Jess W. Rainer. *The Millennials: Connecting to America's Largest Generation*. Nashville: Broadman & Holman, 2011.

Raschke, Carl. *The Next Reformation: Why Evangelicals Must Embrace Postmodernity*. Grand Rapids: Baker Academic, 2004.

Ray, Donna E. "Aimee Semple McPherson and Her Seriously Exciting Gospel." *Journal of Pentecostal Theology* 19, no. 1 (2010): 155–69.

Redekop, John H. "Is Canada Becoming a Post-Christian Country?" *Canadian Christianity*. http://canadianchristianity.com/canada-postchristian-country-3625/.

Reed, David A. *"In Jesus' Name": The History and Beliefs of Oneness Pentecostals*. Journal of Pentecostal Theology Supplementary Series 31. Edited by John Christopher Thomas, Rickie D. Moore, and Steven J. Land. Blandford Forum, UK: Deo Publishing, 2008.

Reeves, Thomas C. *The Empty Church: The Suicide of Liberal Christianity*. New York: The Free, 1996.

Reimer, Sam. "A Generic Evangelicalism? Comparing Evangelical Subcultures in Canada and the United States." In *Rethinking Church, State, and Modernity: Canada between Europe and America*, edited by David Lyon and Marguerite Van Die. Toronto: University of Toronto, 2000.

Reimer, Sam. *Evangelicals and the Continental Divide the Conservative Protestant Subculture in Canada and the United States*. Montreal: McGill-Queen's University, 2003.

Report of the Discipleship Commission. Pentecostal Assemblies of Newfoundland and Labrador, 2012.

Richardson, W.R. "Methodist Revivalism and the Baptists of Eastern British America in 1858." In *A Fragile Stability: Definition and Redefinition of Maritime Baptist Identity*, edited by D.T. Priestly. Hantsport, NS: Lancelot, 1994.

Rideout, F.D. *History of Pentecostal Schools in Newfoundland and Labrador*. St. John's, NL: Good Tidings, 1992.

Riss, Richard M. *A Survey of 20th-Century Revival Movements in North America*. Grand Rapids: Hendrickson, 1988.

Robeck Jr., Cecil M. "Seymour, William Joseph." In *The New International Dictionary of Pentecostal and Charismatic Movements*, edited by S. M. Burgess and E.M. Van der Mass 1053–57. Grand Rapids: Zondervan, 2002.

Robeck Jr., Cecil M. "An Emerging Magisterium? The Case of the Assemblies of God." *Pneuma* 25, no. 2 (2003): 164–215.

Robeck Jr., Cecil M. *The Azusa Street Mission and Revival: The Birth of the Global Pentecostal Movement*. Nashville: Thomas Nelson, 2006.

Robinson, Judith. *Working Miracles: The Drama and Passion of Aimee Semple McPherson*. Canmore, AB: Altitude Publishing, 2006.

Rocca, Francis X. "Pope Francis Discovers Charismatic Movement a Gift to the Whole Church." http://www.catholicnews.com/data/stories/cns/1303443.htm.

Rollins, Peter. *How (Not) to Speak of God*. Brewster, MA: Paraclete, 2008.

Rorty, Richard. *Philosophy and the Mirror of Nature*. Princeton: Princeton University, 1979.

Rorty, Richard. *Consequences of Pragmatism: Essays, 1972–1980*. Minneapolis: University of Minnesota, 1982.

Rorty, Richard. *Objectivity, Relativism, and Truth*. Cambridge: Cambridge University, 1991.

Roxburgh, Alan and M. Scott Boren. *Introducing the Missional Church: What It Is, Why It Matters, and How to Become One*. Grand Rapids: Baker, 2009.
Ruby, Clayton and Gerald Chan. "Clayton Ruby and Gerald Chan: A Law School at Trinity Western University Will Impose a Queer Quota." http://fullcomment.nationalpost.com/2013/07/29/clayton-ruby-and-gerald-chan-a-law-school-at-trinity-western-university-will-impose-a-queer-quota/.
Rudd, Douglas. *Aimee Semple McPherson*. Belleville, ON: Guardian Books, 2006.
Rush, Nate. "The Impact of Postmodernism on Pentecostal Churches." Assemblies of God Theological Seminary, 2009.
Sagers, Robert. "The Emerging Church and Salvation." In *Evangelicals Engaging Emergent: A Discussion of the Emergent Church Movement*, edited by W. Henard and A. Greenway. Nashville: Broadman & Holman, 2009.
Sawler, David. *Goodbye Generation: A Conversation About Why Youth and Young Adults Leave the Church*. Hamilton, ON: Ponder Publishing, 2008.
Schaeffer, Francis A. *The Church at the End of the Twentieth Century*. Wheaton: Crossway Books, 1994.
Scott, Eleonora L. "A Theological Critique of the Emerging, Postmodern Missional Church/Movement." *Evangelical Review of Theology* 34, no. 4 (2010): 335–46.
Shelhamer, E.E., ed. *Finney on Revival*. Minneapolis: Bethany House, n.d.
Sheppard, Gerald T. "Pentecostals and the Hermeneutics of Dispensationalism: The Anatomy of an Uneasy Relationship." *Pneuma* 6, no. 1 (1984): 5–33.
Sidwell, Mark. "The Dividing Line: Understanding and Applying Biblical Separation." http://www.itib.org/articles/dividing_line/dividing_line_10-3.html.
Simms, Shane A. "Moving Forward in Mission: Introducing Missional Life to a Rural Newfoundland and Labrador Pentecostal Church through Shared Narratives and Missional Experiments." DMin diss, Tyndale Seminary, 2011.
Slick, Matt. "What Is the Emerging Church?". http://carm.org/what-emerging-church.
Smith, Christian. *Souls in Transition: The Religious and Spiritual Lives of Emerging Adults*. New York: Oxford, 2009.
Spittler, Russell P. "Theological Style among Pentecostals and Charismatics." In *Doing Theology in Today's World*, edited by John D. Woodbridge and Thomas Edward McComiskey. Grand Rapids: Zondervan, 1991.
Stark, Rodney and William Bainbridge. *The Future of Religion: Secularization, Revival, and Cult Formation*. Berkeley: University of California, 1985.
Stark, Rodney and Roger Finke. *Acts of Faith: Explaining the Human Side of Religion*. Los Angeles: University of California, 2000.
Stetzer, Ed, "First-Person: Understanding the Emerging Church" http://www.sbcbaptistpress.org/bpnews.asp?ID=22406.
Stiller, B.C. *Was Canada Ever Christian?* Markham, ON: Faith Today Publications, 1996.
Stillman, David and Lancaster Lynne. *When Generations Collide: Who They Are. Why They Clash. How to Solve the Generational Puzzle at Work*. New York: Collins Business, 2002.
Strauss, William and Neil Howe. *Generations: The History of America's Future, 1584 to 2069*. New York: Morrow, 1991.
Strauss, William and Neil Howe. *Millennials Rising: The Next Great Generation*. New York: Vintage Books, 2000.
Stronstad, Roger. *Charismatic Theology of St. Luke*. Peabody: Hendrickson, 1984.

Stronstad, Roger. *The Prophethood of All Believers*. Journal of Pentecostal Theology Supplementary Series 16. Edited by John Christopher Thomas, Rickie D. Moore and Steven J. Land. Sheffield, UK: Sheffield Academic, 1999.

Studebaker, Steven and Lee Beach. "Emerging Churches in Post-Christian Canada." *Religions* 3, no. 3 (2012): 862–79.

Sutton, Matthew Avery. *Aimee Semple McPherson and the Resurrection of Christian America*. Cambridge, MA: Harvard, 2007.

Sweet, William Warren. *Religion in the Development of American Culture: 1765-1840*. Gloucester, MA: Peter Smith, 1963.

Synan, Vinson. *The Holiness-Pentecostal Movement in the United States*. Grand Rapids: Eerdmans, 1971.

Synan, Vinson. *Charismatic Bridges*. Ann Arbor, MI: Word of Life, 1974.

Synan, Vinson. *The Twentieth Century Pentecostal Explosion*. Altamonte Springs, FL: Creation House, 1987.

Synan, Vinson. *The Century of the Holy Spirit: 100 Years of Pentecostal and Charismatic Renewal, 1901-2001*. Nashville: Thomas Nelson, 2001.

Taylor, George Floyd. *The Spirit and the Bride: A Scriptural Presentation of the Operations, Manifestation, Gifts and Fruit of the Holy Spirit in Relation to His Bride with Special References to the 'Latter Rain' Revival*. Dunn, NC: George Floyd Taylor, 1907.

Telford, John, ed. *The Letters of the Rev. John Wesley, A.M*. London: Epworth, 1931.

Thielman, Frank. *Ephesians*. Baker Exegetical Commentary on the New Testament, edited by Robert W. Yarbrough and Robert H. Stein. Grand Rapids: Baker Academic, 2010.

Thiessen, Joel and Lorne L. Dawson. "Is There a 'Renaissance' of Religion in Canada? A Critical Look at Bibby and Beyond." *Studies in Religion/Sciences Religieuses* 37, no. 3-4 (2008): 389–415.

Thiselton, Anthony C. "Postmodernity, Postmodernism." In *A Concise Encyclopedia of the Philosophy of Religion*. Oxford: Oneworld, 2002.

Thiselton, Anthony C. *The Holy Spirit - in Biblical Teaching, through the Centuries, and Today*. Grand Rapids: Eerdmans, 2013.

Thistlethwaite, Susan Brooks. "The U.S. Is Post-Denominational." *Washington Post* (February 27, 2008). http://newsweek.washingtonpost.com/onfaith/panelists/susan_brooks_thistlethwaite/2008/02/the_us_is_postdenominational.html.

Thomas, John Christopher, ed. *Toward a Pentecostal Ecclesiology: The Church and the Fivefold Gospel*. Cleveland, TN: CPT, 2010.

Thompson, J. A. *The Book of Jeremiah*. The New International Commentary on the Old Testament, edited by Robert L. Hubbard, Jr. Grand Rapids: Eerdmans, 1980.

Thompson, Matthew K. *Kingdom Come: Revisioning Pentecostal Eschatology*. Journal of Pentecostal Theology Supplementary Series 37. Edited by John Christopher Thomas, Rickie D. Moore and Steven J. Land. Blandford Forum, UK: Deo Publishing, 2010.

Torrey, R.A. *The Person and Work of the Holy Spirit*. New York: Fleming H. Revell, 1910. Reprint, Grand Rapids: Zondervan, 1974.

Torrey, R.A. *The Holy Spirit: Who He Is and What He Does*. New York: Fleming H. Revell, 1927.

Trites, Allison and William J. Larkin. *The Gospel of Luke. Acts*. Cornerstone Biblical Commentary, edited by Philip W. Comfort. Carol Stream, IL: Tyndale House, 2006.

Twenge, Jean. *Generation Me: Why Today's Young Americans Are More Confident, Assertive, Entitled - and More Miserable Than Ever Before.* New York: Free, 2006.

Tyerman, Luke. *Wesley's Designated Successor.* London: Hodder & Stoughton, 1882.

Urback, Robyn. "Girls should not be segregated on public school property." Maclean's http://www.macleans.ca/education/uniandcollege/girls-should-not-be-segregated-on-public-school-property/.

Valdez Sr, A.C. *Fire on Azusa Street: An Eyewitness Account.* Costa Mesta, CA: Gift Publications, 1980.

Valpy, Michael and Joe Friesen. "Canada Marching from Religion to Secularization." *Globe and Mail*, December 11, 2010.

Van Gelder, Craig. "Postmodernism as an Emerging Worldview." *Calvin Theological Journal* 26, no. 2 (1991): 412–417.

Van Gelder, Craig. *The Essence of the Church: A Community Created by the Spirit.* Grand Rapids: Baker, 2000.

Van Gelder, Craig and J. Zscheile Dwight. *The Missional Church in Perspective: Mapping Trends and Shaping the Conversation.* Grand Rapids: Baker, 2011.

Vondey, Wolfgang. *Beyond Pentecostalism: The Crisis of Global Christianity and the Renewal of the Theological Agenda.* Pentecostal Manifestos 3, edited by James K.A. Smith and Amos Yong. Grand Rapids: Eerdmans 2010.

Wagner, C. Peter. *Apostles and Prophets : The Foundation of the Church.* Ventura, CA: Regal, 2000.

Ward, Pete. *Liquid Church.* Grand Rapids: Baker, 2001.

Warnock, Adrian. "The Toronto Blessing." http://www.patheos.com/blogs/adrianwarnock/2005/05/toronto-blessing-11-years-ago-this/

Wayne, Frances. "Healer Visits Denver Underworld to Seek Saving of Souls." *The Denver Post*, July 2, 1921.

Webber, Robert E. *The Younger Evangelicals: Facing the Challenges of the New World.* Grand Rapids: Baker, 2002.

Webber, Robert E. *Ancient-Future Faith: Rethinking Evangelicalism for a Postmodern World.* Ancient-Future Faith Series. Grand Rapids: Baker, 1999.

Wesley, John. *The Works of John Wesley.* Vol. XI. London: Wesleyan Conference Office, 1872. Reprint, Grand Rapids: Zondervan, 1978.

Westerlund, David, ed. *Global Pentecostalism: Encounters with Other Religious Traditions.* London: I.B. Tauris & Co., 2009.

White, Adam. "Knowledge and Transformation: Towards a 'Pentecostal Paideia.'" *Australasian Pentecostal Studies* 14: 111–20.

White, James Emery. *The Church in an Age of Crisis: 25 New Realities Facing Christianity.* Grand Rapids: Baker, 2012.

Willard, Dallas and Don Simpson. *Revolution of Character: Discovering Christ's Pattern for Spiritual Transformation.* Colorado Springs, CO: Nav, 2005.

Witherington III, Ben. *Conflict and Community in Corinth: A Socio-Rhetorical Commentary on 1 and 2 Corinthians.* Grand Rapids: Eerdmans, 1995.

Wolterstorff, Nicholas. *Reason within the Bounds of Religion.* Grand Rapids: Eerdmans, 1984.

Wright, Christopher J.H. *The Mission of God: Unlocking the Bible's Grand Narrative.* Downers Grove: InterVarsity, 2013.

Wuthnow, Robert. *After the Baby Boomers: How Twenty- and Thirty-Somethings Are Shaping the Future of American Religion.* Princeton: Princeton University, 2007.

Young, Howard. "Pentecostal Ministry in a Postmodern Culture: Preserving Pentecostal Vitality in an Ever-Changing American Culture." http://enrichmentjournal.ag.org/200501/200501_031_culture.cfm, (2012).

Zemke, Ron, Bob Filipczak, and Claire Raines. *Generations at Work: Managing the Clash of Veterans, Boomers, Xers, and Nexters in Your Workplace.* New York: AMACOM, 2000.

www.ingramcontent.com/pod-product-compliance
Lightning Source LLC
Chambersburg PA
CBHW070237230426
43664CB00014B/2330